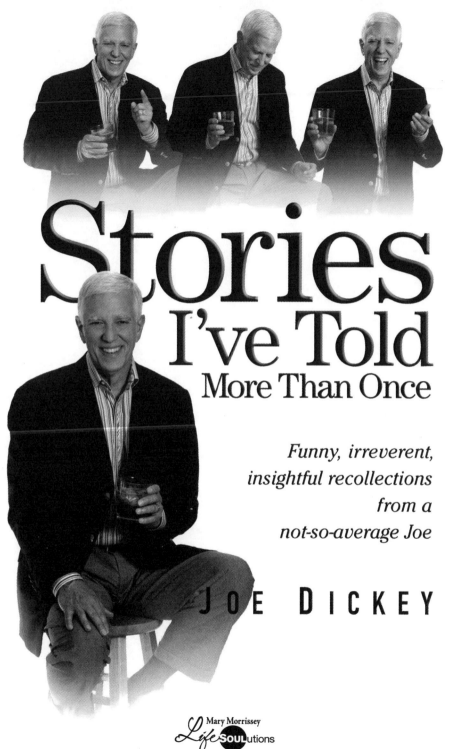

Stories
I've Told
More Than Once

*Funny, irreverent,
insightful recollections
from a
not-so-average Joe*

JOE DICKEY

Mary Morrissey
Life **SOUL**utions

Simi Valley, California

For information address: LifeSOULutions.

Published by

Mary Morrissey
*Life*SOULutions

LifeSOULutions That Work, LLC
PO Box 630269 • Simi Valley, CA 93063
503-922-3460
www.LifeSOULutions.com

ISBN 978-0-9842225-1-3

Cover Design & Book Design ©2012
Judi Paliungas, Susanne Abraham, PalimorStudiosDesign.com

Photography ©2012
Jim Paliungas, PalimorStudios.com

Back Cover Portrait Illustration ©2012 by Joe Dickey

Printed in China

TABLE OF CONTENTS

"Writing is an adventure."

Winston Churchill

"Know something, sugar? Stories only happen to people who can tell them."

Allan Gurganus

"A writer is someone who stands outside in the rain hoping to be struck by lightening."

James Dickey (no relation)

"You can be a little ungrammatical if you come from the right part of the country."

Robert Frost

"Write what should not be forgotten."

Isabel Allende

"Writing is a sweet, wonderful reward. . . ."

Franz Kafka

"There are three rules for writing. . . . Unfortunately, no one knows what they are."

Somerset Maugham

"To read fast is as bad as to eat in a hurry."

Vilhelm Ekelund

"There is, then, creative reading as well as creative writing. When the mind is braced by labor and invention, the page of whatever book we read becomes luminous with manifold allusion.

Ralph Waldo Emerson

"I liked the last story best. Too bad it didn't come sooner." (Paraphrased Cartoon)

Cartoonist Unknown

ACKNOWLEDGMENTS

I'd like to acknowledge my parents, Betty and Frank Dickey, for providing a great life for me, one that became full of great stories. I'd like to thank my sixth grade teacher, Mr. Cox, for nicknaming me "Joker," and giving me some recognition as a laugh producer. I say thank you to my three children, Jennifer, Blaine, and Bridges, who have not only endured my stories but have added to the list with their antics, insights, and good humor. I save my biggest gratitude to my wife, Mary, who saved me from despair, who listens as if I've never told these stories before, who encouraged me to put these stories in writing, and who continues to build me up to imagine that I'm a first-rate writer. Even *that* is a pretty good story.

INTRODUCTION

Ever since I realized in the sixth grade that I could get a lot of attention by getting people to laugh, I have developed a huge repertoire of jokes, knowing one (or two) for nearly any topic. Evidently, the same part of my brain that remembers jokes, remembers stories and events.

Somewhere along the line my brain decided to not remember the awful things that happened to me, or the sad stories, or even the negative aspects of things that took place to or around me. It's been a huge blessing. Oh, I guess I can recall some of the less wonderful situations, particularly if prompted, but for the most part I just don't have any readily accessible memory of them. Plus, I have no real interest in dredging them up—they are literally in the past and I give them little or no importance in my life today. Nevertheless, I not only remember lots of stories, I tell them.

I suppose when you get right down to the truth of everything, each one of us is affected differently by each moment. The reason for this seems obvious: we are all unique individuals, with individual capacities, individual feelings, and individual histories. My view of a past event will not be identical to that of someone who might have been standing right beside me. That's one of the reasons I'm always suspicious of "history books." We tend to believe that history books (particularly the ones we have to read in school) present truth. Who says? Were you there? Did anyone else have a slightly different opinion of what happened? Hmmm.

When one considers "history" as a subject it brings to mind all kinds of responses. To an eighth grader it can not only be sleep-inducing lectures, but show up as the incredible boredom of having to memorize facts and dates that seem to have absolutely no relationship to anything. To a college sophomore it can merely be a means to a degree in a different discipline, having to endure the dark, cold walks across campus at 7:30 on a wintery morning to make it on time to the one class where if you're tardy you're considered absent. To a real historian, it can be a joy, a treasure of information, a veritable freeway to the most vivid recollections of events that have literally molded the human condition, and a display of images that open the amazing world that used to be.

For me, history is personal. It is a compilation of all the events that help me understand why I do things a certain way, and why I think the way I do, and why I react to certain situations the way that I do.

This book is part of my history.

This is a collection of stories (all of them true) that either happened to me or to someone close to me, or they're just bits and pieces of humor, pathos, provocation, or astonishment that have been part of my life in some way or another. Basically, they're anecdotes, that is short narratives of interesting, amusing, or biographical incidents. History.

There may be a tale (or two) in this collection that has been embellished a bit. That's what happens to stories over the years. (I'm a much better high school basketball player now than I was when I was in high school, and I'm pretty sure that my Little League batting average is higher now than it was then, as well.) Some of the stories may not have happened exactly as I remember them to have happened. Nevertheless, it's nice to have any memory at all. I realize that autobiographies are distorted. Even autobiographical vignettes are distorted. However, the distortion is not intentional and if you've ever told a story yourself, you know that occasionally a little "distortion" makes it a much better story.

Most of the names are real and some I've "changed to protect the innocent," but they're all stories that I enjoy telling and re-telling. Because I've been alive a pretty long time, and because

I've lived what I consider to be a pretty interesting life, I have *lots* of stories. Some of them are *not* in this book either because they are parts of my life that I choose to not dwell on, or they might be embarrassing to someone as a result of my telling them. I hope no one about whom I care is embarrassed by any of these stories—I would never want that. Some of them are tales of my own stupidity. Some of them are typical of the way parents brag about how cute their children are. (I don't know if recounting the darlingness of one's children in print is any kinder than showing photos at lunch, but I hope you will indulge a proud dad who thinks his kids are remarkable and can be very, very clever.) A few of these stories are dog tales, and some of them are "big picture" examples (by which I mean there's probably a lesson in life that can be learned by reading or hearing or telling it). But most are just "stories."

I'm a pretty good talker. It sounds more erudite to say I'm an outstanding conversationalist. But the truth is, I just talk a lot. To repeat what I wrote as I began this Introduction, I have a joke for practically any situation and I can remember stories with equal facility. Even as I wrote this book, more stories came to mind.

I've told them all more than once.

(A Few Facts So I Don't Have To Repeat All This Stuff)

PREAMBLE I

I was born a skinny white child to attractive, healthy, intelligent, Caucasian, English-speaking, upwardly mobile, middle-class parents. I was delivered at 1:23 am on July 6, 1945, in the Alachua County Hospital, near Gainesville, Florida. (If you're an astrologer, go ahead and check out my chart. You'll probably know immediately why I love to tell stories.) My father was in the Army and my mother had dropped out of college to be a homemaker. My parents named me Joseph Terry Dickey: Joseph after my father's father, Joseph Stone Dickey; Terry after my great uncle, Leslie Terry Dickey.

I was a few days early, weighed only 6 pounds, 12 ounces, and was 21½ inches long, so it was hard to keep diapers on me—they kept slipping off my little snake-like body.

I have a brother who is two years and three months older than I, Frank Graves Dickey, Jr., and I have a sister, who is two years and three months younger than I, Ann Elizabeth Dickey Haynes. Each of them was divorced once. My brother remarried. My sister has not remarried. I was divorced twice and had one wife die, and I have been married four times. (See PREAMBLE II)

My wives names were (are) Julianna Sparks, Diane Arnold, Robin Timm, and Mary Morrissey. I was with Juli for seven years, with Diane for four years, with Robin for twenty years, and I intend to be with Mary for at least another forty years.

I am the father of three children: Jennifer Drymon Dickey Barnes, born in 1968, whose mother is Juli; Sarah Blaine Dickey, born in 1990, whose mother is Robin; and Thomas Bridges Dickey, born in 1994, whose mother is Robin.

Juli and Diane are both still living. Robin died in 1999, at the age of 40, from colon cancer.

My childhood was spend in Lexington, Kentucky; college in Atlanta, Georgia; and except for brief stints in Colorado and Mississippi, the remainder of my life has been in Nevada and then California. I have lived at 40 different addresses, one of them for 12 years and another for 7. Do the math. That's 38 addresses in 47 years. I should've owned a moving company. And I am happy to report that I've never been evicted. I have lived in seven states, have been in 49 states (Alaska has eluded me, so far), and am currently in a state of contentment and happiness.

PREAMBLE II

I once had dinner at the home of a famous film director who had been married five times. I knew three of his adult children and they had invited me. At the time I had only been married once, but that marriage had failed and I was curious about his five marriages.

He explained that the first four had not worked well for several reasons: he was young, he didn't know how to be loving or how to accept love, he was a poor communicator, and, "perhaps" he explained, "I just hadn't found the right person." He had no children with any of his first four wives. His fifth marriage . . . he "got it right." It had already lasted 44 years, they had five children, and it was a bond of great beauty.

My second marriage didn't work out well either, but my third lasted twenty years, until she died at the age of 40 of colon cancer. It was a tragedy of great proportion, but I eventually recovered from it and am now married for a fourth time and feel like a very, very lucky man to have found true love more than once.

My point is that not all divorces are bad. Not all marriages are made in heaven. Not all tragedies last forever. We must have enough information about situations to make valid judgments about them, and, oddly enough, when we get enough information, our judgments seem to become more rare.

Foster Brooks used to joke about the deaths of his three wives: "The first died from eating poison mushrooms; the second died from eating poison mushrooms; the third died of a fractured skull—SHE WOULDN'T EAT HER MUSHROOMS!"

KLURG

Early in the morning, a few hours after I was born, my father called his mother to tell her that she had another grandson. It was a bad telephone connection and when she asked what they had decided to name me she didn't hear his answer correctly.

"Joseph Klurg! You named him KLURG? What kind of name is THAT?"

"No, Mother. It's Joseph TERRY. His middle name is Terry."

"KLURG? I just can't imagine why you would name him Klurg! How do you SPELL it? Does it start with a C or a K? In the middle, is it with an E or a U? KLURG!?"

After a few more tries, my dad gave up, telling her he'd call her again later. It took two days before she knew I had a fairly normal middle name.

A HAPPY DRUNK

I was two. I had whooping cough. It was the middle of the night.

My mother, after treating me to no avail, called our pediatrician. Since all the pharmacies were closed, the doctor said a homemade prescription would probably work just fine.

"Combine a half teaspoon of lemon juice, a teaspoon of honey, and a half teaspoon of bourbon. Give this to him and the lemon and honey will soothe his throat and the bourbon will calm him down."

My mother was sleepy and didn't get the right amounts written down. She gave me a tablespoon of honey, a tablespoon of lemon juice, and a tablespoon of bourbon. About fifteen minutes later she gave me the same thing again. For the "detail" reader, two tablespoons is equal to an ounce. Sometimes a thrifty bartender will pour you only an ounce when you ask for a drink.

I have been told that I was the happiest little drunk that ever ran up and down a crib. Twice back and forth and then a big wave of my arm, a little bounce, a big grin, and a loud, "HI, MOMMY!" Then a repeat performance. More bouncing. More smiling, Another jog up and down the crib, another big wave, and another loud, "HI, MOMMY!" It went on for almost thirty minutes before I wore out. My parents were greatly amused even though nowadays it might be labeled child abuse.

I've always believed that neither money nor alcohol actually changes people. More money and more alcohol only make people become more of what they already are, deep down inside. Give a jerk a lot of money and he just becomes a rich jerk. Give a happy guy a few drinks and he becomes an even happier guy. That drunken little two-year-old was happy! Not that it has happened very often in my later years, but I'm ALWAYS a happy drunk.

∞

NAMING MY SISTER

I was two years plus almost three months and I was about to be getting a new sibling. My mother told me that if we got a baby sister the baby's name was going to be Sarah Elizabeth Dickey. After thinking about it for a while I came back to my mother and told her that I didn't like the name.

"Why not?" she asked.

"'Cause I can't fay Farah."

"Oh, then what do you think you WOULD like to name her?" not really imagining that I would know OR that she would change her mind.

"Just pwane Ann. ANN Ewibadawiss. That would be OK."

My mother had heard me, but knew that one day I'd be able to pronounce Sarah, and nothing more was said.

After the baby girl had been born, the nurse came to my mother's hospital room and asked, "What are you going to name this child? We need to put the name on the application for the birth certificate."

Under the influence of ether, my mother said, "Her name is Ann Elizabeth Dickey." The nurse departed.

Two days later when my mother was being discharged from the hospital and she was gathering her belongings, the nurse brought in the paperwork for my parents to take home. My mother was shocked. "This says her name is ANN. I didn't name her Ann. I named her Sarah. Sarah Elizabeth Dickey." The nurse said, "No, ma'am. I heard you clearly. You even spelled it without an "e." You said 'Ann Elizabeth Dickey.' That's what we submitted and it's in the records." It was going to be VERY difficult to alter "the records."

My mother resigned herself to a different name than she had chosen: Ann. Ann Ewibadawiss.

3

NAKED ON MAIN STREET

Some of the things we think we remember are merely stories we've heard other people tell about an experience we had, particularly when the experience happened to us at a very early age (like the two stories that immediately preceded this one). I seem to have a partial memory of certain events, but I'm certain that my memory seems clearer because I've heard my mother recount an event a number of times. Nevertheless, I include a few of these as if they are my own vivid memories.

We moved from Ransom Avenue when I was around three years old. One of my mother's favorite tales of our days on Ransom is about when I "escaped" from the back yard and took a walk by myself. It wouldn't be much of a story except for the fact that I was naked.

She had dressed me in a pair of brown overalls and hooked the shoulder straps to a rope, which was attached to a long clothesline. Though many might consider that to be treating me more like an animal than a child, I don't think I have suffered any long-term effects. *Rrrrufff* I guess I got tired of going back and forth across the back yard and climbed out of my overalls and just "took off."

Down the side of the house, a right turn at the sidewalk, a whole block down Ransom to the Presbyterian church on the corner of Main Street. I suspect there was no hesitation—left turn, cross the street, pass directly in front of the showroom windows of Goodwin's Dodge/Plymouth dealership and on down the block past the A & P grocery store.

It was at that point that a cashier saw me. She recognized me from previous visits, clothes or no clothes, and was familiar enough with our family to know our name. (In those days, everybody knew everybody's names, ya know?) She ran out and brought me inside, called my house, my mother came tearing down to retrieve me, and aside from my mother feeling somewhat neglectful, everything turned out just fine.

Just for the record, I have no lingering nudist tendencies. *Rrrrufff.*

AUNT BEULAH'S LAME ADVICE

When I was little I used to be in such a hurry to get places that my head would get in front of my feet and quite often I'd end up falling. I don't think I got hurt any more than any other little boy, occasionally falling out of a tree or off a ladder or out of a car (See A PURPLE BISCUIT, next) but evidently my Great Aunt Beulah thought so.

Aunt Beulah and Uncle John Willie Jones had a farm not too far from Lexington and we'd go visit them every once in a while. It was always a great trip because we had to go through three covered bridges to get there (proving that my childhood was pretty much "back in the olden days").

Once after I'd fallen out of a tree and hurt myself, Aunt Beulah took me aside. She knew if I stayed on the ground I'd stop falling out of trees, so in a very serious and stern voice said to me, "Joe, if you don't want to get hurt so often you should remember to keep both feet on the ground at all times."

I nodded, understanding her clearly, and responded, "Kayyyy."

I sat there for about twenty minutes thinking about that. Finally I realized that if I kept both feet on the ground at all times I couldn't even walk.

That was the end of my taking advice from old people.

A PURPLE BISCUIT

My grandparents were over for dinner one summer evening and while the adults were either preparing the meal or sitting on the front porch chatting, I went out and got in my grandfather's new Oldsmobile, which was parked at the curb. Everyone knew I was in the car, and it was OK with them—I was three, I couldn't reach the pedals, they had the keys, and they were pretty sure I wasn't going anywhere.

When it was time to eat my mother asked my brother to go out to the car and bring me in to supper. As he approached the car, I was leaning against the front passenger door from the inside and as he opened the door, I fell out. My mother said she heard, from the kitchen in the back of the house, what sounded like a gunshot. It was my head hitting the curb.

Everyone came running. They carried me inside, put cold compresses on my forehead, kept me awake in case I had a concussion (which I did), and read Alice In Wonderland to keep me awake, occupied, and still. Dinner got delayed a bit. The adults took turns reading to me while the others ate, but after a few hours I felt like getting up and it seemed like an OK thing to let me do.

I went outside and rode my tricycle up and down the sidewalk showing all the neighbors "my purple biscuit." It was an enormous swollen bruise on my forehead, about two or three inches in diameter, raised up and sticking out about a half an inch, and I was quite proud of such a physical anomaly.

Some time during the ensuing year, I was at our pediatrician's office for a checkup and she rather calmly and simply asked my mother, "Betty, when did Joe fracture his skull?" My mother's reply was equally calm and simple. "Oh, I guess it was when he fell out of the car and hit his head on the curb. He probably had a concussion, too, but we didn't see any point in taking him to the hospital. They wouldn't have done anything different than we did."

Of course she was correct. But Dr. Scott reminded her that brain hemorrhages could be fatal if left untreated. I still have a slight ridge of calcification from the middle of my forehead to the top of my skull. It would still be there even if they HAD taken me to the hospital. The best part about not going to the emergency room was that I got to show off my purple biscuit.

ALMOST FALLING AT NIAGARA FALLS

This is another one of the stories that I don't recall clearly, but have conjured up pictures in my head about it because I heard my parents talk about it a number of times. Our family went to Niagara Falls when I was three or four years old. I believe they might have higher fences now, but in those days there was just a fairly short fence or railing, and not very much separating viewers from a long fall into the churning river below.

At some point, my parents and my brother and sister got a little ahead of me, and when they turned around, they saw me sitting atop that fence, teetering back and forth. Not a bit scared. Totally unaware of how close I was to testing one of Newton's most important laws.

They rushed back to remove me from my perch, got me back on terra firma, and held tightly to my hand for the next few hours.

This is one of those tales that between my mother and me may have gotten "enlarged" a bit over the years. At least it hasn't become, "I toppled backwards off the fence, fell a hundred feet, was caught by the talons of a swooping eagle, was carried thousands of feet into the air, then down again, and gently deposited on top of the car in the parking lot."

Hmm. I like that one even better.

THE ICY PIT

Every few winters in Lexington we'd get some extra cold weather and a couple of really good snows. The winter of 1950 was severe. It snowed and then it thawed a little, then all of the slightly melted snow re-froze and it snowed again. After playing outside for an hour or so, Frank and I were looking for something else to do besides throw snowballs. As we went around the corner of the house to come inside, we noticed that the outside steps down to our basement, which had became laden with ice and snow, looked like a perfect slide.

Down we went. A fast, thrilling slide. "Let's do it again." But try as we might, we couldn't get back up the incredibly slippery slope. We'd get about three feet up and slide back. Neither of us was tall enough to reach the railing up above, and neither of us was strong enough to hold the other one, or push the other up. We tried to open the basement door, but an ice dam had formed in front of it and it wouldn't budge. We hollered for help but our dad was at work and our mom was in the front part of the house. We yelled and yelled to no avail. Now we were starting to get cold.

FINALLY . . . our mother walked into the back of the house and heard us hollering. She came out and by this time we were REALLY cold. She couldn't reach us with her hand, so she went and got a rope and tossed one end of that down. Our hands were so numb by now that neither Frank nor I could hold on to the rope and we weren't able to even tie a knot to loop around our waists.

She pushed a broom handle down and we could reach it but couldn't hold on to it. Now SHE was getting cold. Finally, in a very fine bit of observation she spotted a mop by the back door. Using an even finer piece of imagination she knew what to do with it. It was totally useless as a mop at this moment because the strands of the head of the mop were completely frozen. But as a tool to get two freezing boys up a frozen flight of steps, it was perfect. She pushed it down, holding on to the handle. Frank gave me a little boost and following her instructions I put my stiff fingers as far into the frozen mop as I could and she pulled me out. Then, since Frank was just enough taller to reach it by himself, she pulled HIM out, using the same fingers-in-the-frozen-strands-of-cotton technique.

We were rescued. (Just one of many times we were "rescued" by our mother, I'm sure, but this time it was literal.) We went inside, got a hot bath and some warm clothes on, and expressed great thanks that neither of us had any frostbite.

Later that week, our mother suggested that we write an article for the newspaper describing our harrowing experience. We did, it got printed, and it was entitled, "The Ice Pit." Edgar Allen Poe had nothing on us.

DUMMY RIFLE

Brothers fight with each other. Not all brothers fight. And not all brothers who fight, fight all the time. But every now and then my brother and I would fight. He was bigger and older than I, and he always won if the fight was fair, but one time when I was five I decided I needed a little extra help.

I don't have any idea why I was so mad at him. Even he doesn't remember what it might've been about. But man, I was REALLY mad. Whatever he had said or done to me had made me furious. (It could've been one of the times he referred to my kindergarten girlfriend, Anne Core, as Apple Core. That used to REALLY tick me off.)

He had been given a dummy M-1 rifle as a gift. An adult friend had carved it in his woodworking shop. It didn't have a bored muzzle, so it wouldn't fire anything, but it was a full-sized replica of a rifle. I told Frank that I was going to kill him and ran over and picked up the rifle. He knew it wouldn't shoot a bullet, so for a moment he wasn't scared. But when I turned it around in my hands he could see that I was going to hit him with the butt of the gun. It had suddenly become a formidable weapon.

He knew I was serious. He climbed to the top bunk thinking I was too small to carry the rifle and get up to the top at the same time. I fooled him. I was really mad, and I was going to kill him. A bunk bed was not going to stop me. TEN bunk beds couldn't have stopped me. I was almost onto the top mattress when he spied a pillow in the middle of the bedroom floor. He decided to dive for it. (It was a fairly small bedroom so he thought he could make it.) I think JUMPING for it would've been a better idea, but fear had overcome any logic and he dove. He missed. His mouth and chin hit the hardwood floor, and between the crying and the bleeding I lost all my anger at him. Our parents came running, took care of him, took care of me later, and another fight ended without me winning.

Funny, this is the first time I've ever realized that I never did win any fights with him. Had I known I'd never win one, I'd have probably never started one. Hmmm.

HENRY CLAY SAID . . .

We called one of our grandmothers "Toots," pronounced Toots-as-in foots, not Toots-as-in hoots. She was my father's mother. For most of her adult life, Toots taught second grade at Arlington Elementary School, after having lost a 6-year-old daughter and a husband in the same year, 1929, going back to college to get a Master's Degree, and pulling up on some pretty heavy bootstraps. She reared a great son all by herself.

For her retirement her former students all pitched in and bought her a television set. She was a beloved teacher and much later became even better known throughout Lexington for her less-than-stellar driving techniques. (Other drivers would spot her little yellow car coming down the street and just pull over. We finally had to take her car keys away when she was in her late 80s.)

She was also a very proud woman: proud of her son's accomplishments, proud of her own abilities, and proud of her incredibly brilliant and almost unbelievably personable grandchildren. One fall when I was four years old she got the idea that she could "show me off" at school to her seven year olds. For almost a month she coached me about Henry Clay, Kentucky's renowned Representative and Senator. One of his most famous quotes was, "I'd rather be right than President." She had me memorize that sentence and repeat it over and over to her.

On the day that she took me to school with her, I sat at a desk at the back of the room and was quiet and apprehensive all morning. I kept getting nervous about when she might call on me to act smart. I got more nervous as the day wore on.

After lunch, she got into her history lesson and at one point she said to the class, "Henry Clay was a very wise man, and a very honest and humble man. Joe, what did Henry Clay say that

14

really impressed YOU?' I couldn't answer. I couldn't REMEMBER! I couldn't breathe either. If four year olds can break out in a sweat, I probably did. She repeated, "Joe, what was it that Henry Clay said that became so famous?"

I blurted, "I'd rather be right than wrong." Close. But not NEARLY close enough to keep her from being totally mortified. Apoplectic might be another appropriately descriptive word. I knew the moment the words came out of my mouth that they were wrong, but it was too late and besides I STILL couldn't remember exactly what he'd said. I shrank in my seat, wishing I could actually disappear.

She, without reprimanding me, told the class, "Well, that wasn't quite what he said. His precise words were, 'I'd rather be right than President.'" They already knew the quote and I was most certainly the only fool in the room.

I don't remember any more about the rest of the day. I know Toots repeated the incident to my parents, but they never mentioned it to me. Mostly, I knew that I'd let her down terribly, that she was embarrassed beyond words, and I wished she had never tried to pass me off as somebody special. A small admonition to all proud grandparents.

NO SANTA

I stopped believing in Santa Claus at a pretty early age, even before my older brother. I was six.

I had asked for a football jersey. My parents had given me clues that it was probably a gift that Santa could bring, and my wish had grown into an expectation. What they didn't know, though, was that I didn't know what a jersey was. I thought a jersey was an entire uniform: helmet, shoulder pads, pants, and shirt.

So, on Christmas morning when I got a helmet, shoulder pads, and a jersey, instead of being thrilled at all the "extras," I was almost devastated that the pants weren't there. It didn't take long for my parents to question my lack of gratitude, and it was then that they learned what I didn't know.

"Well, yeah, I got the shirt and the helmet and the shoulder pads, but where're the pants? I asked for a whole JERSEY!"

They explained what a jersey really was, and I finally understood my vocabulary deficiencies. I got over it by lunch and went out that afternoon to play football in my new partial uniform. However, later that afternoon I had time to rethink the whole thing. I asked my parents some important questions. "Hey, if Santa is so smart that he knows everything—I mean, if he knows if you've been good or bad, and all of the other stuff you're doing or not doing—how come he's not smart enough to know that I didn't know what a jersey was? How come he didn't know that I thought a jersey was a helmet and shoulder pads and pants and a shirt? I don't get it." It was a question they couldn't answer satisfactorily. Either by that night, or at least by the next day, I'd figured it out. It was MY PARENTS who didn't know that I didn't know what a jersey was. The jig was up.

It took a few days to get over that shock, but Santa continued to visit our house until all the kids actually moved out.

The burning questions still remain:

    1) When do we tell our kids about Santa?

    2) HOW do we tell our kids about Santa?

    3) Is Santa real?

My answers are:

    1) When they ask.

    2) Very gently.

    3) You bet!

You never know what they know and don't know.

PEABODY SCHOOL

When I was six, my dad was a professor at the University of Kentucky and was, and continued to be throughout the rest of his life, one of the two or three smartest people I've ever met. (And after writing that, I can't actually think of ANYONE whom I would consider smarter than him.) That year, he was selected to be one of a handful of scholars from all over the world who received a fellowship to attend Harvard University for two semesters and be allowed to study anything. ANYTHING. Didn't matter what you'd studied before. If you were a biologist and wanted to go to a class in aeronautical engineering, you could. If you were an authority on Chaucer but thought it might be nice to learn more about DaVinci, no problem. It wouldn't matter what grade you got. They weren't even required to take the tests if they didn't want to. As much or as little as you wanted. It was an amazing offer. He was going to get a chance to go to Harvard for free, actually be paid enough to take his wife and three kids to Cambridge for a year, and just try to soak up as much knowledge as possible in any field(s) of study that struck his fancy. What a deserved honor! What an opportunity! (As it turned out, he did as well at Harvard as he'd done in all of his other academic endeavors. He never made less than an A in any class he ever took. ALL As: Grade school, high school, college, master's work, doctoral work, and now POST-doctoral work, at HARVARD! It wasn't too many years after his year at Harvard that he was appointed President of the University of Kentucky, the youngest major-university president in the country.)

So we went. We bought a little one-wheel trailer from an uncle-in-law, packed it full, and drove to Massachusetts just in time to get three kids registered in Peabody Elementary School. It was an old red brick building, with a big blacktop playground, fenced all around with chain link. The front said it was built in 1889. The back said it was built in 1898. Never got that. Didn't know if the dates were correct and it was built in two stages, or if someone let a concrete engraver's dyslexia slip by unnoticed. As we stood in a block-long line to register, it was my first time to ever get close to ethnicity. I'd been in Lexington, Kentucky for seven years, attended an all-white Christian church, an all-white elementary school, and had all-white friends. I'd never seen a Jew, a Muslim, a Hindu, or a Buddhist. I'd seen black people but they lived on the other side of town. We'd had black ladies clean our house, and black men shovel coal into our basement, but I'd never talked to one. All of a sudden I was IN LINE with them: blacks, Hispanics, Asians. And with a seven-year-old's greatest degree of puzzlement, I looked up at my mother and asked, "Are you sure we're in the right line?" She assured me that we were and that I would even have some of these kids in my class. I was amazed but don't recall giving it another thought.

The first day of school I discovered that the steps to the second floor sagged and creaked. They looked and sounded scary. I was glad my classroom was on the bottom level.

My teacher's name was Miss Pulsford. I thought her to be one of the oldest ladies I had ever met. But it was a really old school, so. . . . Her very first assignment was for each student to come by her desk and get a sheet of paper, take it back to our desks, and then get ready to write all of our letters in cursive. Evidently, these kids had all learned to write in cursive in first grade. I hadn't. I raised my hand to tell her that I didn't know how to do this work, but she must've known what I was going to say because she announced, "For anyone who hasn't learned how to write cursive letters, look at the big letters around the top of the room and copy them and just do your best."

I was about as nervous as a "new kid" could get. I heard her say to write our names at the top of the paper and start by putting a capital "A" and a little "a" on the first line. The paper we'd received was the kind that lots of elementary schools use.

Computers now refer to that view as "Landscape." It was turned sideways with lines and wide spaces beneath an extra wide space at the top of the page. Evidently there were thirteen lines because she explained that we would put letters "A through M" on the left and letters "N through Z" on the right. I was so nervous I didn't quite understand her instructions and put my "A's" in the first SPACE. I sort of thought that extra wide top space was for headings and names and stuff and my "a" in the first space looked right to me. Working very hard to copy those cursive letters as nicely as I could, I didn't notice that when I got to the bottom of the page I was putting the letter "L" in the final space, and my "M" went (in the first SPACE) on the right side of the page.

So, you may have already guessed that when I got to the bottom of the page, I was two spaces short. I had "Y" and "Z" left over and no place to put them. I began to silently cry. A tear hit my desk. Thank God it didn't hit the paper. Miss Pulsford almost immediately saw my distress and came quietly to my side. She leaned over very close to me and whispered, "What's wrong?" I sniffled and took a couple of halting breaths and showed her my page. "My paper doesn't have enough lines." I was really crying now. It must've been VERY important to me that I make a good first impression. She put her hand on my shoulder and very quietly (so no other student could see or hear), and very gently, said that it would be OK for me to just turn the paper over and put the "Y" and "Z" on the back this time. She also showed me that I had put the "A" in the first space instead of on the first line, and that was why I'd run out of space at the bottom.

Her loving calmness helped me get through that first hour in an ancient school with odd-looking classmates. That's the only thing I remember about being in her classroom; except for the POSTURE LESSONS.

POSTURE LESSONS

Walter Shugrue had the worst posture anyone had ever seen. He was only seven but he looked like an 18-year-old horse that been worked too hard, fed too little, and ridden every day by someone who had weighed 350 pounds. He was the poster boy for swayback therapy. The middle of his spine was about 3 inches closer to the direction he was walking than his shoulders or his butt. When he was just standing, it looked like he was always trying to stretch something between his neck and his knees.

Once a month, we would get a visiting adult who had us walk around the room, sometimes with books on our heads, and we would get graded for posture. Most of us got excellent grades for posture. It was the only good grade that Billy Taylor EVER got. But Walter would fail in most of his subjects, and in the posture tests every time. F in September. F in October. F in November. I'll bet when Viet Nam draft time came along, he was *at least* 4-F.

During the first few weeks of school, I became best friends with Walter and Billy. They had been best pals in first grade, and they decided that they liked me and the three of us would hang out together on the playground. What I didn't know was that these were the two toughest boys in the class. I was not a fighter. I was not a tough game player. I was, if anything, more the opposite. But I was labeled by my classmates because of the ones with whom I had become friends.

One day in September (I remember not only was it early in the school year, but the ginkgo leaves were all over the ground where we lived.) Walter walked home from school with me. We were outside playing and got into some kind of argument. He wanted to fight me. I had absolutely no desire to fight him. By this time I had begun to sense a little danger whenever Walter was around. But he insisted that we fight and I didn't think running indoors was going to get me any points at school, so I sort of stood my ground.

Fortunately for me, Walter had a very strange way of fighting. He would charge his opponent and dive to tackle him. After tackling him, he would then quickly roll over and pummel the other boy until mercy was begged for, or blood was drawn, whichever came first. So, Walter charged and me and dived. I nimbly jumped out of the way and he landed in the leaves. Unhurt, he tried the same thing again. Once more, I stepped out of his way at the last moment. This time he landed a little harder. Walter barely made better grades than Billy Taylor, and I would never say that he might be close to the upper 50 percentile of his class. He tried this same tactic three or four more times, failing on each occasion to tackle me. Finally, sore and tired, he gave up. We remained friends. The next day at school, evidently he told Billy and a few others that he and I had had a fight at my house the previous afternoon and that he hadn't been able to beat me up. His listeners misinterpreted that to mean that I had beaten HIM up. Now, not only was I associated with the two little thugs, I was considered to be King of the Little Thugs. I can't remember if it ever became fully apparent that I WASN'T a thug. It's probably a good thing that we moved back to Kentucky and I didn't proceed into the third grade with them.

LANGUAGE ARTS

It was during my first week in Cambridge that I learned something very interesting about skin color and accents. Having lived in the South all of my young life, I assumed that everyone in the United States talked like we did. Oh, I knew that black people and white people had different speech patterns, but I didn't know anything about accents in other parts of the country. The very first day we lived there, I met a kid who lived across the street. He had medium tan skin—and in retrospect was probably of Puerto Rican descent—but I had no thoughts about where he might have hailed from. I could hardly understand his accent OR his choice of words.

We got to talking about this and that, and then he asked me in a decidedly Bostonian accent, "Whadya have fuh dinnuh last night?"

I said, "We had a pot roast, with carrots and potatoes. How about you?"

He replied with a lot of speed "I et a whole tinna tomahtas." I didn't understand one syllable of that sentence, and asked him to repeat it. He did. "I et a whole tinna tomahtas."

I quizzed him, "Are you saying 'ToMAYtoes'?"

"Yeah! Tomahtas."

OK, I'd gotten most of it, but I needed him to repeat it again, much slower. "I ET . . . A WHOLE TIN . . . OF TOMAHTOES!"

I cocked my head a bit, squinted my eyes a little (as if that would give me greater insight) and said, "You ate a whole TIN of tomatoes?"

"YEAH! Exactly!" He was happy I knew what he was talking about, but I DIDN'T know what he was talking about. I had no idea what a "tin" was.

"You ate a whole tin of tomatoes. OK, what the heck is a 'tin'?"

"A can. A tin. It's what you buy tomahtas in at the market." I nodded, realizing that I'd never eaten a canned tomato before, but also realizing that not only did these people talk funny, they had different words for things.

Later that same week, my older brother and I were walking a few blocks to a market to bring back a few grocery items. Coming toward us, on the opposite side of the street, was a tall teenage black boy. About 25 or 30 feet in front of us was another teenage black boy. The boy across the street spotted the boy in front of us, and apparently being a friend shouted in one of those same decidedly Bostonian accents, "Hey, Jahjy. Whatcha doin'?"

The boy in front of us hollered back, "Nuttin!" followed by a response from across the street,

"Same hee-ah."

I looked in every direction to see who else might be doing the shouting in this very, very Boston accent. No one else was in sight. It was pretty obvious by now that it was the two boys closest to us who were making this "verbal nonsense" and I had my first revelation that all African Americans did NOT speak like the Southern African Americans I had known.

Several months after that, we were in a drug store that had a soda fountain with stools to sit on and my mother asked my brother and sister and me if we'd like to have something to drink. We all said yes, knowing that it was a rare occasion to get a treat like that. When the waitress took my order, I asked for a chocolate milkshake. A few minutes later, I got a glass of chocolate milk with a lot of froth on top. It wasn't what I'd ordered. I told my mother that all I'd gotten was chocolate milk and that there wasn't any ice cream in my milkshake. She called the waitress over and mentioned it to her.

The waitress, though not actually indignant, was a little put out. "You ordered a chocolate milkshake and that's what you got."

I timidly interjected, "But there's no ice cream in it. It's just chocolate milk."

"Well, that's what you ORDERED. It's chocolate milk, shaken up. What you meant to order was a frappe."

"A frappe," I asked?

"Yeah, honey. A frappe is milk and ice cream all mixed together."

"OK, I'd like a chocolate frappe, please."

"You got it, sweetheart." She swiftly picked up my glass, poured it into the chrome canister, threw in a few scoops of ice cream, turned on the motor, poured it back into my glass, set it down in front of me, and exclaimed, "Here ya go, little guy. And THAT, my dear, is a FRAPPE!"

Wow, I might as well have been in a foreign country.

MIDNIGHT TIGER

Many years ago, Art Linkletter had a television show called, *Kids Say the Darndest Things*. They sure do.

I have a younger cousin, Mary. My grandmother was her great aunt. Though we called my grandmother "Toots," her real name was Katherine. Some people called her Kate, and Mary called her "Aunt Cake."

Mary was around five years old and was spending the night at her great aunt's house, the first time she had done that. My grandmother's loud snoring woke Mary up in the middle of the night. Having never heard a noise like that before, she crept across the hall into her aunt's room, and with great concern, gently shook her awake. "Aunt Cake, Aunt Cake," Mary whispered loudly, "I think you should wake up. There's a tiger under your bed."

"YA CAN'T NOT WANT WHAT WE AIN'T GOT"

During my father's tenure as a Dean and as the President at the University of Kentucky, he was called on numerous times to give commencement addresses all over the state, and often throughout the country. On one such occasion, he drove into the mountains of Kentucky, and before he arrived at the designated high school, he stopped for dinner at a local diner.

He told the waitress that he would like the Special—the chicken-fried steak, the French fries, and the house salad. "But I don't want the brussels sprouts, please. Just leave them off the plate because I won't eat them."

She replied, "We ain't got no brussel sprouts today."

He said with a smile, "That's just fine, because I don't WANT the brussels sprouts."

To which she retorted, "But sir, ya cain't not want what we ain't got."

Head-scratching time, huh.

REALLY BIG MAN

When my brother and I were ages ten and eight, we traveled with our grandmother to Texas to visit her sister. We thought it only right to bring our parents back some gifts. They always brought us things when THEY went away, so we wanted to buy something for each of them. Adding together the money that our grandmother, our aunt, and our parents had sent with us, we had $10.

We found a set of wooden coasters for our mom. They were natural wood with roosters painted on them. As the years rolled by, those coasters got even more ugly, but she kept them. (As this is written she is 90, and I'm pretty certain she still uses them. The roosters themselves, thankfully, may have chipped and faded completely off the wood.)

Our father was a little more difficult to buy for. We went to a men's clothing store and needed to find something for under $8. Now, remember, this was 1953, so $10 then is worth almost $85 today. It wasn't that we didn't have enough money; it was that we didn't know any of his sizes. We finally decided that a belt would be a nice gift, partially because we didn't know that belts had sizes.

The salesman was very attentive and showed us to his best belt rack. Hickock made the really good ones. When he asked us what size we wanted, we said we didn't have any idea.

"Well, is he a big man?"

Frank said, "Yes sir, he's a big man."

"Well, is he a REALLY big man, or just a big man?"

After a moment of conferring, we both agreed that our dad was "a REALLY big man."

So, the salesman put a size 44 in a box, we took it home, and found out some years later that our dad wore a 34. He could have taken it to almost any men's store and gotten the correct size, but he kept that belt, always hanging ten inches longer in his closet. Turns out that our dad, at 5'11", 165 pounds was, indeed, a REALLY big man. He always was until he died: 91 years old, size 34 belt, really big man.

BOBBY BIG-EARS

We had a neighborhood friend named Bobby Hawkins. I don't actually remember his ears, but I know we called him "Bobby Big-Ears" and made fun of him all the time, so I guess his ears must've been pretty big and they must've stuck out pretty far. We teased him so much that when he would come around he would put his ears under his cap so they couldn't stick out.

The old saying "Boys will be boys" is such a horrible acceptance of the insensitivity attributed to the young males of the species, but we always seem to live up to it's lowest levels of predictability. We just couldn't let Bobby be one of the guys and we learned that if we stole his cap, if we took it off his head and tossed it around playing keep-away so he couldn't get it, it made him furious. When he would finally retrieve it, he would immediately jam it down on his head as fast as he could, ears tucked under the edges.

One summer, a few days before July 4th, some of us had firecrackers. We made a plan for when Bobby Big-Ears would come down to our house that day. The plan was for one of us to steal his cap, we'd toss it around for a while, as another of us lit a firecracker. The plan was to put the lit firecracker in his cap, give him back the cap, and then watch what happened when he jammed it down on his head and the firecracker exploded.

The plan worked perfectly.

It was a BIG explosion!

It wasn't funny.

First, we were scared that we'd blown his head off, and when we discovered that his head was still attached we were scared we'd at the least blown his ears off. He didn't appear to have any outward damage, but I know that his ears must've rung for days. I moved away that year, but I don't remember him coming back to play any more.

I still feel really bad about doing that.

∝∾

GERONIMO!

It's a wonder most of us survive into adulthood: teenage drinking and driving; setting little fires in the garage; manufacturing homemade gunpowder in the basement; climbing to the small branches of a fifty foot tree; playing ball in the street; boxing in the attic; and trying to parachute off a garage. Only two of the these events made their way into this book (see KNOCKOUT IN THE ATTIC). I'll now recount the embarrassingly stupid act that came last on that little list of inane thing I did.

One afternoon when I was home by myself—still living on Cooper Drive, so I had to be younger than 10—I decided that it would be fun to parachute off the edge of the garage. I got an umbrella and a ladder. I climbed to the side of our garage, opened the umbrella, and jumped. I had no fear. (This was long before Mary Poppins had been made into a film, but I was certain that I would just float to the ground.) Thank God it was only an eight-foot drop. There was no floating. As a matter of fact, the umbrella turned inside out, and I hit the ground almost before my feet left the asphalt shingles. I was surprised, but not hurt . . . and undaunted.

"Well, THAT didn't work very well. I need a bigger parachute and a higher place to jump from." (If you are a mother, or a potential mother, this is how boys' minds work. You have now been forewarned!) I went upstairs, got a clean sheet out of the linen closet, unfolded it so I was holding the four corners in one hand, and climbed the ladder again. This time, I carefully moved up to the peak of the garage and inched my way to the front. I couldn't jump off the back because there was a tree in the way.

I looked down at the blacktop driveway, and it looked a LONG way down there. This time I WAS scared. It looked like it was 50 feet. I suppose when I think about it, it was only 19 or 20 feet, but it sure looked like a long way down. On the other hand . . . it would give my sheet plenty of time to open and I would just float down onto the macadam instead of the grass. One more big breath and . . . "GERONIMO!" I jumped.

Another big surprise. The four corners of the sheet remained firmly in my grip and not one cubic foot of air had gotten under the rest of that sheet. I went straight down as if I were holding a lead weight instead of a sheet. I hit the driveway, hurt my feet and ankles, fell and banged my forehead, and lay there for a few seconds. Eventually, after registering the shock and the surprise, and coming to grips with my own stupidity and hence my own mortality, I got up. It really hurt but I didn't cry because there was no one there to comfort me.

Unbeknownst to me, our across-the-street neighbor, Mrs. Livesay had been looking out of her kitchen window and had seen my leap . . . and my fast descent . . . and my hard landing. She later said that for a moment, until she saw me move, she thought I'd killed myself. As soon as my mother got home, Mrs. Livesay called our house to tell my mother what I'd done. As soon as she hung up the phone, my mother ran out back to confront me with my dangerous act. I was playing in the back yard by this time, sheet folded and put back in the linen closet, umbrella properly collapsed and put back in the umbrella stand.

She demanded to know what had happened and then I cried. I told her how much it had hurt to hit the driveway so hard, and how my head had a bump on it, and how much it hurt to hit the driveway so hard, and how my head had a BIG bump on it, and how much it REALLY hurt and on and on . . . and she rubbed it and held me and let me cry. I think I remember her being mad at me, but mostly I realize that crying is pretty much a social thing. I don't think I've ever cried when I've been hurt unless there was someone else around. I've cried from grief when I was alone, but not from physical pain. Oh, I've had tears come to my eyes from physical pain, but never real crying. I wonder why that is? If you know, email me. I'm curious about a lot of things and that's one of them.

When I read those last three sentences to my eldest daughter, she said, "Trying to be Andy Rooney, huh?"

Maybe.

"OH, LAWDY, OH, LAWDY"

Our regular baby-sitter's sister, Addie, was staying with us for the afternoon. Frank and Ann and I were all home, ages 9, 5, and 7 respectively. Frank was playing some songs from "H.M.S. Pinafore" on the piano, but I wanted to go outside and play baseball. He wouldn't come with me, so I started banging on the piano. He asked me to stop but I wouldn't.

He stood up from the piano, threw me on the den floor and started choking me. Addie was sitting on the stairs reading her Bible. As Frank choked me she looked up from her reading and as I began to sputter and turn blue she exclaimed, "Oh, Lawdy, oh, Lawdy, he's hurtin' him," and began to read her Bible again.

As I began to turn grey and lose my ability to struggle, she once again let loose with another, "Oh, Lawdy!" and went back, even more earnestly, to her Bible. I think I heard somewhere that good Christians believe there's always an answer in the Bible. I've just never heard how long it takes to FIND it.

Finally, the youngest person in the house saved my life. Ann yelled, "FRANK! STOP IT! YOU'RE KILLING HIM!" Frank suddenly realized that he WAS killing me, and loosened his grip on my throat.

I don't remember what happened after that. Maybe we went out and played ball.

BITE YOUR (R)EAR OFF

My sister was six and thought she owned every inch of property between the street and our front porch. That included the sidewalk.

One afternoon a boy who lived around the corner rode his bicycle past our house . . . on the sidewalk. Our afternoon babysitter was in the house, Ann was in the front yard alone, and decided that she needed to give that boy some important information.

"Hey, you're supposed to ride your bicycle in the street, ya know!"

By the time she was finished he was already so far down the street he probably didn't hear anything more than, "Hey."

But twenty minutes later when he came riding back UP the sidewalk, she was ready for him. Pedaling up a slight incline, he wasn't riding nearly as fast, and she got out on the sidewalk and stood in his way. He stopped, and she straddled his front tire and fender, putting her hands on the handlebar.

"I told you that you're supposed to ride a bicycle in the STREET, not on a sidewalk. Now, you get off the sidewalk!"

I'm certain this boy couldn't believe what he was hearing, but she was being the consummate bully and even if he'd agreed with her, he was twenty feet from a driveway and couldn't get his bike in the street. Instead of moving his bike, he told her to mind her own business and to let him pass. She didn't budge, and he jerked the handlebar hard enough to force her to let go, and pedaled off as fast as he could go. As he rode away from her she heard him yell, "I'm going to tell my father about you, and he'll come down here and bite your rear off."

When my parents came home a few hours later, they asked the babysitter where Ann was and she didn't know. Neither Frank nor

I had seen her and could offer no clues. Everyone immediately went on a girl hunt, hollering for her in the house and in the back yard. Finally, my mother found her, crouched down in her bedroom closet, behind as many clothes as possible. When she was coaxed out of the closet my mother also discovered that Ann had a dictionary in the back of her underpants, a pretty difficult placement to maintain.

My mother announced to the rest of us that the search could be called off, and we all went into Ann's bedroom to find out what was going on. She told my parents about the boy, about her insistence that he get off the sidewalk, and then confided her fear that the boy's father was going to come down to our house and bite her rear off.

My parents knew the family, so my dad quickly got on the phone to find out more about what was happening. He hung up the phone in a gale of laughter. The boy had, indeed, told his father what had happened, but the neighbor had no intention of following up on his son's threat. Besides, his son hadn't said he would come down and "bite your REAR off." He had said, "My father will come down and bite your EAR off."

Ann had hidden in the closet for almost two hours, with that huge book in her pants. Even if it's a misquote, fear can create pretty drastic reactions.

A BEATIFIC SMILE

Ours was a very musical family. My mother had sung in a professional quartet while she was in college. My dad had earned money while going to college by playing the organ at Kerr Brother's Funeral Home. They were both staples and soloists in the Woodland Christian Church choir. My brother played baritone horn, trombone, tuba, piano, organ, and guitar. My sister played clarinet and piano. I started out on the clarinet, switched to oboe, switched to baritone horn, and also learned to play the trombone and tuba, as well as struggling with the piano for many years.

When I was eight my parents agreed that our family would sing a song at a Sunday night service. Ann and I were to sing the melody on top. Frank would sing alto. Mother could sing tenor. And, Daddy Sang Bass (uh, sorry). We all practiced and learned "Fairest Lord Jesus." It wasn't bad for a group whose median age was 10.

Comes that fateful Sunday night and the five of us are in the choir loft, behind the pulpit, looking out on a small group of faithful worshippers. Time to sing. We stand. I hear the musical introduction, and all of a sudden I can't breathe. Literally. I could not get a breath. Two more bars of introduction to go and unless I get a breath soon I'm not going to be able to even stand up, much less SING. Panic! Real panic! The possibility of breathing became even more remote.

Then . . .

Our family always sat on the "stage left" side of church, in about the fourth row of pews. There was a family we knew pretty well that always sat on the "stage right" side of the church, about three pews back. They were the Bryant family: Vernon, Jo, I can't remember the older brother's name, but the younger son, Terry, was in between Frank and me in age.

Anyway, I don't know if all of them were there that night or not. I only saw *Mrs*. Bryant. In my tortured state of no breath, I looked out toward the right side of the church and there she was, smiling at me. Smiling the biggest, most beautiful smile.

Instantaneously, I could breathe. OHMYGOD! What relief. I took a second big breath and came in perfectly on the first note of the song. We got through it.

Many years later, I wrote her a letter thanking her for being responsible for my singing career, telling her that if she hadn't smiled at me that night, I'd have never been able to sing, I'd have been totally embarrassed and probably wouldn't have ever wanted to sing in public ever again. So, without ever knowing it, she was the one person I could thank for a really great life.

I saw Terry at my dad's memorial service, 56 years after "the smile," and about 25 years after the letter. I asked him if he knew that I'd written his mother a letter "many years ago." Not only did he know about the letter, he told me that she had kept it in her wallet and referred to it fairly often. I guess my letter to her was meaningful. Learning that she appreciated my letter was REALLY important to ME.

A smile she hadn't known was important. A letter I hadn't known was important. Lives touched in important ways. Who knows what we do that we never know about?

TWINKLE, TWINKLE

My four-year-old niece was out in the driveway playing with the two little boys who lived next door. They began to tease her about something and as it got a little more intense, one of the boys, to absolutely prove his superiority, blurted, "You don't even have a twink!" To which she replied, "Oh, yes I do. But mine is up inside so YOU can't SEE IT!"

NEVER MOVE A PILLOW

When I'm asked what kind of church I went to when I was young, I always say, "It was a Christian church: Woodland Christian Church."

Most people reply, "Well, of course. All Catholics and Protestants are Christians. Which denomination?"

I say, "It's actually called Disciples of Christ, but all the churches are named, 'Christian,' like 'First Christian,' and 'Bel Air Christian,' and 'Woodland Christian.'"

They rarely get it, but it's never important. I no longer believe everything that church espouses, anyway. It's a denomination that was established in the early 1800s, in Kentucky and Pennsylvania at the same time by two different men, and is mostly found in the mid-south, but there are around 3600 churches of this denomination all across the country.

At Woodland Christian Church, Sunday school started at 9:30, was over at 10:30, and church started at 11:00. Our family (two adults and three kids) always sat together in church, nearly always in the same spot, in the fourth pew, on the right side as we faced the pulpit, mid-way between the far right isle and the middle right aisle. It wasn't a huge church but it seemed pretty big to me.

One Sunday, when I was seven or eight years old, after we'd gotten to the church around 9:25, I decided for some reason that I would skip Sunday school. I didn't have any malicious or delicious plans—like go to the corner drugstore—I just didn't want to go to Sunday school that day. So, I went outside for a while, I think I walked around the block, and then went, very early, into the sanctuary.

I went to our regular spot and, being alone in the sanctuary, decided that it might be nice to sit a little close to the center. I slid over a few spaces and then noticed a large, black satin pillow a few feet from the center aisle. I pushed it over to the end of the pew, and sat quietly for about 30 minutes.

Then all hell broke loose!

Unknowingly, I had moved MRS. THOMAS' cushion!

I sort of knew that we always sat in about the same place, give or take a few spaces, but I didn't know that people had a sense of *ownership* about where they sat. So, I'd pushed her pillow over a couple of feet.

I was just sitting there, totally minding my own business, looking up at the stained glass windows, wondering how long it would be 'till my parents got there, thinking about how boring Rev. Hayes Farish was, and suddenly I was being attacked. This ancient, loud, overbearing, deeply wrinkled, wide-brim-hatted, bass-voiced woman was standing beside me, yelling. I heard, "MOVED MY PILLOW, in MY seat, how DARE you, just who do you think you are!" It was a real tirade and it scared the hell out of me. (I guess that's what churches are *supposed* to do.) I almost started to cry. I could just see one of those long hatpins going deeply into my shoulder if I didn't move fast enough.

I moved. Fast.

I slid down way farther than I needed to, and began to intently stare at the windows to my right, so I wouldn't have her in my sight. When my parents arrived, I let them climb over me to sit between Mrs. Thomas and me. I didn't say anything to them until we were on our way home—I was still too scared of her to even THINK about discussing a church-related near-death experience.

But after a few minutes, I opened my conversation about what had happened by saying, "I thought people came to church to be better people." My mother asked me what I meant by that, and it all came pouring out—the "moved my pillow, in my seat, how dare you, just who do you think you are!" I almost cried again.

My parents were very supportive, and explained how old people sometimes can be unreasonable, and how we *do* come to church to be better people, but sometimes some people just don't listen, and many most certainly don't practice what they learn.

It was the beginning of my desire to find more meaning in my church experiences. By the time I was twelve, and my grandmother and I had a debate about who does and does not get into heaven, I was ready to go elsewhere. But it took another five years for that to happen. (See LEAVING CHRISTIANITY)

AMERICA'S GAME

I have no idea where my love of baseball came from. My dad was most definitely not an athlete. Once, when he tried to play basketball out back with my brother and me, he could barely shoot the ball. We both truly appreciated his effort to come out and play with us (he was a very busy man, working more hours a day than anyone we knew), but he didn't have any ability or interest in sports. Both my brother and I became avid baseball card collectors before we were even six or seven years old. Though it's an exaggeration, we practically learned every statistic about every player. We were amazingly knowledgeable about all aspects of the game.

Frank tried out for Little League the first year he was eligible and made the team. He played for the Cardinals. Two years later, when I turned eight, I also tried out. I, however, did not make a team and was severely disappointed. Not discouraged, though. I still wanted to play and improve.

They had an organized league called Little Minors, and I suspect *everybody* could make a team in that league. I first played for the Hawks. We didn't have pants and stockings, but we wore burgundy shirts and caps with an H on them. My coach was only a year older than my brother, but we all called him Mr. Sullivan. Ten years later, he and my brother would join the same fraternity, I went to some of their parties, and it was difficult for me call him Pat. I was seventeen, he was twenty, and he was still Mr. Sullivan to me.

THE PERFECT GAME

The next year I *still* didn't make a Little League team. I had to play in the Little Minors again. Though it's not etched in my mind, I suspect I felt a lot of embarrassment that summer, playing for the Spiders. We had green caps with an S on them.

I recently learned that in 1899 the Cleveland Spiders lost so many games that they were kicked out of the Major Leagues, and relegated to the minors. I had no idea when I was nine that I was playing for a team with such negative historical significance.

Our games were six innings long, and early in that season I pitched a four-inning, rain-shortened perfect game. For the first three innings I had not allowed a runner to reach first base and we were leading 8 or 9 to nothing. It began to drizzle. Our coach knew that a game could be called complete if four full innings were played, so he instructed our batters in the top of the fourth to go up to the plate and swing and miss the first three pitches. He wanted to speed up our half of the inning so I could go out and get three quick outs and the game would be over. It began to rain a little, but our batters struck out quickly, I took the mound and struck out all three of their batters, the game was over, and I'd pitched a perfect game. Only four innings, Little Minors, but perfect nonetheless.

LITTLE LEAGUE LEGEND

Late in the summer that I was playing for the Spiders, I got "called up" to Little League. I didn't get to play very much but I was happy to be in the BIGS. The following two seasons proved to be some of the most funs months of my whole life.

The year I turned eleven I got chosen in tryouts by Shorty Reeves, the coach of the Giants. Mr. Reeves was a vice president of a local bank. He and his wife were childless. I would only see him on the baseball diamond two or three times a week, but he turned out to be a major influence in my life. He was a great Little League coach. He knew baseball and he knew how to teach kids how to *play* baseball. I made the All-Star team both years, played third base, batted over .300, and in my last season went 11-0 as a pitcher (including a no-hitter). Our catcher (who later became a third team all-SEC basketball player for the University of Georgia) could throw the ball back to me harder than I could throw it to him, but I had great control, learned how to throw a tiny little curve without hurting my arm, and I was tough to hit.

It's funny what kind of memories we have and how not all of them have anything to do with monumental events. I remember making a running, diving, facing-the-wrong-direction catch of a little bloop fly ball, hit by a friend of mine in a practice game. I remember, on my birthday, getting hit in the jaw by a throw as I was sliding into third base. I cried. I was embarrassed to cry, but I cried anyway. It really hurt. (I have a theory now that we only cry to get attention. If we're alone we don't cry, at least we don't cry when it's *physical* pain that might cause it. We might involuntarily have tears, and might cry when we're alone from grief, but if it's just physical pain and we're alone, we seem to bear it. I know this is repetition of something I wrote in my JUMPING OFF THE GARAGE story, but for some reason I think it's important.) I remember the game that was broadcast on a local radio station and I had asked my grandfather to listen in. I was pitching that day. The biggest boy in the league came to bat and I made a poor pitch to him, which he blasted over the center field fence. We still won the game, but all I could think about was that my grandfather had listened to that game and had heard C. J. Miller (See, I even remember his name!) hit a home run off me.

A GAME OF STATS

As the children of the Dean of the College of Education (the job my dad had before he because President of the University of Kentucky, UK to us) it was only right that we kids should attend the elementary, junior, and high school on the UK campus. The elementary school was in the North wing, the junior and high schools were in the South wing, and the college was in between. My dad's office was right inside the middle front door.

One day when we were in fifth and third grades respectively (for what reason I cannot recall), my brother and I had to do something on the high school side. As we were walking back to our classrooms we had to walk down the hallway of the college students. Moments after we passed an open door, we heard Dr. Sorenson call our names, "Frank! Joe! Would you boys come in here for just a minute?" We turned around and went to the door of his classroom, filled with 20 or 30 college students. "Frank, what did Ted Williams bat last year?"

Frank replied, ".407, but it wasn't a whole season."

"Joe, what was Warren Spahn's record last year?"

I replied, "23 and 7."

"Thanks, boys. You can go on back to your classes now." And we left.

That night at dinner we told our dad the odd thing that had happened that day with Dr. Sorenson. None of us could figure it out. So the next day, our dad called Dr. Sorenson into his office. "Herb, my boys tell me that you stopped them the other day in the hall and had them come into your classroom to answer some random baseball questions. Is that true?"

Dr. Sorenson had a perfect reason. "Yes, it's absolutely like they told you. You see, I'm teaching this elementary education class and I had just gotten to a part of my lesson plan where I was trying to explain to my students that kids could learn nearly *anything* if they were truly interested in the subject matter. Just then Frank and Joe walked by and I knew how much they knew about baseball, so I quickly told my class to pay close attention to what was about to happen. I ran to the door and called the boys back in. Then I asked them each to give me a statistic that would be almost impossible for most baseball fans to know, they gave what I figured were the right answers, and as soon as they left my class expressed astonishment. It was a perfect example of what I was trying to teach."

Our dad agreed, said, "Good job, Herb," and explained it all to Frank and me that night. No big deal to us.

UNITED STATES SENATOR JIM BUNNING

One of the games I won when I was twelve was a no-hitter. It wasn't a perfect game—I think I either walked a batter or someone made an error, but it was a complete game, no-hit shutout and it was a pretty big deal.

Fifty years later, at a cocktail party, my mother was introduced to one of the Senators from Kentucky, Jim Bunning. Jim Bunning was one of the greatest pitchers of all time, one of only seven major leaguers to win over 100 games in each league. He pitched no-hitters in each league, including one against the Mets in 1964 that was a *perfect game*. He is a Hall of Famer, and was one of my baseball card heroes. During their brief conversation my mother bragged to him, "My son pitched a no-hitter."

He was curious. "Really? When did he do that?"

My mother replied proudly, "When he was in Little League." (This seems funny in writing it, but she wasn't trying to be funny. She was proud of her son's accomplishments and thought it was a way to have an interesting bit of conversation with a famous ball player.)

His response was a verbal sneer. "Who gives a shit!" And he walked off.

When she told me that story her disappointment was evident. Her disdain was greater.

BALLS ARE TO BE PLAYED WITH

The University of Kentucky had two of the greatest coaches to ever coach college athletics—at the same time! Paul "Bear" Bryant was the football coach for eight years, between Maryland and Texas A&M, and Adolph "The Baron" Rupp held court there for forty-two years, between zero and 879 wins. Coach Bryant gave my brother and me a practice football and we were allowed to play with it. Coach Rupp gave my brother and me a basketball, autographed by what was then called "The Fabulous Five," and unfortunately, we played with it. Our parents never dreamed that we would take it outside and use it on the blacktop. It was *autographed*, by Ralph Beard, Alex Groza, Wah Wah Jones, Kenny Rollins, and Cliff Barker. Those five guys had won the Olympics. But we didn't know. We were only, like, eight and ten years old. It wasn't worth anything extra to us. We just knew it was a leather ball and it was cool to play with a leather ball. We wore the signatures totally off.

There's no way to know what that ball might be worth today had it remained in perfect condition. All I know is that it would be worth way more than a brand new leather ball every year for the rest of our lives.

FIFTH GRADE UPGRADE

One of the people I need to thank for my singing career is my fifth grade teacher, Mrs. Barrett. She wouldn't know this though.

Our elementary school had a music teacher named Ruth Osborne. Now, she's a teacher I *really* had to thank, (and I did, years ago) but Mrs. Barrett was the one who told Mrs. Osborne that I could sing, so. . . .

I began going to this school when I entered the third grade, and Mrs. Osborne would come to our classroom once a week to teach singing. In third and fourth grades Mrs. Osborne had a group of four boys who were the best and who got to sing as a quartet and do special songs. I didn't know that I could sing as well as them, so I never asked to "audition."

In between Mrs. Osborne's weekly visits Mrs. Barrett would have us tap out songs with our pencil erasers as we spoke the words in rhythm. Evidently, I could do this very well. By the third or fourth week of class in the fifth grade, she told Mrs. Osborne that "Joe Dickey knows all of the songs and he has an especially good sense of rhythm. And he seems to have a very pretty voice. I think you should listen to him."

The very next week, the little group of four expanded to five, and Mrs. Osborne always included me in those kinds of groups from then on. By the time I was fourteen or fifteen, I was singing most of the solos, but it was Mrs. Barrett, several years earlier, who got it all started.

Today, there's hardly any music in our schools. Just like so many other things these days, our youth have to find out about so many things . . . all by themselves.

MAXWELL PLACE

I had a charmed childhood. I had two great parents (still have one of them), a terrific brother, and a terrific sister. When I was ten, my father became the President of the University of Kentucky. At only 36, this was an appointment that made big headlines and meant big changes for our family. We moved to the UK campus and took up residence in the president's home, Maxwell Place.

It was a large, brick house built in 1872, with twelve main rooms and thirty-three total rooms, counting the basement, the attic, the halls and bathrooms. It had small verandas and trellises, which served as occasional exits and entrances to my bedroom (see TRELLISES ARE MEANT TO BE CLIMBED ON), it had circular driveways in the front and the back, there was a three-car garage with a residence above for our gardener and cook, we had two other permanent employees, as well, and all-in-all it was a great place to live for the seven years of my dad's presidency.

I had many privileges that most teenagers don't have. Our family didn't have very much income, but we had lots of privileges. We were awarded a country club membership, but drove two Plymouth station wagons. We had a huge garden (until they built a new physics building and took away the garden and about half of our yard). We had a great place to play basketball out back. We had two refrigerators and two freezers and a butler's pantry and an extra large cook-top on the back porch. We needed all of that extra kitchen equipment because there were lots of functions with lots of people in the house.

Many afternoons I would come home from school and find the house full of people, attending a reception at our house. One day I went upstairs to find a lady looking in one of the drawers of my dresser. She was embarrassed to be caught going through my things. I was just happy she wasn't looking under my mattress.

JAMES GARTH

My mother was hosting a small tea to recognize and entertain a group of students and dignitaries from Uganda. There were about forty of them. As they entered the house, all dressed in their colorful native garb, she shook hands with each of them, introducing herself and asking their names. Each one spoke his or her name with a heavy accent, and without exception every name was distinctly different than what we are accustomed to hearing in this country.

The final man to come in shook her hand and said, "Hello, my name is James Garth."

"Oh," my mother replied, "Mr. Garth, you speak such perfect English and your name is not difficult to pronounce. I'm delighted to meet you."

He answered her, "Yes, ma'am. I'm from Mobile, Alabama. I'm the tour guide."

"But . . . I don't understand. You're dressed just like they are," she remarked.

"Yes, ma'am. I discovered a few weeks ago that if I dressed like the Ugandans, I could go any place they went, especially into restaurants. If I dressed like a man from Mobile, I was kept out. It didn't take but a few seconds to figure out which I liked better."

This was the late 50s. Segregation in the South was still rampant. It was not present in our house that day, or ever.

THE WHITE K'S

Another time, during one of the big teas downstairs, I was in my room studying and a lady walked in. I suppose she thought it was OK to just wander all over the house. UK's colors are blue and white, and I had two blue bedspreads and three blue cornices, all with large white K's on them. This lady stared at them for a while and asked, "What are the K's for?"

Without a pause, I replied, "K is my middle initial."

"Oh," she said, and left.

THE RIOT

We had a full-scale mob scene once at Maxwell Place. It was scary. We referred to it as a riot but nothing got destroyed so I guess it was just a near riot. But it definitely was a mob and with that also comes a mob mentality. That was the scary part.

The UK football team had won, beating Tennessee, the archrival. Governor Chandler, becoming part of all the celebrating, went down on the field and declared the next Monday to be a school holiday. Because of accrediting regulations that wasn't really possible, so my dad had to countermand the governor's declaration, telling the students that there would be classes as usual on Monday.

Now, part of what goes on at football games has nothing to do with the field of play. There is plenty of "playing" in the stands, most of it having to do with sipping, imbibing, guzzling, and just plain chugalugging. Forty or fifty of those in attendance who had done a good job of doing just that, decided they should protest the President's decision and marched across campus to our house. As soon as the news was broadcast on local radio stations that there was a mob in front of the university president's home, every young person in central Kentucky wanted to descend on Maxwell Place to see what was going on.

By nightfall there were at least several hundred students out front (it seemed like thousands). They built a bonfire whose flames eventually got over twenty feet high. (I know it was at least that high because we got scared and went up to the third floor of the house and peeked out the front window and the flames were as high as the window.) Then at one point they began to shout, "Let's go in! Let's go in!" There wasn't anything to prevent them from breaking down our front door had they decided to carry out that chant.

Then the police arrived *and* it began to rain. The rain dampened both the fire and the spirit of the crowd. The threat of arrest sent them on their way. Though the whole thing had been extremely frightening to our family, and the event made the newspapers the next day, there was no residual damage, other than the big circle of charred ground out front.

DOCTOR DICKEY

One night our family was eating dinner when the phone rang. Our maid answered it.

"Dr. Dickey's residence . . . yes . . . yes . . . Oh, no, no. He's the kind of doctor can't do you no good!"

For the remainder of his life, we laughingly reminded our dad of that particular opinion of him.

PRESIDENT LINCOLN

In our side yard we had a lovely fishpond. It was big enough that I learned to ice skate on it. Not big enough to do anything fancy, but big enough to go in small circles. We never thought about it being a public nuisance until one day my dad looked out the window and saw five or six little boys and girls trying to swim in the pond. He quickly went down to "run them off."

He succeeded in getting them out of the water and told them to go away. As they were leaving one little girl asked, "Are you the president?"

My dad replied, "Yes."

She followed with, "Is your name Lincoln?"

My dad answered, "No." They ran off, and even though he knew he was the youngest university president in the country, he was surprised by how old he felt.

KNOCKOUT IN THE ATTIC

Maxwell Place had 12 little rooms in the attic. I guess they weren't *that* little. One of them, Frank and I turned into a boxing ring. It wasn't a full-sized ring, but it was big enough for two boys to box in and pretend it was bigger.

While we were constructing it, with thin wooden posts on stands and strands of copper wire, Frank cut his wrist on the wire and we thought we were going to have to go to the hospital to stop the bleeding. (That should have been a sign to us to not proceed with this athletic project, but we were not exactly observant of "signs" in those days.)

We didn't go up there to box very often, and we never went up there to "settle" anything, or to actually try to beat each other up. It was just fun to box. Frank was always a little bigger and more athletic—I suppose being two years older helped him in that regard—so, I rarely beat him in any game in any sport and can't remember ever beating him in the boxing ring.

One time, when we were probably twelve and fourteen (and it may actually have been the *last* time we ever boxed), he caught me on the chin with an extra hard punch and knocked me out cold. I was lying there on the floor, completely motionless. He shook me and I still didn't move. He thought he'd killed me. He said later he didn't have any idea what to do, but he was scared! Before panic could completely set in, my eyes fluttered open and he knew that I was going to survive.

What relief for him. I didn't care one way or the other. I didn't even know where I was for about ten minutes.

Yeah, I'm pretty sure that was when we both decided to hang the gloves up and get our boxing kicks by watching Cassius Clay (later to become Mohammed Ali) every Saturday evening, on *Tomorrow's Champions*.

COPPERHEAD

The University of Kentucky owned a rustic property in the Eastern Kentucky Mountains, called Camp Buckhead. A number of sleeping cabins and a dining hall, maintained so engineering students could learn surveying skills in rough terrain. Our family drove up there for a few days when I was around twelve.

We shared the camp with a group of college students (most of them young men), the Dean of the College of Engineering and his family, our family of five, and, of course, the people who cooked and cleaned. Since my dad was the President of the University, we always got deferential treatment. (I sort of knew it in those days, but wasn't always aware of it.)

One morning, I was asked if I'd like to go out on a surveying expedition with the college boys. Of course I did. I was told it would be a little tough keeping up with them, climbing the mountainsides and all, but I thought it would be fun to hang out with big guys. As we were about to depart, Mrs. Shaver, the Dean's wife, called out to me. "Joe! Bring back a rattlesnake so your mom can make some earrings out of the rattles."

My mother shushed her. "Franny! Don't tell him that! He's just liable to *do it!*"

I heard her, but had no real interest in meeting up with a rattlesnake. However, as we pulled out of the camp, one of the students warned us all to be very careful, that there were *plenty* of poisonous snakes in these mountains.

So we drove, maybe five or six of us, for about ten or fifteen minutes, to the foot of a really steep hill that was part of a larger mountain. They were going to climb it and survey it, and I was going to try to just climb it. As we started up, grabbing saplings and bushes to pull ourselves up the incline, another student warned me again, slightly differently. "Joe, be really careful about putting your hand on top of a rock if you can't see what's above you. A lot of snakes will sun themselves on these flat rocks and if you startle them, they'll strike." It was enough of a warning to frighten me a little, at least enough to make me more cautious when I was about to pull myself up on a big rock.

After a pretty tough climb, we were about three fourths of the way up the hill and I was ready for a rest. I saw a large, flat rock about ten feet away and climbed toward it. Forgetting for a moment about the earlier admonition, I pulled myself up on one end of a long piece of limestone. On the other end, curled up, was a *big snake*. I very quickly and very quietly retreated from the rock and whispered as loudly as I could, "There's a snake on this rock." The student nearest to me came quickly with a machete.

As he moved onto the rock, the vibrations alerted the snake and it began to move. I suspect that we must've jumped or hollered or something, because the snake began to move away faster. My rescuer swung his machete as hard as he could but partially missed and only cut the snake's tail off. It darted off the rock into the bushes. We all began to look for two things at once—the snake and the rattles. In a few minutes another student spotted the injured snake and killed it. We started to continue the search for its rattles when another surveyor identified the snake as a copperhead, not a rattler.

We picked up the snake (I think I told them I wanted it), and I kept it beside me all the way back to camp. As we disembarked from the back of the truck, and Mrs. Shaver and my mother met us, I held up what was left of a four-foot copperhead, hollering to my mom, "I couldn't find a rattlesnake. A copperhead was the best I could do."

They both came very close to fainting.

ALL MY MARBLES

As a young teenager I asked for—and my parents bought me—a big, heavy umbrella tent. That's the only kind they had in those days. My cousin, Steve, and I used it several times when we went camping on the island in Strodes Creek. And I once loaned it and set it up for a night and got a huge payoff for my efforts.

My mother was a member of the Junior League. One of this chapter's service projects was to sponsor a weeklong day camp for kids with Cerebral Palsy. At the end of the week, the boys and girls were to spend the night, in tents, at the Lexington Reservoir. So, my mother asked me if we could take my tent out there on Friday and if I'd be willing to set it up for six kids to sleep in. I, of course, agreed. (I was the only one who used the tent, but I hadn't paid for it. I figured the tent belonged to my parents.)

So, we went out there, I set up the tent, and we had to hang around for a while. Many of these kids were in wheelchairs, others were barely able to walk, most had great difficulty in being understood when they talked. But I knew a little about CP and understood that their mental capacities were not to be compared with their physical incapacities. For a fourteen year old, I had a lot of compassion for these slightly younger kids.

I noticed that one of the boys, maybe eight or nine years old, carried a wooden box with him everywhere he went. It was a beautiful, inlaid box, with a sliding lid, and it rattled noisily each time he moved it. I asked one of the camp counselors about it and she told me, "I think you should ask him about it. If you engage him in a conversation and he trusts you, he'll tell you about the box."

So I went over to him and we began to talk. A few minutes later we sat on a log, looking out at the water, and I finally asked him, "What do you have in the box?" He cocked his head, and with a huge twinkle in his eye, slid the top back so I could see inside. It was loaded with marbles.

In words that were tremendously impeded by his lack of muscle control, he told me, slowly, one word at a time, "This . . . is so . . . nobody . . . can say . . . I haven't got . . . all my marbles." As soon as the sentence was finished, he looked at me to get my reaction. I laughed and I've never forgotten his little joke on the world.

Many years later, when I was one of the hosts for the Las Vegas portion of the United Cerebral Palsy Telethon, my memories of his courage and his sense of humor were primary factors in keeping me going for the entire twenty-four hours of fundraising.

LYING TO THE MINISTER

In our church, Disciples of Christ, most of the kids got baptized when they were in their early teens. It was thought that we could finally comprehend what it really meant to take Jesus as our Savior if we were in double digits. Most of the baptisms were at Easter, and to get baptized you had to attend six classes with the minister, one a week for six weeks. My brother and I decided that we should do this together.

So, once a week, our mother would drive us to the church on Wednesday afternoons. After four weeks, Frank and I didn't want to go again. (The minister, Hayes Farish, was old and *really* boring. We weren't all that concerned about salvation. Those classes were just the pits.) So, that afternoon, after my mother dropped us off at the side door of the church, we went into the room where the classes were held and told our minister that we weren't going to be able to stay that day, that we had to visit our sick grandfather. Then we left the church and walked two blocks to the corner drug store. We hung out for an hour, then walked back to the church to be picked up by our mother.

The next day, Dr. Farish called our home to ask my mother if her father was feeling any better. Not understanding the question, my mother listened to him as he told her that we hadn't been able to stay at our class the previous day because we'd told him we had to visit our sick grandfather.

One of my mother's favorite admonitions was, "The truth will out." Frank and I had no idea that it could out in less than twenty-four hours! Or that it would out with such force. We were in *huge* trouble. Not only had we lied, we had lied to our minister! And we had lied during the six weeks of class leading up to our baptism, which would ensure our immortality.

This was a real problem. It was not only going to take contrition and remorse and begging for forgiveness on our part, it was going to take compassion and understanding from a man who shook his fist and pointed fingers at us every Sunday from the pulpit.

This was a real problem. Frank and I were scared to death.

Our parents made an appointment for us with Dr. Farish. They drove us over to the church the next Monday afternoon. We had to go into his office with them, and talk about this lying stuff. I don't remember if I cried or not, but it scares me now just to think about that hour.

He forgave us. We promised we wouldn't lie again. We said that we understood the magnitude of the promise. We got baptized the next month. I'm still not certain about my immortality..

SURF'S UP

During our baptismal ceremony that year there were nine children to be baptized. I don't know how the order was determined, but Frank was second and I was next to last. Ours was a church that believed in full immersion, that is, we had a big bathtub called a baptismal font, it got filled with warm water, we wore seersucker slacks and short sleeved white shirts, we were to walk down a few steps into the water where the minister was standing. We sat on a little stool, we put a handkerchief over our nose and mouth and he put his hand on top of it. Then he recited a short piece that ended with, "I now baptize you in the name of the Father, and the Son, and the Holy Ghost." Then he'd dip us backwards, under the water, pull us back up, and that was it. We were saved.

After baptizing six kids Dr. Farish was tired and evidently got a bit confused. As I was standing just on the other side of the top of the steps leading down to the baptismal font, watching the boy in front of me get baptized, I experienced a bit of terror through his terror. The boy sat on the stool, put his handkerchief over his mouth, Dr. Farish covered the boys face with his hand, dipped the boy under the water and only then proceeded to recite the declaration that ended with "I now baptize you in the name of the Father, and the Son, and the Holy Ghost." By the time he finished, the boy was struggling and writhing about and came up sputtering and gasping for air.

As a witness to that mistake, and as the next one to go "in," I almost couldn't make myself walk down those steps. Did I *really* need saving, after all? I'd only lived eleven years. How bad could I have been already? Just as I was about to talk myself out of salvation, Dr. Farish motioned for me to come on down. I was not about to disobey him now.

I crept into the water and sat. All went well. I walked out and got dried off, and didn't feel any different than an hour before. Somehow I thought being saved would give me a sense of confidence, or maybe just a feeling of well-being. The only thing I know about that day was that a kid nearly got drowned thirty seconds before my turn. And I think the only thing that saved him was good lungs

LEAVING CHRISTIANITY

The year I was 12, the year after I got baptized, I had a terrible disadvantage in Sunday School. My grandmother, Toots, was my teacher. I not only had to be extra good and extra smart, I was also afraid to ask any questions. At some point, though, she finally made a few statements that demanded more explanation, and I confronted her in the classroom. That Sunday morning we got into a discussion about heaven, and more importantly, who would get in and who wouldn't. It was her contention that "only Christians can get into heaven." Here was an intelligent woman with a Master's degree in education. She was the mother of the President of the University of Kentucky. But I couldn't let her get away with such a specious argument.

"So, no one except those who have been baptized in a Christian church will get into heaven?"

"That's right. It's in the New Testament. Jesus said it."

"So . . . what about all the Buddhists, and Muslims, and Hindi, and Confucians and Jews? If one of them is living a really, really good life, doing good deeds all the time, they're not going to get into Heaven?"

She paused for just a moment but answered, "If they've heard of Jesus and reject Him, they won't go to Heaven."

"OK, then what about Africans, in the middle of the jungle, who've never heard about Jesus? Will THEY be able to get into Heaven?"

She waffled a bit. "If they've never heard of Jesus, then they could get into Heaven. But if they've heard about Jesus from one of our missionaries, then they won't get in."

I was flabbergasted. "You really MEAN that? You really believe that if I'm a Buddhist, and I live one of the most exemplary lives that anyone on the planet ever lived, or I'm a devout Hindu, say

I'm Mahatma Gandhi, I won't get into heaven?"

She shook her head. "That's not what it says in the Bible."

"Well," I responded vehemently, "I think the Bible is WRONG!"

She was shocked. "Why, Joe! You can't say that!"

"Yes! I CAN say that! And I also say that I can't believe that you BELIEVE that! Not one Buddhist? Not one Hindu? Not one Jew? Not one Native American? Wow! Any one of them could live a perfect life and NOT get into heaven? Unbelievable. Yeah, that's exactly what this is. NOT believable. There's nothing about this part of Christianity that I can understand or agree with."

There was more argument, but it had no conclusion and no winner. She knew she was right and I knew she was wrong.

After that, I was pretty certain that there was stuff in the Bible that just didn't stack up to anything that seemed rational (I was already a confirmed Evolutionist), and I was totally certain that Christianity was not going to be the only religion for me.

I may have had no idea where heaven was (I later read in Luke that the Kingdom of Heaven was within me), but I was pretty darned sure that the gates were open to more than just Christians, and only BAPTIZED Christians, to boot. I stopped going to Sunday School after that. For a very, very long time I declared myself to be a full-blooded agnostic and a borderline atheist. It took a lot of study to find a peace-filled spiritual path.

THE BIG POOL TABLE

I was still twelve. I didn't believe in Santa, but Santa still brought us presents. I liked that.

I had a friend, Lyle Walker, who owned a tiny little tabletop pool table. It was probably 14" wide and 28" long and had little cues, and balls that were considerably smaller in diameter than golf balls. Every time I'd go to Lyle's house we'd play on that little pool table. We always had fun and I wanted one. I asked Santa for a little pool table for Christmas.

It was always my habit to awaken very early on Christmas morning, quietly go downstairs and check it all out. I would then climb back in bed and be unable to sleep. I'd stay awake until it was OK for us to go downstairs and "see" what Santa had brought. At our house Santa didn't wrap his gifts—they were laid by the fireplace, near our filled stockings.

This particular Christmas I was expecting to get a little pool table, like Lyle's. I awoke about 4:30 and crept downstairs and into the library where our fireplace was. I turned on a lamp and could hardly believe what I saw. It was a pool table, but it had LEGS, and it was WAY bigger than what I'd asked for. Don't get me wrong, it was nowhere near a full-sized pool table, but it was probably two feet wide and four feet long, on legs, with cues and balls that were much bigger than anything I'd imagined I could have. I was happy. I was excited!

I ran back up the stairs as quickly as I could, taking two steps at a time. I rushed into Frank's and my bedroom and shook him awake. "Frank, Frank! You've gotta come down and see what Santa brought! Wake up! You've gotta see this!"

He was a heavy sleeper and I saw his eyes just barely open. "What!" He didn't want to know. He didn't want to wake up.

"FRANK! He brought a BIG pool table. It's not a little one. It has

LEGS! You've gotta get up and come see it."

He rolled over, pulled the covers up higher, and mumbled, "Yeah, I know. I helped 'em pick it out."

"WHAT? You helped them PICK IT OUT?"

"Yeah. We bought it last week. I'm goin' back to sleep."

I remember having a lot of mixed emotions right then. There is no logical reason for it, but I felt betrayed. A few minutes later I realized that I felt like a little kid who was now sharing a room with a big kid. No, not just a bigger kid, he was now more like an adult. His participation in selecting and purchasing a gift from Santa had placed him in the "adult" category.

Later that year, Frank requested of my parents that he have his own bedroom, that he and I no longer share a bedroom, something we'd done all my life. His was a reasonable request. We had two more bedrooms in the house that weren't being occupied and we only needed one guest bedroom. But it hurt my feelings. I felt really rejected—by my own brother!

A pool table that had been one of my best Christmas gifts ever turned out to be the focal point of other emotions that had nothing to do with sports or entertainment. I loved the pool table. I learned to deal with the other stuff.

"HEY!"

I had a two-year-old nephew who was extremely bright and precocious. He had gotten in the habit of crying every night when his parents put him to bed. They had always catered to his demands, and finally grew weary of it. Using some information they'd just gotten from *Parents* magazine, they decided to just let him "cry it out." So, that night they laid him in his crib, went into the living room, and sure enough, before they could even sit down, he started wailing. Though it proved difficult for them, they heeded the instructions in the magazine and let him cry. About ten minutes later, he stopped.

"Wow! Great! That worked!" They were both elated.

A moment later, however, he began again. They repeated their restraint. It was noisy and they were feeling guilty, but they stuck it out.

About ten minutes later, he stopped again.

"Finally. He wore himself out. Poor little guy. This was good."

A moment later it all started again! They were certain that this couldn't last much longer and they remained true to their plan.

This time, after only crying for about another minute or so, he stopped, waited about five seconds, and then hollered as loud as he could, "HEY! Doesn't anybody out there HEAR ME?"

PRINCE HOTEL BEATING

In the summer of 1959, our family drove to Monterrey, Mexico, so our father could evaluate an extension program that the University of Kentucky had initiated at the university in Monterrey. During that two-week jaunt we spent two nights in Mexico City, which turned out to be the opposite of Philadelphia, The City of Brotherly Love.

We had reservations in Mexico City at the Prince Hotel, a six-story, somewhat upscale, downtown hotel. They didn't have a room big enough for the five of us, so they put us in the two penthouses. One bedroom, living room, kitchen and bath on the east side of the swimming pool, and one bedroom, living room, kitchen and bath on the west side. Frank and I got the west side, which also included a giant stone fireplace. Nice digs.

The first night, we turned out the light, and immediately heard a squadron of B-52s buzzing around us: loud mosquitoes, big mosquitoes, hungry mosquitoes. They had exited their home in the chimney of the fireplace. Most of the time when a mosquito bites me, I get a welt that's at least the size of a dime and sometimes the size of a quarter. By the time we got the light back on, I had already been bitten twice. We didn't quite know what to do about this, but Frank had a plan. "We turn the lights back out, and if you feel one on your back or shoulders, tell me, I turn on the light and whack it." Seemed reasonable to me. I was twelve years old and trusted my fourteen-year-old brother.

A few minutes later I reported, "There's one on my back NOW!"

Frank flipped on the light and WHACK, he slapped my shoulder. "Darn! I missed."

About thirty seconds later I whispered loudly, "There's another on my back."

He flipped the switch, and pounded me on the back. "I think I missed that one, too."

After four enormous whacks on my shoulders and back, I suddenly realized that I was giving him permission to beat me up. I hollered at him, "Hey! You are beating the crap out of me and enjoying every minute of it! I hate you!" I pulled the covers up to my chin and hoped the mosquitoes wouldn't be able to find my face.

The next morning I had welts from mosquitoes and sore shoulders and back from getting whacked. I told my parents how Frank had laughed at his "dirty trick," they scolded him for it, and I still felt hurt both physically and emotionally.

The next day he got what is commonly called Montezuma's revenge, but instead of being just a stomach disorder, it affected all of Frank's body. He had such pain in his legs that he was afraid he had contracted polio. He lay in the back of the station wagon, moaning, and was in real agony.

I was happy he was miserable. I hoped he would die. And when he finally began to recover a few days later I was sorry he was getting better.

Years later I still felt stupid for being tricked so easily in Mexico City, but only felt slightly guilty about wanting him to die. I've quizzed a number of friends who have siblings. A lot of them, at one time or another, wished bad things on each other. Makes me feel a little more normal. No guilt remains. We talk on the phone a couple of times a week and end nearly every conversation with, "I love you." "Me, too."

"HUP, HUP, HUP"

My dad taught the kids in our family to drive. He was a logical, intelligent man and he taught us well. However, he did something very odd that amused the entire family. (I had heard him do it when he had taught my older brother to drive, so it wasn't unexpected when he did it with me.) Whenever the student driver would do something that alarmed our dad, he would quickly utter, "Hup, hup, hup." I don't believe it was ever just one or even two "hups," and it was never four. As I recall it was always three. "Hup, hup, hup." It meant, "Watch out!" But we never knew what to watch out for. Were we in the wrong lane? Were we too close to the curb? Were we too far from the curb? Were we going too fast? Were we about to crash?

"Hup, hup, hup," became a byword in our family for, "Careful, you're about to do something." Or sometimes it meant, "Too late, now you've done it." In the car, during a driving lesson, under the tutelage of our father, it was never funny. Thereafter, however, it was *always* funny..

THE BIRDS AND THE BEES

(I related this story during the eulogy for my father's funeral.)

Every now and then my father would take either Frank or Ann or me on one of his commencement address trips. A few hours of riding in the car, a dinner out, sit through a really boring commencement ceremony, a long drive home late at night. It was a good opportunity to spend time together.

One such trip occurred when I was around thirteen. As we headed out of town, no more than ten minutes into our trip, my dad asked me, "Do you know everything about the birds and the bees?"

In an instant I realized that he and I were supposed to have a father/son talk about sex. I paused for a moment and answered, "Yeah, I guess so."

He blurted, "GOOD!"

That was it.

THE LAST SPANKING

Even when Frank and I got into a fight it was never violent. It was mostly just a shoving match with an occasional headlock, and I always caved in, in the end. Our last "fight" occurred when we were both too old to do that any more. I suppose we were 14 and 16. We were upstairs in my bedroom, making a lot of noise—sounding from downstairs like a fight—and our mother stormed up and demanded we stop immediately. We had interrupted something she was doing and she was pissed that she had to come upstairs to break up a fight.

As she was about to leave, she rebuked us with, "You both ought to be spanked," and she gave me a little swat on my behind. Frank, across the room, made a face at me and I laughed. Unfortunately—*very* unfortunately—my mother thought I was laughing at HER. Without a moment's hesitation she walked over to my closet, got out a belt, and proceeded to thrash my behind with a heavy leather strap. It hurt. I think she whipped me till her arm got tired. When she was finished, she left the room and Frank and I laughed about how he had just gotten me in such trouble.

Skip ahead about 35 years.

Our family is sitting in the living room of my parents' summer home in Blowing Rock, NC. It is around 10 at night, my mother has had about one glass of wine too many, which sometimes brings about maudlin tears of guilt or regret about any number of sundry memories. This night she is feeling guilty about "the last spanking." Remorsefully, she remembers that she had really beaten the heck out of me with that belt and she felt bad about it, and then she said, "Will you ever forgive me for that?"

I shouldn't have been surprised that she remembered it—she remembered nearly everything negative that ever happened to her—but Frank and I laughed and I responded, "Do you want to know the truth about that?"

"What do you mean, the truth? The truth is that you two were fighting and you laughed at me when I smacked your bottom and it made me mad and I beat you with the belt."

By now Frank and I were really laughing. I replied, "Well, all of that is true, but the *reason* I laughed was because Frank made a face at me. So, when I laughed you thought it was at you, and it really pissed you off, and I got the bad end of that deal."

"Oh, no! Oh, no. Why Frank! Now I'm mad at *you!*"

I jumped in. "Well, I'm not mad at him. I'm not mad at you. It's a long, long time ago, and now it's just funny."

"It's not funny to *me*," she insisted. Tears began to run down her cheeks. "I've felt bad about this for years. I need you to forgive me for hurting you. Please."

"Well, OK. I'm happy to forgive you. I think I forgave you years ago, but if you need to hear me say it, 'I forgive you'." She sank back in her chair and felt much better.

Skip ahead another five years. Same situation. Same location. A little more wine.

"Do you remember the last time I spanked you?"

"Yeah. It was way more than a spanking."

"Yes, I know. I am so sorry about that. I think about it a lot. I would like for you to forgive me for hurting you."

"But we've already been through this, five years ago."

"I know, but I feel like you didn't really mean it. I need your forgiveness for that."

"But I *did* forgive you. I don't ever think about it any more. And when I do, it's just funny."

"It's not funny to *me*."

"OK, OK. Here it is for the final time. I forgive you. Really. Honestly. I forgive you. I have absolutely no anger, no hard feelings of any kind. I have no energy on it. You are totally forgiven."

Since then it's never come up again. Thank goodness. (Except when Frank and I laugh about it.)

I suppose there are two things I learned from this story over the years. One: it's not healthy to hang on to regrets, particularly if one has asked for and been granted forgiveness. And two: when you're about to get your ass whipped, close your eyes.

TRYING

We had a small high school, only 90 kids in the upper three grades, only 45 boys. Only about 15 of the boys were athletic in any regard. The majority of those fifteen were "country club" kids who became good golfers and tennis players. Our school competed very well in golf and tennis, but had no football, had to drop baseball when I was a junior, and won very few basketball games, ever.

So even though I wasn't a very good basketball player, I got to be on the team. And even though I wasn't a very good player, I was a smart player: when I was in the game I knew where to pass the ball, and I knew what plays to call. When I was sitting on the bench, I was aware of what was going right, and wrong, on the floor.

One afternoon during practice I did something that irritated the assistant coach, and he took me out of the scrimmage. As I trotted to the bench, I said, "I'm *trying*, coach." He gave me one of "those" looks and said, "Yes, Dickey. You are *very* trying.."

Coach Thornton: 1.   Player Dickey: 0.

BLOCK BOTTOM

During an afternoon basketball practice when I was a junior in high school, and still playing "way down on the bench," I went in for a layup and got upended, falling about four feet onto my tailbone. It really hurt. I couldn't continue.

The next day my mother took me to the doctor and had it x-rayed. I had a cracked and bent coccyx. Two weeks later the doctor gave me a cortisone shot to relieve the pain, but he cautioned me that any future injury like that could be much more serious and he encouraged me to stop playing basketball.

Well, I didn't want to quit. I sat on the bench almost all the time, but I loved the camaraderie, I was actually a good student of the game, and I most certainly didn't want to be labeled as a wimp or, worse yet, a quitter. Besides, it was a very small student body and I wouldn't have made the varsity basketball team at any other high school, so it was pretty cool for me to just be on a team. Even though we hardly ever won any games, it was still fun to be part of an organized sport.

The doctor told me that if I was to continue playing I would have to guard that part of my body from further damage and that I would have to find a piece of padding, like foam, to cover my tailbone. There was no medical device shaped to cover that particular part of a body, so we had to improvise. I got an 8" x 8" x 3" piece of foam, and taped it to the top of my butt. It was a daily ritual before practice and before games.

I felt stupid and *looked* even more ridiculous. It was bad enough to have to wear it in practice, bad enough to have to rip adhesive tape off my butt every evening after practice, but to wear that thing under my uniform in front of hundreds of people. Man, I had to swallow a lot of pride every time I went out on the floor. The guys would occasionally tease me, calling me "Block

Bottom." But I could only imagine what people in the stands were saying, and what they might be calling me. The imagination of an embarrassed teenager can be pretty powerful. The worst night was when we played in the District Tournament in Memorial Coliseum, the home of the Kentucky Wildcats, seating about 600,000. OK, it just seemed like that many that night. It was probably more like 12,000.

(I can still feel the embarrassment in my chest as I write this. Wow! What a strong, lasting memory. I had no idea this would happen because it's a story I hardly ever tell, and I don't recall having this much of an emotional response when I recounted this story many years ago. I have some work to do on this.)

After high school I never played organized basketball again, so some time around the end of March in 1963, I tossed that piece of foam rubber in the dumpster behind the gym. Not anything I'd want to keep with my annual, or Senior Prom dance card, or SAT scores.

CHIP AND DALE REUNION

I had two schoolmates, boy and girl twins, named Landy and Jeannette Dale. They lived on a really nice farm—cattle, tobacco, sheep, horses, chickens—and they also had a number of sheepherding dogs. One spring they announced at school that they had puppies to give away, did any of us want one or two or four? By the time our family had agreed to get a new puppy, there were only two left, brothers, and none of us wanted to break up the duo so we took both dogs. They were a mix of border collie (the mother) and some other kind of medium-sized, black, long-haired something or other, like Australian Shepherd, that must've closely resembled the mother.

We named them Chip and Dale.

They were pretty dogs, similar markings, but much different in size. Chip was about 20" at the shoulder and longer than he was tall. Dale was shorter in height and length, but had a bigger chest and weighed more. We had a bricked in part of our back yard that had at one time been a clothes drying yard, with the eyebolts still embedded in the brick walls. It was a perfect place to keep dogs safely.

Every once in a while the dogs would "escape" if the person who opened the gate wasn't careful. They loved to run, and they would head out across the UK campus. On one such occasion we got a call from the campus police who had what they thought was perhaps a rabid dog: OUR dog. We asked them to keep him in the truck until we could come get him. By the time we arrived, he had calmed down, had stopped foaming at the mouth, and the next day we learned that Dale was epileptic. He didn't show any symptoms of it when his life was normal, but when he got out, he was so excited that he would have a seizure.

After this had happened three times, we, as a family, decided to give him away, and we found a farmer in the neighboring county who was hoping that Dale would be a good sheepherder. As it turned out, Dale was an *incredible* sheepherder. It came naturally to him and the farmer loved his new dog.

Chip was lonely at first but eventually got used to being by himself.

Two years later my father resigned his position at UK and we were moving to Atlanta. We didn't see it as a possibility to move Chip. It seemed like a big adjustment for everyone to make, and a dog felt like a little too much. So, we called the farmer in Scott County and asked if he'd like to have the brother of the dog he now possessed. "WOULD I! ABSOLUTELY! Dale is the best sheep dog I've ever seen. I'll bet his brother is just as good. Yes, absolutely. Bring him over."

The next week we took Chip to Scott County. When we let Chip out of the car and he and Dale saw each other, you have never seen such joy! The dogs ran toward each other and leaped into the air, bumping into each other like professional football players after a wild touchdown. They did this over and over, eight or ten times. Then they yelped and talked and whined and ran in circles and flipped and jumped some more. Then they did the chest bumps some more, until they were exhausted. Finally, they lay down beside each other, panting, bodies touching, faces close enough to feel each other's breath.

As we departed left, knowing we'd done the right thing for both dogs, the farmer told her, "After seeing this I don't really care whether Chip can herd sheep or cows. Just watching their reunion was good enough for me to keep them together forever."

And believe it or not, there are actually some people in the world who still say that animals don't have emotions.

∞

BALCONIES ARE MEANT
TO BE CLIMBED ON

Boys will be boys. Girls will be girls.

By the time I turned sixteen, I'd been living at Maxwell Place for six years. By then I'd learned that the trellis beside the veranda off my bedroom would easily support my weight of 135 pounds. It was possible to get out of the house, let the car coast down the driveway to the street, and start the car without being heard. It was a little more difficult to get the car back where it had originally been with equally low decibels, but I learned that I could shut off the engine part way up the driveway and coast to a stop in front of the house. The trellis climb was totally silent and the door never squeaked.

Some of my friends knew about my escapades. One night, as I was studying, I heard a tapping on one of my bedroom windows. It was the older sister of the girl I was dating. She was very attractive, she was very popular, she was a "college girl." And she wanted to come in. I didn't know what to do. While we were debating, I was certain that our whispers were going to be heard throughout the house. I was at great odds with myself. The excitement (and to be honest), the thrill of having this "older" girl approach me, were making me crazy with desire. The terror I felt at the possibility of being caught, though, overrode everything else. I finally got her to climb back down and go away.

Fear can sometimes be one of our best forms of protection.

ANN MILLER AT TUTS

My first real job in show business was an Equity summer stock job in Atlanta in 1964. Getting an Equity card (being allowed to join the union that has jurisdiction over theatrical work) when you're only 18 years old is something to be proud of and something that would be considered pretty lucky. I auditioned to be part of the chorus (6 men and 6 women) for Theater Under the Stars, to perform six shows in Chastain Park throughout the summer, and I got the job. It was a GREAT summer. We rehearsed a show during the day while we were doing a different show at night. It was rigorous and exciting and most nights we'd have thousands of audience members.

The lineup of shows was outstanding: "My Fair Lady," "West Side Story," "The Sound of Music," "Bye, Bye Birdie," "Tovarich," and "La Traviata." (The only show we weren't ready to stop performing after a week was "West Side Story." By the end of that week we all felt like we had barely scratched the surface of the musical version of Romeo and Juliet.) That summer I got mononucleosis and had to miss the last two weeks of the season, but all in all it was a wonderful experience.

One story I remember clearly was about Ann Miller. She came to star in "The Sound of Music." She was a bit long in the tooth for the role of Maria, but she was a real star and the producers knew she would fill the seats. On opening night, after our final bow, the curtain had just come down and she turned to all of us, still standing on stage, and shouted, "Watch this, kids!" With that, she parted the curtain and stepped onto the apron to tell the audience, "Atlanta has always been my favorite city. You were, tonight, one of the greatest audiences I've ever performed for and . . ." (she began to cry) "I cannot even begin to tell you how touched and happy I am to be here this week. It's one of the highlights of my entire career." She went on, talking, crying gently, big tears running down her cheeks. We could hear the emotional reactions of the huge audience. She finally finished her curtain call speech, got another standing ovation, took a last deep bow, turned and came back through the curtain. With a jubilant look on her face, she pumped her fist into the air and shouted, "HOW WAS THAT?"

TOOTS' TIME OF DEATH

I've had a few personal instances of knowing that there's more to this world than meets the eye, particularly in the specific areas of pre-cognitive dreams, extra-sensory perception or at-a-distance awareness, and out-of-body experiences. I suspect that nearly everyone in the world has some of these some times. I know a few people who are able to do this sort of "stuff" any time they choose. I have, jokingly (but I really do think it could be true) often said that I think aliens come to earth, look at the way earthlings behave, shake their antennae and admonish the human race for not knowing its potential. They observe us like we might observe ants, saying, "Look at how they run to and fro. Poor things. I wonder if they know what they're doing? I wonder if they have any idea of their potential? Let's come back in about 5000 years."

I was living in Tennessee when my paternal grandmother died in Kentucky. She had been sick and we knew she was on her way out of this life, but no one was thinking that her death was imminent. I awoke one morning at 6:05 and knew that Toots (It's so funny we called her Toots—a woman who lost a husband and a 6-year-old daughter in the same year, went back to college to get a Master's degree, singly raised a brilliant and successful son, taught elementary school all of her life, was totally revered by thousands of students, and we called her Toots. Go figger.) had died. A few hours later I got a call from my parents informing me that Toots had passed away earlier that morning. When I asked if the time of death was a little after 6am, my dad replied, "The time of death was 6:05."

SATURN ROCKET BURNS ON LAUNCH PAD

The only way I know what year things happened during my four years in college is by knowing where I was living at the time. So, I guess this happened in early 1967 because we were living in the Decatur Arms Apartments. I can "see" the kitchen and the dining room table—where this next event occurred—in my mind. I was starting breakfast, around 6:30 in the morning, getting ready to go to an eight o'clock class when I got a terrible feeling and a vision of a Saturn rocket, sitting on the launch pad, burning. All day long I was aware of tremendous sadness, distress, and even fear, but I didn't know these feelings were related to my vision earlier in the day. That evening, when I read the evening edition newspaper, the headline was "Saturn Rocket Burns on Launch Pad: 3 Astronauts Die." It happened at the exact same time I became aware of it.

I've always wondered how many things are "known" as they happen, but we assume they are just our random thoughts rather than a significant documentation of events happening at a distance. The ALIENS know!

CANDY CANES AT CHRISTMAS

Thousands of books have been written about dreams: their significance, the symbology, their power to inform us of our subconscious thoughts and feelings. Most dreams seem to be a way for us to "work out" the problems and dilemmas that our conscious mind is unsuccessful in dealing with. But some dreams turn out to be pre-cognitive. Deja vu all over again.

I've never kept a dream diary. I've thought many times that it would be a good idea, but it's just another good idea that I haven't acted upon. I actually don't even remember very many of my dreams. But when they occur just before I awaken, and they are clear, and they are silly enough to amuse me, and there's somebody close at hand to tell them to, then sometimes they get "documented."

This was one of those pre-cognitive dreams that was "provable."

In maybe August or September, the dream was . . . We were at the Kelly's house sometime near Christmas. It was decorated with bows and garlands and lots of red and green plaid table covers. The Kellys were the parents of my wife's brother's wife. I had only met them once before. I was sitting in a wing-back chair, unwrapping candy canes and tying little bows on them, I reached over and put a piece of cream-filled chocolate candy in my mouth. Mrs. Kelly walked into the room holding a tin in her hands and said, "Here, Joe, do try this peanut brittle. It's delicious." My reply was, "I can't. My mouth is full of chocolate candy." That was the end of the dream. I told it to my wife, Juli, and neither of us ever mentioned it again . . . until the next Christmas.

In December, in real life . . . We had traveled to Arkansas for the holidays, and had been invited to the Kelly's for dinner. The house was decorated just like in my dream, but I had no conscious memory of it as we entered. Shortly thereafter, as any good guest should, I asked, "Is there anything I can do to make myself useful?" Mrs. Kelly said, "Yes, as a matter of fact there is. Do you see that bowl of candy canes over there? And the pile of little red ribbons beside it? Would you be so kind as to unwrap the candy canes and put a bow on each one? That would be a great help to me." I said, "Sure," and plopped down in the wingback chair and began this mindless little task. About five minutes later, still unwrapping and tying, I spotted the box of candy to my left and put a piece of cream-filled chocolate in my mouth. No sooner had I done that than Mrs. Kelly walked into the room with that tin of peanut brittle and said the exact same phrase I'd dreamed about months earlier. "Here, Joe, do try this peanut brittle. It's delicious." I started to say, "I can't. My mouth is full of chocolate candy," but since I knew I'd already said it once before it seemed ridiculous to say it again.

Instead, I apologized for not being able to accept the peanut brittle, and went into the bedroom to ask Juli if she remembered that dream I'd had about Mrs. Kelly and the candy canes and the peanut brittle. She was vague about it at first, but as I went into slightly more detail, she remembered it more clearly. Her recollection was the same as mine.

At dinner, we told everyone around the table about the dream and the actual event. No one was impressed. There'd been a lot of alcohol consumed that evening, and it seems there were no extra senses available or interested.

2.7 GPA

During high school I got accepted into several outstanding universities and chose Emory. My SAT score was well above average and I had graduated second in a small high school class. I knew college would not be a piece of cake, but I expected to do well.

My second week at Emory, I was scheduled to meet with my advisor. He counseled me in depth about my course of study and what classes I should be taking in the future, but I only remember one thing about that meeting. Toward the end of it, while he looked in my folder at my high school records, he remarked, "You did very well in high school and your SAT scores are outstanding, but our freshman class here at Emory is the best we've ever had, you will be competing with some very, very bright students, and we expect your overall grade point average, when you graduate, to be 2.7."

I was shocked.

I didn't say anything. I probably nodded my head and said, "Uh huh," but was thinking, "REALLY? That's it? 2.7?"

Four years later, when I graduated, my overall grade point average was . . . 2.7. Was the counselor uncannily accurate, or did I somehow cut enough classes and drink enough beer and just barely skate by on enough tests to eke out at 2.7 overall grade point average?

In retrospect, I hate that I made them right on that one.

What if that counselor had told me that Emory was filled with bright, talented students but the school thought, based on my test scores and academics, that I would do very well in my four years there. "We can't predict how well our students will do. It all depends on how hard they work and how much they want to succeed, but we have great expectations for you and it will be a pleasure for me to not only watch your progress during your tenure here, but I will be happy to see a very high grade point average on your transcript for graduate school."

What if he'd said THAT? Could I just as easily have made him right on that one?

MICHELANGELO'S DAVID

My first church singing job was at a Christian Science church in Atlanta. It paid $10 a week and required me to sing a solo on Sunday, and lead three hymns on Sunday mornings and Wednesday nights. When I auditioned for and got the job, I had no knowledge of the fact that my father had been a Christian Science soloist, and his mother had also been a Christian Science soloist. No one in our family was ever a Christian Scientist; we all just SANG for them.

The church allowed me to wear a bone colored suit in the summer instead of the prescribed white, as it would have taken the entire summer's pay to buy a white suit. It was a congregation of very loving people, many of them little old blue-haired ladies.

I was nineteen, naive, and very nice.

One Sunday after church, one of the aforementioned ladies came up to me and said, "Oh, Mr. Dickey, I was sitting in the back today, and the entire time you were singing all I could think about was how much you reminded me of Michelangelo's David."

I must have blushed crimson. I didn't know whether to be complimented or just cover my crotch with my hands.

FIRST HAIRCUT

It was 1967 and I got to spend the next four years in the military, through the height of the Viet Nam War. It was an unhappy time in the United States of America, and it was an unhappy time in my life. I was "eligible" for the draft. If I'd had any idea that a D in French in my sophomore year would put me on academic probation for a quarter, which would mean that I'd be eligible for the draft the moment I graduated, I'd have practiced more Edith Piaf songs, eaten more escargot, and dressed more like Marcel Marceau. When I discovered that it was either four years in the Air Force or three years on the front lines of Viet Nam in the Army, I chose the extra twelve months with fewer bullets and no mud. Besides, I thought it would be a whole lot of fun to be a pilot, particularly if Uncle Sam was going to be paying for my flying lessons. But my eyes were less than perfect and I had to opt for navigator.

But when my medical records showed that I had had four concussions in my life (falling out of the car, hitting my head on the curb as a three-year-old; getting pushed off the top of the slide onto the blacktop in the second grade; banging heads at first base in a sandlot baseball game as a twelve-year-old; cracking heads and getting stitches in my eyebrow in a backyard, pickup basketball game as a fourteen-year-old) I became ineligible for Navigator's School.

It still seemed smarter to go for the four years in a cleaner, safer environment, and to help me make that decision they promised I could either be a Logistics Officer (which matched up with my BBA) or I could be in Special Forces as a singer, which matched up with my dreams and abilities. As it turned out, both choices were lies to get me to sign up.

In May, I learned that Officers Training School didn't begin again until June, so I would get to spend four weeks in Basic Training before my ten weeks at OTS. A group of recruits flew from Atlanta to San Antonio and then got on a bus to Lackland Air Force Base. There were a few boisterous ones, but most in the group were somber if not actually sullen. The afternoon we arrived, our identities became numbers, we were given clothes that would distinguish us even less one from another, and then we were herded to the base barbershop to get all of our hair cut off.

The Beatles were still a force in the world at that time, so a lot of us had long hair. Maybe not long compared to the way some kids wear their hair today, but way longer than the 40s and 50s. The line wound clear around the building and we waited thirty minutes before discovering, as we got to the door, that there were twelve barbers working furiously. A few expletives from the chairs were proof that the ones with the clippers in their hands didn't care about soliciting return customers.

I watched the awful transformations. Some were crying. I saw young men who had looked like everybody else go in, and I saw young men who only looked like each other come out. No hair, no egos, no strength. I thought briefly about Samson, and the Bible that had been given to me by the church where I'd been a regular paid soloist. I thought, *"I really don't want my hair cut off,"* which led to, *"I really don't want to be here,"* which led to, *"This war sucks,"* which led to, *"I am serving my country, regardless."*

"NEXT!"

That meant me.

I walked the length of the barbershop, sat in the chair, and let him fasten the plastic cover around my neck. He was a sergeant, four stripes on his sleeve.

He leaned down and asked in a rather cheerful voice, "Well, how would you like it today?"

I paused for just a moment, not certain if it would be appropriate to be funny. But since he was obviously being facetious I decided, *"What the hell, things can't get much worse than this,"* and answered, "Why don't you take it all off of this side, and then take it all of the other side, and then go ahead and take it all off the top?"

He and the barber at the next station both laughed out loud. My barber sergeant patted me gently on the shoulder and said, "Buddy, you're going to do just fine around here."

BASIC TRAINING

My four weeks in Basic Training, prior to my transfer to Officer Training School, were a real test. My barracks NCO was a Staff Sergeant, past an age where he would ever get promoted again, short, Hispanic, profane, understood his job clearly, and had absolutely no use for young would-be officers. Out of the forty new recruits in his barracks, only one of us was going to be an officer. He knew me by name within minutes of my arrival.

I have conveniently forgotten his name, one of those people that I'm better off not remembering clearly.

We were told that we could bring a Bible and two paperback books with us, along with one set of civilian clothing, and our toiletries. He was strolling around with his hands behind his back as we were putting our personal belongings in our footlockers. He stopped behind me, saw my books, and demanded to know what I'd brought. I showed him. *A Thousand Days*, by Arthur M. Schlesinger Jr., and *The Kandy-Colored Tangerine-Flake Streamline Baby*, by Tom Wolfe.

He picked them up. "I know what this one is—about Kennedy. What's this crap?" He put Wolfe's book in my face.

I replied with what might've seemed a bit of haughtiness. "It's a first-rate commentary on American mores, on society's strengths and ills, and it's recommended reading by many of our nation's best literary critics."

He threw it against the wall at the end of the room. "Eet's trash! I don't have trash in my barracks."

I stood up and began to protest, saying things like, "My recruiter said I could bring a Bible and two other books as long as they weren't pornography, and these most certainly are not . . ."

He was about to win, no contest. "I SAY EET'S TRASH. THIS EES MY HOUSE, AND I DON'T HAVE TRASH EEN MY HOUSE! THAT EES

ALL, AIR-MAN DEEEKY.

Round One: The Sergeant

Later that evening, we were given very specific instructions about how to fold each shirt, each handkerchief, each sock, where each item would go in the footlocker, and, of course, how to make a tight bed. We wrote all the instructions in a little notebook that we had been furnished.

The bed next to mine was occupied by Sonny Waterfield. He was from Kinston, North Carolina, and had never been out of the state of North Carolina in his entire life. He had joined the Air Force to become a butcher, so he could go back to Kinston after his four years and work for the Kroger store there. (From what I later learned, that is exactly how it all worked out for Sonny—a Cinderella story of a sort.)

To say Sonny was unsophisticated would be a use of that word that exceeds its limits. A heart of gold, a brain of lead, and so little life experience that it was a wonder to me that he was able to do *anything* correctly. After attempting to fold his clothes and put them away, he realized that he wasn't doing it properly and leaned over to ask me for help.

I wasn't anxious to do it for him, but asked him what he needed help with.

"I can't figger out how to fold my white tee-shirts."

"Did you take notes, Waterfield?" I asked him.

"Yeah."

"Well, get out your notebook and look at your notes. That's what the rest of us are doing."

So he dug into his pile of stuff and got out the notebook, opened it and studied it intently for well over a minute. Finally he looked up and said, "Naw. This is for handkerchiefs."

I folded his shirts for him.

The first Sunday we were there, they held three worship

services. Catholics went at 8am. Jews were to go at 9am. And Protestants were to go at 10am. At about 8:55, someone downstairs told Waterfield to tell the Jewish guys to get ready. Waterfield hollered, "All you Jewish guys get ready to go to church!"

Immediately he was corrected. "You don't call them that, Waterfield. You call them synagogues."

"Oh. OK. ALL YOU JEWISH SYNAGOGUES GET READY TO GO TO CHURCH!" We all died laughing and never knew if he did it on purpose or not.

The next day my sergeant tested me again. I don't remember how it started, but he got really mad at me about something and threw my footlocker down the stairs and yelled, "Get that cleaned up in five minutes, or else!"

I ran down the stairs, not even considering what "or else" meant, piled everything into my arms, carried the footlocker back up the steps, and got it all put away perfectly in five minutes. I never considered for a moment that he could have been court-martialed for doing something like that. It was most certainly against U.S.A.F. regulations. In retrospect, I realize that he had already accomplished what Basic Training was for. I was totally compliant. I didn't question his right to do that. I didn't give him anything less than full allegiance, full authority, and full disdain. He could have been severely disciplined for an action like that, but I didn't know it, and I wasn't about to test *anything*.

Round Two: The Sergeant

Some time during the month, in a very close face-to-face, loud monologue, he told me with a great deal of venom that I would never make it through Officer Training School, that I would never become an officer, and he'd see me back in basic after I washed out of OTS.

Round Three: The Sergeant

At the end of those four miserable weeks, I transferred across the base to OTS. I never saw any of those guys again, except for the sergeant.

I did my ten weeks at OTS. They were tougher—for a number of reasons—than Basic Training had been. (I have more stories about OTS. See MORALE CHECK and SIDEWINDER.) One of the things that made it especially tough was after I'd been there for four weeks, my wife, Juli, told me she wanted a divorce, and I cried myself to sleep for several nights, hoping my bunkmate above was already asleep and didn't hear me. But I made it through, graduated in the top 10% of my class, being honored as a Distinguished Graduate, and I felt proud to begin wearing that single gold bar. I wasn't happy to be in the military, but I was happy about what I had accomplished.

The morning before I left to drive to Denver, to go to Avionics School for six months, I crossed the base to my old barracks. My breathing quickened as I got closer. I didn't know why I had come over there, but I was there and I was going to speak with my old training instructor. I knocked on his office door, and he, thinking it was one of his recruits, yelled, "Get your ass in here!" I entered and closed the door and took the two steps it took to get to the edge of his desk. He stood and showed his awkwardness by not knowing what to do with his hands. At first he wanted to salute, but it was his office and we were indoors and he was not required to do that. Then I saw that he considered shaking my hand, but I was not offering my hand to be shaken, so he just stood there.

"Sergeant, do you remember me?"

"Yes, sir. I remember you."

"Sergeant, I have very little to say to you except to let you know that not only did I make it through OTS, I was a DG. And Sarge, for all of the ways that you mistreated me, all I am going to do right this minute is require you to stand at attention for the remainder of the time I'm in this office, and then salute me before

I leave. Both requests are within my prerogative."

His body tightened to a position of attention, his arms stiff at his side.

"Sergeant, I will never know why you berated me so by telling me I'd never make it. If it was to motivate me, you failed. I am not motivated by fear or degradation, nor is anyone else I know. If you really meant it, you were way beyond wrong. I will be a good officer, but not because of anything positive that I learned while I was under your command. On the contrary, I will be a good officer by showing RESPECT for those with whom I serve. I probably could say a lot more, but it would be a waste of my time. I just want you to know what a poor job you did with me, and as far as I can tell with every other man I served with in this barracks. I'm leaving now. We won't see each other again. I believe, according to my Customs and Courtesies Manual, you are to initiate the salute. You may now do that, Sergeant. Good bye."

He put his flat hand to his right eyebrow, I snapped a return salute, did a very crisp about face, walked out of his office, and that was that.

The Fight: The 2nd Lieutenant

I felt like raising my arms like Rocky. But Rocky hadn't been written yet. It seemed like I'd only been in his office for a few seconds. It seemed like I'd been in the Air Force a really long time.

MORALE CHECK

USAF Officer Training School is ten weeks of hell. The first five are much more difficult because you're an "underclassman." An upperclassman has the authority to ask you to do almost anything, to demand answers of you about almost anything, and to generally give you a load of shit any time he (or she) feels like it. Thinking back on it, no female officer candidates ever gave me any grief. It was just the guys.

It was around my third week there and I was just coming out of my room. An upperclassman approached me, I saluted him, he said, "Mister, I want a morale check." The correct response to a morale check was to tell him how much I loved OTS, how I adored the upperclassmen, and generally how much fun the entire experience was proving to be.

I hesitated, and he demanded, "Mister, I want a morale check. NOW!"

I blurted out, "I hate this fucking place!"

He was not to be dissuaded. "Mister, I want a POSITIVE morale check!"

To which I quickly replied, "I POSITIVELY hate this fucking place!"

He died laughing, wrote me up for five demerits, and went his merry way. I felt like we had both won.

SIDEWINDER

It must've been in my eighth or ninth week of OTS because I remember feeling quite confident about everything, pretty certain I was going to graduate. I was walking back to our barracks (which was actually more like a college dormitory: a set of bunk beds in each room, lockers, desks, a big bathroom in the middle of each wing of the three story brick building) one hot afternoon. About two feet off the edge of the sidewalk I spotted a small sidewinder. I was dressed in fatigues and felt no hesitation in stepping over and putting one of my boots right behind his head. I stood there for a minute or two before I saw some underclassmen approaching. They saluted me and were going to walk on past, but I stopped them.

"Gentlemen, I am standing on a rattlesnake. Would one of you please go into the storage shed and bring me a hoe so we can chop his head off?" You'd have thought I'd told them I was standing on an armed atom bomb. They looked down at my boot and took off like my foot WASN'T on the rattlesnake.

In fewer than two minutes there were ten or twelve underclassmen on that sidewalk, and two of them had hoes in their hands. I was being so cool. I thought, *"This is good. I'm setting a great example of bravery, and calmness, and authority. Perfect. Just what an upperclassman should be doing."*

"Thank you for getting the hoes, gentlemen. Now, would one of you be so kind as to chop this snake's head off so I can get back to what I was doing?"

No one moved.

"Guys! I'm standing on a rattlesnake! Will one of you PLEASE cut his head off?"

No one moved.

I wasn't actually certain I had the authority to order one

of them to do something that might be perceived as being dangerous. I mean, even though this was wartime, we weren't IN it. So, I reached for a hoe.

"OK, just give it to me, dammit! I'll do it myself!" I grabbed the hoe and said, "Everybody get back." They all moved like they'd been choreographed. I lifted my boot off the snake, took a quick step back and swung the hoe blade in a swift, perfect arc. That little sidewinder never had a chance. He was in two pieces, the longer part of him still writhing about, as I tossed the hoe back to the one who had been holding it before.

"Gentlemen, please clean this little mess up. Wait till he stops moving, throw the snake in the Dempsey Dumpster and put the hoes away. I have better things to do."

I walked off without looking back. I felt like John Wayne. When the word got around during dinner, I think that snake had grown by at least a foot.

SKIING BRECKENRIDGE

One of the only good things about being in the Air Force in Denver was that I got to go skiing a couple of times. Once I went alone, to Breckenridge. It's a very large ski area with many slopes and many levels of expertise. I was a true beginner and tried to stay on really easy hills.

Toward the end of the afternoon I made a mistake on one the lifts and found myself near the top with only two choices of runs to go down, each of them a double black diamond slope. I knew that if I tried either one I would surely die. Luckily, I spotted a ranger, pushed myself over to him, and explained my predicament. He was sympathetic; I suspect he didn't want to have to pick up my remains on such a steep hillside.

In almost a whisper, he told me, "Now, you can't tell anyone I told you to do this. I'd get in big trouble. But if you look over there to your left you can see two posts and a chain in between them. That's a fire road. It goes all the way to the bottom of the mountain. There's not supposed to be anyone skiing on it, but since you're in big trouble otherwise, I'm suggesting that you climb over that chain while I'm not looking, and take the fire road down."

I thanked him, not nearly profusely enough, and headed for the chain. As soon as I got past it I was out of sight of the rest of the world. For what seemed like forever I skiied alone, with just the sound of my shushing skis, on what would be considered less than a bunny slope—hardly any pitch, gentle curves, wide enough to make snow plough turns—and it was just me and virgin snow. Wow. What a treat. Picturesque. A lifetime memory. Safe.

All baseball inferences aside, sometimes angels appear in ranger uniforms.

∞

"GOD DANNIT!"

On a Sunday afternoon in the fall of 1970, I was driving home from the Commissary with some groceries, and my barely two-year-old daughter Jennifer was standing on the front seat next to me, arms spread out across the back of the seat. (Those were the days before seat belt enforcement.) I decided to drive by the base hobby shop to check on a wooden candlestick that I'd turned on the lathe and then stained.

As I turned onto the street where the hobby shop was located, I saw no cars in the lot and realized it was a Sunday and the shop was closed. I said, "Aw, man, it's closed," and continued to drive by.

Jennifer said very definitely, "God Dannit!"

I said, "What did you say?"

She answered, "I said 'God Dannit.'"

"Why'd you say that?"

She replied, "'Cause the hobby shop is closed."

She wasn't quite certain how to pronounce it, but the inflection, the meaning, and the justification for it were spot on! It caused me to wonder how many times she had had to hear it in order to know how to properly repeat it.

MANAGING A MALCONTENT

By the time I became a 1st Lieutenant I was not quite as green or naïve or incompetent. Though I still had a lot to learn as a manager, I was beginning to get the hang of it. I had 135 men working under me, about half of them older than I was. During each inspection by the Inspectors General we had garnered all Outstandings and my commanding officers had nothing but praise for me and my guys. However one of my new troops was proving tough to manage. It seemed that out of the 135 he was the only one who needed to have his butt kicked every day. He just wouldn't do the work unless somebody came down real hard on him.

It was not my management style to be mean or ugly, and I didn't like for my sergeants to have to manage that way either. Each week I would hold a 20-minute inspection of all the personnel in the Avionics Branch, looking at uniforms, haircuts and mustaches, shoes, etc. I would go up and down the rows checking everything out. One morning, after I'd been thinking about this particular airman who needed extra discipline to stay in line, as I passed him during inspection, I whispered, "See me in the corner of the hangar right after this is finished."

I dismissed the troops and walked to the end of the huge hangar to meet with Airman Shertoff. He and I arrived at the same time and though he came to attention, I put him at ease and said, "We need to talk." He didn't know what I was going to say, and quite frankly I didn't either. But I began by saying, "You don't like being in the Air Force, do you?"

He quickly answered, "No Sir, I don't."

I waited for him to go on, but he didn't. He wasn't dumb. He probably knew the less he said the better. So, I jumped in.

"Ya know what, Airman Shertoff? I don't like it either!"

I could see the shock on his face. I think he assumed that all officers were Lifers (personnel who stayed in for at least 20 years).

I went on. "You probably had to join the Air Force because you were gonna be drafted and you thought this was a better choice than being on the front lines in Viet Nam, right?"

"Yeah. Uh, yessir."

"Well, I'm in exactly the same boat as you, except I have a bar on my shoulder instead of a stripe on my sleeve. I had the same choice you did, except I was lucky to have earned a college degree and could become an officer. But I'm not certain being an officer is much better than being an airman. I have to serve a whole year longer than you do, and I've got responsibilities that you can't imagine, and I've got guys like you to deal with, and I've got my own dislike of the military in general, and I've got a ton of disdain for this war we're involved in. But I still have to do my job because I AGREED to do it. I just didn't have enough guts to go to Canada. So, let's understand each other, OK? We both are unhappy with where we are and what we have to do. What are we gonna do about that?"

He was silent. He looked down. I let the moment be awkward.

I finally spoke. "I've watched you for quite some time now. I've discussed your performance and your crappy attitude with your NCOs. They tell me that you need more discipline and they're fuckin' tired of spending all their time on one soldier. I don't appreciate having to spend my time on one guy either. I have *a hundred and thirty-five guys* to be in charge of, and you're wasting everybody's time. If you actually need to have your butt kicked every day, I'll do that. But trust me, I'll kick it so hard you won't know where it came from. I'll kick it so thoroughly that you'll think a HUNDRED lieutenants were kickin' your butt. But I think I have a better idea. Because I don't like kickin' butts, and because I think you have a lot of intelligence and a lot of talent, and you're just testing all of us, here's my plan, Airman Shertoff. Every week, after inspection, you and I will meet right here. We'll talk about what's going on with you, about how your NCO's think you're doing, and if you need for me to, I'll kick your ass. So, for now, let's just pretend that I kicked your ass, and you hated every minute of it, and you feel like crap, and you can go back to work now and do a great job this week. And I'll meet you right here in another week. OK? You don't have to answer."

He gave me a salute and went to his job.

The next week he and I met and I asked him how he was doing and he replied, "Better, Sir."

I knew he was doing better. I'd heard nothing but amazement from his NCO's that week. He and I chatted for a moment and I said, "Airman Shertoff, I've got a lot of things to do this morning. Let's just pretend that I kicked your ass again, OK?"

"OK, Sir." He smiled.

The following week, as he approached me at the end of the hangar, I said, "We don't really have to do this any more, do we?"

"No, Sir, I don't think we do."

"Here's the deal, Airman Shertoff. Any time you think you can't stand this military stuff any more, remember that you and I are having the same feelings about it. All I'm asking you to do is to do the best you know how to do. That's what I'm doing, and I think every guy in this Avionics Branch expects that of me. But it sure doesn't make me *like* it. I just do it. So . . . let's keep pretending that I've kicked your ass. Every time you SEE me, just imagine it. I think it'll be good for both of us!"

He laughed. I smiled. I reached out and shook his hand. He saluted. I saluted back. The next time he was eligible for promotion he got his next stripe.

DEMPSEY DUMPSTER: SECOND PLACE? YOU'VE GOTTA BE KIDDING!

It was my first Halloween at George Air Force Base. I've never cared much for Halloween since I've been an adult. I've watched it turn from a fun night for kids into really bad pranks into cruelty to animals into actual criminal acts, all in the name of a holiday. For me, it's not very fun any more.

But at 5pm that evening I discovered the Officers' Club was having a big costume party and there'd be prizes for the best costumes. As of 5pm neither Juli nor I had costumes but I was anxious to go and decided to get creative. The costume judging was to take place at 9pm. I had four hours to get it together.

I drove to the base supply squadron and begged the sergeant for a huge cardboard box. I took it home, painted it white, cut the top at an angle with double lids, painted warning signs on it, and then put two rods through the sides, on the inside, so I could climb inside of it and hold it on my shoulders. What it was, was a Dempsey Dumpster. I was going to the party as a Dempsey Dumpster, and Juli would be a garbage person walking along side. The paint didn't dry until almost 8:30, we barely got the box in the trunk of car with the lid up, and walked into the party at 8:45. Everyone in the ballroom stopped what they were doing when we came in. The place fairly exploded. It was the best costume anyone had seen all night.

Unfortunately, they had decided that no one else was going to show up at the party and had judged the costumes at 8:30. I was ineligible! I was kind of upset about it since the poster had said the judging would be at 9:00 and I was there by 8:45. According to everyone's enthusiasm about the Dempsey Dumpster it was clear that I would've won.

The 1st Place prize, a case of pretty good champagne, had gone to a Lieutenant Colonel dressed as a pirate. It was a darned good pirate costume, but, geez, it didn't come close to a Dempsey Dumpster! And he knew it. Around 10 o'clock he generously offered to give me half of his first prize. I thought that was incredibly noble of him, and accepted with thanks and appreciation.

In the meantime, every woman in the club wanted to dance with me. To do that I had to lift the box up as high as I could, they'd crawl under it, and we'd dance inside the Dempsey Dumpster. Every now and then someone would lift one of the lids and toss in some trash, which would just go through to the floor. It was pretty funny and gave everyone a whole lot of fun.

Since then, I've created a few other fairly good costumes, but nothing that ever equaled that one.

And half a case of champagne is way better than none.

"Thanks, again, Colonel."

U.S.A.F. WORLDWIDE TALENT CONTEST

Remember me writing that when I joined the Air Force my recruiter lied to me? (If you're one of the many millions of men or women who served in our nations Armed Forces, you just laughed, didn't you? Nearly everyone who joins the military gets lied to! Of course, we just don't know at that time that we're being lied to.)

The lies I got were that when my day came to actually be transported to Lackland AFB I would go to Officers' Training School, and that after I graduated from OTS I would either be assigned to logistics or to Special Services.

When I got to Lackland, I went to Basic Training because the next OTS class wasn't starting for four more weeks. And when I got out of OTS, I had to go to Avionics school for almost eight months to learn things about which I had absolutely no interest or ability. It's just that I take tests very well and I scored exceptionally high on a test that would indicate that perhaps I could learn enough about Avionics to become an Avionics Officer. I still think an ohm has more to do with meditation than getting electrocuted.

All that is a preamble to this particular story.

It took me several years of being an Avionics Officer before I found out there was an Air Force Talent Contest. What I found out was that if I could win the base contest I would go somewhere else to compete, and if I were to win there I would go somewhere else to compete. Winning at each level would keep me away from my job for more time. It was very enticing. I felt like I was a good singer. I signed up.

I won the George Air Force Base Contest and joined a group of other base winners at Luke Air Force Base, in Phoenix, to compete in the Tactical Air Command contest. There were a number of categories in which contestants could compete and I won both the classical and the pop singing divisions. I got to go to some base in Florida for the worldwide finals. It was a couple of weeks in my life that are amazingly blurry in my memory. I can't even, for certain, recall the name of the base in Florida. It might have been Homestead. I remember that my mother and my sister made a long drive to come see me perform, but I was so preoccupied with the contest I was particularly ungracious and expressed no gratitude at all for their supportive efforts. I barely remember any part of that entire experience.

What I do remember is that I won the Pop division, and that I was actually a better singer than the young man who won the Classical division, but later learned that the judges just didn't want to give me both trophies.

It turned out to be a good thing for me (as most disappointments eventually are). I had enjoyed the music of opera, but I had never liked the singers very much. So now the universe was supporting me in giving up opera in favor of being a "pop singer."

After winning, I flew to Nellis AFB in Las Vegas, and was picked up by a Lt. Colonel and flown via a single engine plane back to George AFB in Victorville. I remember that he let me fly the plane part of the way home, and I wasn't very good at it.

When we parked the plane on the tarmac, even though it was close to midnight, I got out to find a rather large group of friends, with a big sign congratulating me on being a winner, cheering as I stepped from the little plane. I was touched and appreciated their support. That week, my name was on the base marquee, with the same congratulatory message.

The "fame" was nice. Being crowned as "the best" was nice. Getting to be away from my regular Air Force job for almost a month was way better.

8-MINUTE MILE

While we were in Officers' Training School we had to run a mile three times a week. By the end of the ten weeks we were expected to be able to run it in under eight minutes. Most of us could do that without feeling like we were going to die, but any time you run a mile it hurts. I got my time down to 6:20 but even if I ran it in 7:50 it still hurt.

About three years after I got my commission and had been working at George Air Force Base in Victorville, California, for most of that time, there came a decree from on high that *everyone* would be required to run a mile, each year. Those of us under the age of something-or-other (I think it was 30) would have to run it in under eight minutes. It sent shudders through the ranks. No one wanted to do it, but it was the Air Force's way of trying to get everyone in better shape. The plan was for all of us to run each week, so when testing time came around we'd be able to pass the test easily.

There was a small group of junior officers who hung out together (Lieutenants and Captains, most of us maintenance officers) and we all decided to "go along with the program" and run once a week during the lunch hour, to "get in shape." The first time we all went to the athletic track together, and ran around the oval four times, there wasn't one of us who thought it was any fun, and most of us were ready to throw up.

I decided then and there that I was not going to do this the way the Air Force had intended for us to do it. While the other officers continued to run once a week at lunch, and improve their times so they could pass the test that was to come in two more months, I rejected this method of training. I ate lunch during the eight times they ran.

When the test day came, I ran the mile with all of them. I did it in 7:35. It hurt like hell. But it only hurt once! I had passed. I knew I could do it, but I didn't think I wanted to hurt every week just so I could get my time down to 7:20. Good choice.

But non-conformity was not what the Air Force wanted. It did not bode well for me during my final six months of duty.

YOU'RE FIRED!

I can say several things about my Air Force career that most cannot. Very, very few can say they took First Place in the USAF Worldwide Talent Contest, hardly anyone in my career field (Avionics) could say they didn't have to do a tour of duty in Viet Nam. (That's the next chapter in this "Air Force saga" section; see SANITY PRESERVED) And only a handful had to admit to being fired, perhaps none of them with Outstanding Officer Efficiency Reports. It was all about conforming and non-conforming.

Remember, this was the early 70's. Long hair, hippies, tie-dyed clothes, peace marches. I didn't want to be in the military. But I felt like it was my civic duty, I never considered *not* serving, and it was in my nature to do my very best, no matter how distasteful it was to me, personally. When I was little guy, my mother tells me I would say, "If I got a good gob [sic] I DO a good gob. If I got a bad gob, I DO a bad gob." Meaning, no matter whether the job at hand was good or bad to me, I would, nevertheless, DO it.

But it was a tough time to be in the military. I was spat upon one evening after we had driven down to San Bernardino to go shopping at the Orange Mall. I had a military haircut and a neatly trimmed mustache, and even in civilian clothes it was obvious to everyone that I was in the military. A "hippie looking" guy walking towards me in the mall mumbled something about the war and just spit on me. Right on the side of my face. I couldn't do anything back. I just kept walking. I've had a *lot* of trouble with people during this past decade who have told me I'm not patriotic when I say that I support our soldiers but not the war. I'll NEVER support the wars that that were waged in Iraq, or in Afghanistan, or in Libya, or in Iran (or anywhere else we might be by the time this book gets published) but I will ALWAYS support the troops who are fighting. I was one of them. I KNOW what it's like to serve in a war in which I have no belief. But I digress. Sort of.

During my last year in the Air Force we got a new commanding officer of our squadron. He was a Lieutenant Colonel, and he was a stickler for detail. I was a Captain, anxious to get out of the military and especially tired of short hair. One day he called me into his office and after a lot of extraneous conversation asked me to cut my hair and mustache shorter. I asked why, not understanding his request. He said that he thought I wasn't setting a good example for my men. I replied, "Sir, I am setting a perfect example for my men. There is a regulation stipulating exactly how long hair can be, and how long a mustache can be, and I am exactly at that limit." He argued with me, and I stood firm. Exasperated, he finally demanded that I come into his office every day for the next six weeks, and be personally inspected by him. If he were to find ANYTHING out of place about my personal appearance I would be punished. I did as he demanded, standing at attention each morning at 8am, while he walked around me looking for a hanging thread, anything out of place, a belt loop missed, and especially hair that might be a millionth of an inch too long. It reminded me a whole lot of Basic Training. He never found a discrepancy. It infuriated him. He finally admitted it.

He said, "Captain Dickey, I can find nothing for which to fault you. Your Avionics branch is beyond reproach. Your troops do exemplary work. Your management efforts get a 10 in every category. Your personal appearance is perfect. You are driving me crazy. I can't stand to have you around and I'm going to send you to Headquarters for your last three months of active duty."

"I'm being fired?" I asked.

"Yes, I guess you are. But I have no just cause, so it'll just look like a legitimate transfer on your record."

So, I changed jobs for my final 90 days, literally shuffling papers for three months, all because I felt justified in setting a perfect example for my men.

SANITY PRESERVED

When I became an Avionics Officer it was pretty much a sure-fire thing that I would get a tour of duty in Viet Nam. Everyone in my career field had to go. It was just a matter of time. So, I waited. No orders. Then I found out I was number 2 on the list to go. Then number 1. I prepared to pack my bags, Juli and I talked a lot about it, and I dreaded it. Then, another Avionics Officer, somewhere else in the world *volunteered* to go. A lot of guys, knowing they were absolutely certain to go, would volunteer, just to get it over with, thinking the war was just going to get worse and they were better off going now rather than later. So, I stayed at number 1. Then two more volunteered, and I moved back to number 2. I kept going between "just about to ship out" and "somebody else volunteered."

During these months, I built a patio cover out back. "Yep, just as soon as I fix up this patio, I'll probably get sent away for a year." But nothing happened. Then I bought a new car. Not a *new* car—a used Oldsmobile—but a *nice* car. "Surely, I'll have to go now." But nothing. Finally, it was too late in my four-year career to have to go.

I turned out to be one of very few who didn't have to serve in Viet Nam. Just being in the military during those years was bad enough, but Southeast Asia changed nearly everyone for the worse. In the ensuing years, I have met less than a handful of men who came back from Viet Nam and *weren't* screwed up. Drugs, alcohol, neuroses, irrational fears, rage, Agent Orange, you name it, they had it. But I never had to go.

What a blessing. There are some who contend that I'm not sane. But at least we can't blame it on Nam.

PEACH WINE MIRACLE

When stories about Jesus' miracles come into a conversation, I always remind people that He didn't start out with really big miracles. His first one was merely turning water into wine.

Heck, I turned peaches into wine, once, and that was just the beginning of the miracle. I was out of the Air Force, we'd bought a house in Altadena, California, and we had a backyard with chickens, roses, a vegetable garden and peach trees.

I made five gallons of peach wine in a big Sparklett's bottle, carefully fermenting it, making certain to follow the recipe exactly. It turned out terrible.

But my next-door neighbor loved it and took the entire five gallons. He traded me a refrigerator for it.

Now, *that's* a miracle!

WHITE OPAQUE PANTY HOSE

In the early seventies I was in a musical play called, "Lock Up Your Daughters." It was a bawdy, Tom Jones-ish kind of show, and was a lot of fun. It was set in the 1700s and my costume consisted of a blousy ruffled shirt, knickers, and long white stockings. I couldn't find any white socks that were long enough, so I finally went to the Broadway department store to try and find some heavy opaque white panty hose. After searching for a few minutes, a lady retail clerk asked if she could help me. I told her that I was looking for some heavy, white opaque panty hose.

"What size are you looking for?" she asked.

"I'm not sure," I replied.

"Well, what size is the person you're buying them for?'

"Exactly the same size as me," I said.

I saw her take a little step backwards before motioning toward the Queen Size rack. I thought that had some humor in it, right there.

I picked out a pair, and since the show was going to run Fridays, Saturdays, and Sundays for an entire month, decided to get an extra pair while I was there. As I was paying for them, she asked, "Will there be anything else?"

I leaned closer to her and said very quietly, "No. Two pairs will be enough. I only wear them on weekends."

"I JUST DIDN'T WANT YOU TO BE ALONE"

In the process of a divorce, I had moved out of our house in Altadena about two weeks earlier, and had come back late one night to pick up a few things that I needed. Juli and I had finished talking for the night and I was standing in the kitchen alone, leaning up against the counter in front of the kitchen sink. Jennifer walked into the doorway and stood there in her little pink ankle-length flannel nightgown.

I acknowledged her presence. "Hi. What are you doing up so late?"

Her reply was, "I just didn't want you to have to be alone."

At what age does compassion usually get fully developed? In her case it got expressed in the most complete and mature way before she was even three.

RAINY DAYS AND MONDAYS

Jennifer was four and she and I were driving somewhere on very gray, dreary day. It was raining just enough to have to switch the wipers on every 15 or 20 seconds. It was gray enough that you could only see a few blocks ahead. I had wanted to take her to the park or the beach but the weather was not going to permit it.

"I'm really sorry about this weather," I remarked as we stopped and started in traffic.

She didn't require an apology. "Oh, no. It's OK. I LIKE days like this."

"You do? Why?"

"'Cause on days like this you have to look at things up closer."

THE WOMBAT

I took Jennifer to the Los Angeles Zoo when she was about three and a half. We spent most of the day there, getting a pretty good look at nearly every exhibit. As we were driving away I asked her, "What did you like best today? What was your favorite animal?"

Her answer really puzzled me. "The wombat."

"The *wombat?*" I couldn't hide my surprise. I couldn't even REMEMBER the wombat for a few seconds. Even when I did I still couldn't figure out why the wombat could possibly have been her favorite. I had been certain it would've been one of the more dramatic animals—tiger, elephant, maybe even the giraffes. But the wombat?

"What was so great about the wombat? Why did you like him the most?"

"Because he likes people."

Suddenly I remembered the wombat clearly. He had been in one of the indoor "cages" with a large glass pane between him and us. As Jennifer had paced back and forth in front of him, he paced back and forth with her, following her every move. She was wearing a red overcoat that day and perhaps the bright color had attracted him. OR . . . maybe it was because he liked people.

I wasn't about to try to alter THAT opinion.

BLUE CROSS RUMORS

Upon discharge from the Air Force in March of 1971, we bought a house in Altadena, and—after a few weeks of desperation—I got a job with Blue Cross of Southern California as a Management Trainee in their Claims Department. It wasn't the job I wanted—I wanted to be a singer—but it would pay the bills.

Even though I got immersed in a musical theater workshop that took all of my attention, time, and energy, and even though I decided to get a divorce with all of the ensuing emotional trauma that accompanies that kind of life-altering event, I got quickly promoted a few times.

It was a huge claims department: over five hundred employees who worked in three shifts, in a room that looked bigger than a football field. Most claims adjusters could only get to know those who sat nearby, but as the Manager of the Training Department I made friends with many individuals who sat in different locations. I spoke casually with most, purchased a used Mercedes from one of the men, got interested in a young lady at the other end of the room, and had no idea that anyone was paying any attention to any of my comings and goings.

Every Wednesday afternoon the Claims Department section managers would meet with the "big guy" and we would all sit around a very large oblong table in a conference room. Just prior to one of these staff meetings, two different colleagues informed me that there were rumors circulating among the claims department about me. One of the rumors was that I was "seeing" the man from whom I had bought the Mercedes. (His desk was at the south end of the room.) The other rumor was that I was "seeing" the young lady I previously mentioned. (Her desk was at the north end of the room.)

The staff meeting was nearly over that day when our boss

asked if anyone had anything else to add to the proceedings. After the real business had been finished, I said that I would like to say something. He acknowledged me and I announced, "I have just heard that there are two rumors going around the department about me. One is that I'm seeing John Jacobs, and the other is that I'm seeing Jeannette Richards. I would like for all of you to know that the rumors are only half true."

Amidst the consternation and the laughter, I left the room and went home for the day.

"SCARLETT"

While working at Blue Cross, I got accepted—with a full scholarship—in the Civic Light Opera Musical Theatre Workshop. It was a very intense thirteen weeks; lots of hours of singing, dancing, acting classes, five nights a week. When it was all finished the instructors told me I was one of their favorites. I'd had a very good influence on the younger students. They offered me another thirteen weeks with another scholarship, but if I ever had intentions of working in musical theatre I had to get rid of my rather strong Southern accent. I opted not to do the entire 13 weeks again, but I did enlist a diction coach to help me. He gave me a practice tape and I worked diligently for almost six months.

I had gotten rid of a rather large portion of the accent when I had an opportunity to audition for a big show at the Civic Light Opera. It was called "Scarlett" and was a musical version of "Gone With the Wind." I got three callbacks for the part of Ashley. It was a very good part and what I thought would be a huge career break for me. After the third audition, I was told that they had given the part to another actor.

I was young and naïve and would never do this now, but then I didn't know any better, so I went back to the producers and asked them why I didn't get the part. I will never know if they told me this just to get rid of me or if it was really true, but in either case it was totally ironic. Their reply was, "We didn't think you could sustain a good Southern accent for the entire three hours."

I was so dumbfounded I couldn't even sputter a coherent rebuttal. With only one word, "Oh," totally without accent, I left. I think I'm still confused about the whole thing.

A GOOD GHOST STORY

I was in the middle stages of my first divorce. My decision had become irrevocable some months earlier. The paperwork would not be finalized for several months to come. But I had moved out.

I lived for three weeks in a big house with a friend and his girlfriend and stayed about a week too long. We all needed for me to leave but I really had nowhere to go. At some point of desperation she (the girlfriend) had a brilliant idea.

"Would you mind staying in a house that has no furniture? You'd have to sleep on the floor, but you'd be safe, *and* you'd actually be doing me a favor."

I had no notion what she was referring to, but I said, "Heck, yeah."

It turned out that she and her ex-husband were finally selling a house that they'd owned for many years. It was in a fashionable part of Hollywood, and all she wanted me to do was keep the house available for realtors to show, and make it look to neighbors and strangers like somebody was living there. The next day I took my sleeping bag and all my clothes and moved into one of the upstairs front bedrooms of a beautiful old house on N. Ogden Avenue, in between Sunset and Hollywood Boulevards.

That afternoon I heard the doorbell ring. I went down to the front door and no one was there. I went to the back door, thinking it might have a doorbell and no one was there. I went back to the front door and saw a man walking up the sidewalk toward the house. I noticed a realtor sign on the side of his car. I opened the door, said hello, and asked if he had rung the bell. He said he had not, that he had just now gotten out of his car. He asked if he could look around inside, that he had a prospective client who might be interested in looking at the house.

I said, "Sure," and let him check the place out. He left after a short tour.

The next day, I was upstairs when I heard the doorbell ring again. I went to the front door and no one was there. I went to the back door, and again, no one was there. I went back to the front door and saw a lady sitting in her car parked at the curb. Her car, too, had a realtor's logo on the side. I went out to the car and asked her if she had rung the doorbell. "No," she replied, "but I was just about to come up to the house. I'd like to know if it's OK for me to preview it."

I said, "Sure," and walked her up the sidewalk and through the house.

That evening, I was talking with my friend Gerardine, who owned the house, and told her about these odd experiences. She got a look on her face, and I asked "What?"

She stammered a bit, repeating herself, and rushed as she explained. "Well, we think the house is . . . is haunted, but we didn't want to say anything about it because . . . because we . . . we thought you might . . . you might . . . well, YOU know . . . you might be scared to . . . to stay in a haunted house, and I really do . . . I really do need you to be there, and I hope you'll stay even though it's haunted." I didn't think she was finished, so I didn't say anything. She implored me to stay with her next question. "You're not afraid to stay in a haunted house, are you?"

I was more amused than scared, and replied, "No, I'm not scared to stay in that house. I don't really believe in ghosts, so even though something odd happened, and even though you SAY it's haunted, I wouldn't be so sure about it. Sure. I'll stay as long as it's OK for me to be there. What makes you think it's haunted, though?"

"Well, there've been times when we thought we heard coat hangars rattling in the closet, and chilly drafts sweeping through the house, and sometimes even lights going off and on. Both

Ellen and I have been there when these kinds of things happened. So we think it's haunted." (Ellen was her best friend, and an acquaintance of mine, as well.) "But you'll stay?"

"Sure."

She was quite relieved and that was the end of that conversation.

At that time, I was taking a ten-week Hypnosis class at UCLA on Wednesday nights. That particular week the teacher, Terry Ballard, showed us something pretty remarkable. He told us at the beginning of the class that he didn't believe in ghosts, but he did believe in things that looked like ghosts. He went on to explain a phenomenon called astral projection, and he also went into a great deal of detail about human auras.

He told us what he was going to do and then did it: He sat in a chair, center-stage, put himself into a state of hypnosis, and then increased the intensity and size of his aura. It was a bright yellowish white aura. There were about a hundred students, seated in a steeply banked auditorium classroom, the lights had been dimmed, and it was easy to see Terry's aura. It extended six or eight inches from his head and shoulders, and was a bit smaller around the rest of his body. He then, very slowly moved the aura from his physical body and moved it across the stage, through the wall to his left. A few minutes later, he returned his aura into the room, slowly moving it from stage left and back again into his body. When he brought himself out of hypnosis, a few moments later, he asked, "How many of you saw what happened?" About 80 or 85 of us raised our hands. We didn't even have to ask what his question meant. We had seen the aura go from his body, through the wall, and come back again. It was a stunning demonstration.

"Did it look like a ghost?"

Those of us who had viewed it voiced our "YES!" in one loud response.

"There are some people who just don't see auras, so some

of you don't know what we're talking about right now, but most of you saw it, right?" Again, the room almost shook with the response. We were amazed and impressed.

"Well, THAT'S what I think ghosts are. Just people whose auras have gone someplace else, and they have energy, and we can see them, and I don't know but I think maybe they can even *do* things." Class was over and I immediately went down to the stage and got Terry's attention. He came over, I introduced myself, and asked him if he had few minutes to talk about ghosts, that I was living in a house that some people had told me was haunted. He was interested from the moment I starting talking with him.

After only a few sentences, he *really* wanted to check that house out!

He said he could come over any night that week, but he'd really like to come when the owner could be there, so I called Gerardine the next morning and asked her when she could fit it into her schedule. She said she and Ellen could come on Friday night at 7pm, and I made the appointment with Terry.

I had to be away for the afternoon and pulled my car up in front of the house about five minutes before seven. Terry had parked a few houses up, and was walking up and down the sidewalk in front of the house and also in front of the neighbor's houses.

"How're you doing? What's up?"

"I'm just trying to read some of the energy of these houses, if I can." He motioned for me to come to where he was standing at the north corner of the property. He pointed to the neighbor's house. "That house is pretty normal. I'd bet there are two old people in that house. It just kinda feels 'old' to me." Then he quickly walked us to the other corner of the property, pointing to the house that was neighboring the south side of the lot line. "Now THIS house feels really sad. I can't tell you why but it just feels very, very sad to me."

I confirmed his "readings." "In that house," pointing to the first one, "there are two old people. A very nice old couple, and mostly what they do at night is just watch TV. But THIS house . . . I can see why you think it's sad. There's an old lady who lives there and her husband died about a month ago. She's really sad, and doesn't know what to do about her great grief."

He nodded, knowing that his interpretations of the energies had been correct, and then he paced back to the front of the "haunted house." "But THIS house, WOW! There's something really strange going on in there."

I asked, "How do you *know*?"

He pointed to the roof. "Look at the roofline. What do you see?"

I looked. "I don't see anything. What do you mean?"

"Look carefully at the roofline. Tell me what you see."

It just looked blurry to me, so I took my glasses out of my pocket and put them on. Then I could see what he was talking about. "It looks like heat waves coming up from the blacktop except they're running back and forth along the top of the roof."

"EXACTLY! I think that's ENERGY! We're seeing some kind of energy coming from this house and there's a LOT of it. WOW! I've never seen anything like this. Maybe it is a ghost! Oh, man, this is good. Where's the woman who owns this house?"

Just at that moment, Gerardine and Ellen arrived.

I introduced Terry to them, he repeated what he and I had been discussing regarding the neighbor's houses, and they confirmed my information. We went inside, sat on the floor in the living room, and Terry let Gerardine and Ellen tell him all about the "ghost" and all the things that had gone on in the house during the past year.

Then he asked if he could go through the house and "check it out." They assured him that's why we were all there, and he and I got up and walked through every room downstairs. He looked in closets and cabinets, he opened the oven door, he picked up the corners of the oriental rugs, he opened the front and back doors, he flushed the toilet and turned the faucets on and off.

Nothing.

Then we went upstairs. He was climbing the steps in front of me and the moment his foot hit the floor of the upstairs hall, he froze. "IT'S HERE! It's right here!" I froze, too.

"What's here?"

"THE GHOST! Or whatever the heck it is! I can feel it and I can SEE it! It's right here. And it's NOT a ghost. It's energy!"

He motioned for me to come up the remaining steps and stand beside him. I did.

He asked me, "Do you SEE it?"

I couldn't see anything. "No, I don't see anything. What are you seeing?"

He explained. "Just unfocus your eyes. Don't try to look at anything in particular. Just stand here and be aware of what's around us."

The very moment I stopped trying to see something I saw it. "It's like the waves we saw on the roofline, isn't it? They're all around us aren't they?"

"YES! YES! That's exactly what it is!"

I could hardly believe what was happening. It felt a little scary, but he wasn't scared and I decided I didn't need to be scared either. It WAS exciting, though. I wanted to know what we were experiencing.

"What IS this?"

Terry paused, and moved his pursed lips around like he was searching for something to say but didn't quite know what to say. "I'm not sure yet. I CAN tell you for sure that it's not a ghost. This energy is coming from something that's alive. I think if I'll just be real still, and try to "read" this energy, maybe I can figure out what it is."

He stood motionless. His eyes would close then he would open them again. In the dimly lit hallway I could still see the energy waves rippling in front of us.

After 10 or 15 minutes, I stopped observing carefully, not being actively involved in whatever it was that he was doing. Then he said, "I think I've got a good idea of what this is. Let's go downstairs and ask Gerardine and Ellen some questions."

We hurried down the steps back to the living room where the ladies had been chatting. "Well?" Ellen asked. "What's going on?"

Terry started telling them what he had gotten from his "reading." "I think this energy is a man. He's not dead. He's alive. He lives somewhere else. Feels like far away. It feels like he really loves this house. It feels like he's trying to protect it somehow."

Gerardine and Ellen were listening intently.

"This guy is like an artist or something. And from what I know about astral projection I think this guy is asleep and I think he comes here while he's sleeping."

Ellen clasped her hand over her mouth. "OHMYGOD, Gerardine, he's describing JIMMY!"

Terry stopped talking about the "ghost" and asked, "Who's Jimmy?"

Gerardine answered. "Jimmy is my ex-husband." There was a long pause in the room. She continued. "Jimmy is VERY artistic. He's a director and he lives in Toronto now. He and I lived in this house for many years before our divorce, and . . ."

Ellen interrupted. "And he loved this house more than he loved Gerardine!" They both laughed at that comment, but Gerardine concurred.

"Yeah, he did! He REALLY loved this house. He didn't want to leave, and he still doesn't want us to sell this house. I mean, we HAVE to. But he doesn't WANT to."

Ellen added the definitive piece of information. "And Jimmy

was a Rosicrucian Catholic! Part of what he learned to do was to astral project! OHMYGOD, Gerardine, it IS Jimmy!"

I was silent through all of this. I was glad it wasn't a real ghost, but I wasn't all that happy to have some guy from Toronto astral projecting into this place where I was staying. So, I asked for a solution.

"What do we do now?"

Terry raised his eyebrows and without much conviction said, "Well, I think I'll go back upstairs and try to somehow 'get in touch' with this guy. I have no idea what'll happen, but I'm just going back up there and see what I can do."

I sat down with Gerardine and Ellen as he walked up the stairs. The three of us chatted for about 15 minutes until Terry came back down and quietly announced, "I think I fixed it. I think I actually communicated with him and he's gone."

"What do you mean 'gone'", I asked.

"I mean, his energy's not here any more. Come back upstairs with me and see." He addressed Gerardine and Ellen, "Do you want to come up, too?" They both shook their heads, "No."

I once again followed Terry up the stairs and when we both got into the upstairs hallway he said, "What do you see NOW?"

I purposely unfocused my eyes and did my best to see what I'd seen before. But there was nothing to see, nothing to feel, nothing odd to sense in any way. I said, "It's gone."

"Yeah," Terry said. "I kind of zeroed in on this Jimmy guy. I tuned into his energy, and told him that the house was safe, it was going to be OK, that he didn't need to be concerned about it any more, and that it would be perfectly alright for him to not come here any more. Practically the moment I felt like I was really communicating with him, the energy went away. It was pretty weird, man. It just disappeared."

It sure was gone. We went back downstairs and the four of us discussed how Jimmy must've been trying to thwart the sale of the house. Terry told us his stories about astral projecting, we all told other more ghostly tales, and around 9pm we were ready to depart.

We all went out front, Terry and I said goodbye to Gerardine and Ellen, and he and I stood on the front sidewalk looking back at the house.

"What do you see now?"

I put my glasses on and gazed intently at the roofline.

Nothing.

"Nothing. It's just like a regular house now."

"Yeah," Terry said. "Just like a regular house now."

As he walked up the street to his car, I said, "Thanks for coming over. See you next Wednesday." The next week I would use my new hypnosis skills to quit smoking. Terry was becoming a teacher of great value.

The following Monday night I went to my first acting class with a renowned acting teacher, Curt Conway. My car had broken down and I ended up walking about two miles to the class. As I crossed Sunset Blvd., I thought, "Life is SO great. I am absolutely loving my life right now."

I had a broken down car, I was paying twice as much in alimony and child support as I was collecting from Unemployment, I had applied for and been denied Food Stamps, Curt Conway had "loaned" me the initial $55 for the acting classes, and I was one of the happiest people in all of Hollywood. Go figger. Many years later I learned that circumstances do not determine our feelings. We determine our feelings.

Because the acting class was mostly scenes, I only observed for the first two hours. The final hour was spent on an exercise where everyone had been instructed to bring a prop with them. Each actor was to use the prop as he or she told a story, and then the class voted whether they thought it was true story or one the actor had invented. Everyone had done their piece, and Curt was giving his final comments when I asked if I could do the exercise.

"But you didn't know to bring a prop with you," he explained.

"Well, actually I do have a prop with me." I walked from my seat down to the stage. "Is it OK to take an extra five minutes with this?"

"Sure, go ahead."

I stood in front of this group of actors, and announced that my prop was a ghost. He was with me on stage, and as I sat on the bench, I continued, "And now he's sitting right here beside me." I then proceeded to tell them the entire story about Terry Ballard and Gerardine and Ellen, referring to Jimmy Douglas throughout the monologue.

At the end of my story Curt asked for a vote of the class. They were completely silent. I had believed so completely in my story that it all seemed totally real to them. When Curt asked for a show of hands, every single person thought the ghost was right there beside me. They couldn't see it, but they were pretty sure I *could*. It was a good start to an acting career that never took off.

"STILL ROLLIN' AROUND DOWN THERE"

My two-year-old nephew (the one who hollered, "HEY!") was standing in the kitchen and purposefully put his hand into his pocket. A moment later he announced rather loudly to no one in particular, "Yep, they're still rollin' around down there."

THE RAY CHARLES SINGERS: FIRST DAY

After a number of auditions for musicals, commercials, films, and plays, I auditioned for Ray Charles. Not the black, blind, R&B Ray Charles. The white, arranger, songwriter, special-material writer Ray Charles. We called him the white, deaf Ray Charles. But he does have an exquisite musical ear. His six-part vocals arrangements are still among the best ever written. After many years of being mixed up with the more famous Ray Charles, this Ray Charles registered his name with the unions as "The Other" Ray Charles. I was fortunate enough to be chosen to be one of the twelve new Ray Charles Singers.

The first day of rehearsal with the newest iteration of The Ray Charles Singers was at CBS in the early fall of 1972. Ray had always had "recording groups" but this was the first time he'd ever attempted to put together a group that would perform on stage. We were scheduled to be an opening act and backup singers for Perry Como in Las Vegas, Lake Tahoe, and on television specials. Ray hired three singers he'd known previously, but nine of us were singers he'd never known until we auditioned for him the month before. It hadn't been a particularly rigorous audition but Ray knew exactly what he wanted and conducted auditions that gave him what he needed.

We had to be able to sight-read music very well. We had to have a pleasant voice and sing precisely on pitch. We had to be able to blend with eleven others. And, evidently, each of us had to be a nice person. All of the musical criteria were evident from the first eight bars we ever sang together. The last requirement, that we be nice people, became evident later, but was of greater lasting importance to all of us.

We began at nine in the morning. He passed out charts, we

introduced ourselves, Bob Alberti began playing and we all began singing. It was my first real job as a professional singer and it was (if you'll excuse the play on words) noteworthy. Actually, at that moment in my life it all felt monumental. It was the achievement of a great goal, *plus* it was a glorious, beautiful sound. There's hardly anything more fulfilling than to be part of a group that produces "complete" music: harmonic, in tune, balanced in every way. Oh, what a deep pleasure that first hour was.

I was singing! I was having the time of my life! I was getting paid for it!

Around 10:45, even though he told me later he was reluctant to do so because he was enjoying it so much, Ray suggested that we take a break. Not one of us wanted to. No one even got up out of his or her chair. We wanted to keep singing.

By the end of the day I think everyone knew we were part of something special. And it was. I have more great memories than there will be stories in this book, but we sure did love each other. And many years later, Ray would say that this was his favorite group of all the Ray Charles Singers that ever sang together. It sure was *my* favorite group.

RAY'S SWEATERS

The first day of rehearsals Ray wore a beautiful V-neck sweater. I don't recall the color. (You'll know why in a few more sentences.) The next day he wore *another* beautiful V-neck sweater. The third day (or maybe the fourth) he wore another beautiful V-neck sweater. By this time, I had noticed.

When he showed up in a fourth beautiful v-neck sweater (all of them exactly the same designer and the same cut but different colors) I asked him about them.

"I've noticed all of your beautiful V-neck sweaters, all by the same designer. How many of them do you own?"

"I don't know."

He could see my surprise, and went on. "Bernice and I just returned from a rather interesting cruise. A friend asked us if we'd like to go sailing in the Mediterranean, putting in at every nice port we could sail to. It was an amazing 30 days, six of us sailing with a 10-man crew, an incredible chef, the most accommodating weather, and a trip of a lifetime."

My face was showing all the fascination that I was feeling when I returned to my original question, "But what about the sweaters?"

"Oh, yeah. The sweaters. I can't remember the city we were in, but I went into this clothing shop and saw these beautiful V-neck sweaters. They were on sale. REALLY on sale. I asked the salesman to sell me one of each color. He wrapped them, I paid for them, Bernice packed them, I've been wearing them this week, and I honestly don't know how many colors I have."

He chuckled at his innocence. I laughed at his total lack of information about this incredible exhibit of sartorial splendor. It turned out that he had eleven or twelve of these sweaters. They might've been cashmere. They might've only been very soft merino wool. I don't know. But they were *very* nice, and they were all the colors of the rainbow plus four or five more.

It made a deep impression on me. At first I thought, *"Gee, that's pretty extravagant."* A few days later I realized that he had gotten a good bargain, he had plenty of disposable income, he'd been on a cruise that could've cost tens of thousands of dollars but hadn't had to pay for it and instead of buying trinkets he bought these sweaters, and they were giving him a tremendous amount of pleasure.

Oh, we could probably all do more altruistic things with our money, but we don't always do it.

I have more than twelve sweaters. They're just not all by the same designer and I didn't buy them all at once. In the long run, what's the difference? Way to go, Ray.

I wouldn't be surprised to learn he still has them. They were timelessly styled and impeccably knit. Maybe even a better bargain than he thought when he bought them. Way to go, Ray.

ALL YOU CAN EAT
FOR A WEEK...

The first time The Ray Charles Singers worked live on stage with Perry Como was in 1972, at the Las Vegas Hilton for two weeks over Thanksgiving. We didn't get our rooms paid for, so Rich Maxwell and I agreed to stay together in a little suite with a kitchenette, which was only a few blocks from the Hilton. We figured we could actually go home with some money in our pockets.

The first night we arrived in Las Vegas he and I went to the Thunderbird Hotel for a $2.99 buffet. I had a very fine idea before we left our motel room: I lined the pockets of my overcoat with aluminum foil. We went back for seconds and thirds of everything, then just before we left I went back for a big plate of fried chicken—about 10 or 12 pieces. I put on my overcoat, and one by one, those pieces got placed into my foil-lined pockets. We departed with enough chicken to last the rest of the week.

THANKSGIVING IN LAS VEGAS

On Thanksgiving afternoon, Perry and his wife, Rozelle, invited all of us up to their penthouse for a Thanksgiving dinner. One of the most fun parts of the day was playing the two slot machines that were in the living room. When I arrived, the nickel machine had a tray full of nickels and Perry told all of us that we were welcome to play the machine with those nickels. As my tray dwindled, and it looked like I might have to stop playing after just a few more pulls of the handle, Perry walked over, opened the machine with a key, made a slight adjustment to the mechanics inside, and said quietly, "Now put in three nickels and give it another try." I did as he told me and hit a jackpot that made all the bells ring and poured hundreds of nickels into the tray. It was fun for me to hit a jackpot, and even more fun for him to know how to make it happen.

We had a sumptuous meal, and after we had eaten all we could, Nick Perito, Perry's pianist/conductor sat down at a grand piano and announced that he would be pleased to accompany anyone who wanted to sing something. The group was comprised of twelve very fine singers, all of them more experienced than I. I recall that I sang "My Funny Valentine" and was so very happy to be accompanied by one of the finest in all of show business.

We only did one show on Thanksgiving night and as I was walking backstage with Perry, the stage manager informed him of the "room counts" up and down the strip. The Hilton showroom held around 1400, and that night we had only had about 700. Perry was disappointed until he found out that at the Sahara, Milton Berle had an audience of 85. And at the Tropicana, Jack Benny had only 35. He remarked to me, "You'd think those old farts would get out of the business."

I thought about it for a moment and replied, "But what would they do?"

He didn't pause for a second. "Anything! Anything's better than not having anyone show up."

He didn't get it. I said to him, "But they don't know how to do anything else. Standing on stage is the only thing they know how to do."

He argued that point on his own behalf. "Man, not me! I'd WAY rather be playing golf or taking my boat out fishing."

"Really?"

"Yeah, I only still sing 'cause it's the easiest way for me to make a good living."

It surprised me to hear that. The easiest-going singer in the world was actually happier doing other things! It also surprised me to discover how extremely competitive he was. He wanted to crush Berle and Benny—every night. And he did.

A MAGICAL CHRISTMAS

Perry Como was going to be at Harrah's South Tahoe during the Christmas holidays and The Ray Charles Singers were to be there, as well. Two weeks.

Four of the guys decided that we should rent a four-bedroom house for the two weeks and even though it wouldn't save us any money it would be more fun. After searching the South Lake Tahoe newspaper ads we finally found something that we could afford and sent a deposit.

When we arrived we discovered that one of the "bedrooms" was being used for storage and there were actually only three bedrooms. We drew straws and Rich and I lost. We moved into the largest of the three bedrooms, upstairs. It was inconvenient, especially when my girlfriend drove up to stay for a few days, but it was all so fun-filled that there were no real problems. Janet came up to be with Jim. Cissy came up to be with Steve. Peggy came up to be with me. Rich still couldn't find a girlfriend.

One of the nights at Harrah's there was a storm and the electricity went out in the hotel during Perry's show. Instead of canceling the show, which was already half an hour in progress, the waiters moved all the candles from the tables to the edge of the stage and Perry sat at the front and sang without a microphone, accompanied softly by his great pianist, Nick Perito. On the numbers for which we usually sang backup for him, we came out, sat around him, and sang as softly as you've ever heard any twelve people sing.

I'm certain no one in the audience will ever forget that night. It was beautiful. It was unique. It was memorable. It was magical.

Two days later it snowed so hard that Harrah's *did* cancel the shows for that night. Unexpectedly, we all had a night off. We invited the others in the group to come over to our house. Some of them came and around 11pm we decided to walk down to the payphone so Jim could call Janet, who had gone back to work as a dancer in Las Vegas. There was a full moon and the snow had almost stopped falling, and we were all crunching along in the snow, chatting, laughing, truly enjoying the time off. My reverie was rudely interrupted by a very cold, hard WHACK to the side of my face. A SNOWBALL! I didn't even know who'd thrown it, but the fight was on! No stopping anyone until everyone had been hit at least once. There were no "sides.." It was every man (or woman) for himself (or herself). No quarter given. None expected. We were ALL in it.

I guess there were nine of us. I have no idea how many shots I took or how many hits I made, but we were howling with glee and running and hiding and no group of adults has ever had more fun for ten minutes. It, too, was magical.

NEVER A STRUGGLE

Perry and I were riding the elevator down to the dressing rooms (He had bad knees and didn't like climbing up and down stairs if he didn't have to.) and he mentioned something about the lounge acts in the hotel. "Kinda makes you wonder why they'd want to do something that was so hard for such a small amount of money."

I said, "They're just doing their best to break into the business. I mean, actually, working a lounge in Las Vegas is a pretty good gig considering how many acts are still playing the Holiday Inn in Amarillo, ya know?"

Then I asked him, "How'd *you* start out?"

"Well, it's not a very long story. I guess my first singing job was with a local guy named Freddie Carlone, but the very next year I got a good singing job with the Ted Weems Orchestra. It was the most famous band in the country at the time, and it had a kind of odd feature. There was this guy named Elmo Tanner and he was a whistler. He was really good, so he'd get to whistle all the big hits and I'd sing all the little hits. That job got me started and got me a lot of national attention."

"So your very first job was with the biggest band in the country?" I was almost incredulous. "And then you got a recording career and some hit records, and few movies, and then a television show, and basically you've always been a star?"

"Yeah, I guess so."

"Wow." It was no wonder he didn't understand why anyone would be willing to struggle to make it in show business. He never had to.

His father had been a barber and as a young teenager Perry had obtained a barber's license and worked in his father's barbershop. He actually cut hair, and even sang to entertain the customers, but never actually called barbering a career. One night I asked him if it was true that he still had his barber's license. He admitted, "Yeah, I do. I renew it every year. I figure if my singing career ever hits the skids I can go back to cutting hair."

I thought, *"Yeah, if your singing career ever hits the skids you can go fishing and play golf every day."*

In spite of the fact that he had little understanding of others in his own business, Perry Como was truly one of the nicest men who ever set foot on stage. Oh, he wasn't without faults, but he was more gracious and sweeter and softer than any other big star I ever met.

NECROPHILIA

One of the guys in The Ray Charles Singers was gay. He wasn't blatant about it, but kept it no secret either. He shall remain nameless for this story.

In a rambling dressing room conversation one night a few of us somehow got to talking about necrophilia. From the far end of the room he loudly asked, "What's necrophilia?" The rest of us explained it to him, sparing no details. He gasped. "EEeeyoo! I could NEVER do THAT!"

About twenty minutes later, as we were all talking about something else, from the same far end of the dressing room we heard him say, "Well, I don't *think* I could ever do that."

"THERE'S NO BUSINESS . . ."

One of the jobs with The Ray Charles Singers was to perform for a Writers' Guild Banquet in Beverly Hills. It was to be another ordinary great job, except that by the time the date rolled around all the Hollywood writers were on strike. The event was held as scheduled, to honor their own, regardless of whether any of them were making any money that month, and it was a gala: a posh banquet room in a posh hotel. Dinner was served; short speeches were made. Then it was time for the entertainment.

The orchestra began the intro, the curtain went up, the twelve Ray Charles Singer "marched" from upstage down toward the front of the stage and sang with great gusto, to the well-known tune from "Annie Get Your Gun." "T – H – E – R – E ' S . . . NO BUSINESS!"

BLACKOUT

It's impossible to remember how long the laughter went on, but it was huge and it came in rolls as each group of tables would realize once more, and sometimes even once more, how very funny that was.

Ray Charles has always been known as one of the best parody writers in America, and this turned out to be one of shortest and funniest parodies in many a decade. After the laughter began to wane, the applause began. And IT lasted a long time, as well.

I don't remember anything else about that show. But I'll never forget that opening. I'll bet it's the same with nearly every member of the audience.

SINGING BUSBOY

After my job(s) with the Ray Charles Singers had pretty much come to an end, I found my bank account diminishing quickly and had nothing on the horizon. I scoured the newspapers for temporary jobs and obtained a weekend of very hard work as an inventory clerk for a major department store. But that was only two and a half days of work at very low pay, and I needed something more substantial, or at least something that lasted longer.

I finally found an ad for a busboy at The Great American Food and Beverage Company, in Santa Monica, interviewed for it, and got the job. No experience necessary. It was a nice but casual restaurant where all the waiters and waitresses SANG. Perfect. I could still be a singer and could earn a meager living while auditioning for other things.

First day on the job, though, I discovered that no one was allowed to sing until his or her table chores were complete (at least for the three minutes it took to sing a song), and therefore, no busboy had ever sung a note in that restaurant. Pretty major disappointment.

The next day I thought, "I've got to find a better system to this busboy thing or I'll never get to sing." By the end of the day, I was carrying bread and butter to the table at the same time as the water pitcher and the extra napkins, I was stacking dishes and cleaning and clearing tables in one trip, I was checking on the needs of all my tables before I went into the kitchen for anything so I could get everything everyone needed much more quickly, I knew I could come in ten minutes early the next day and get the watermelon slices cut in advance, and by the end of the second day I HAD A SYSTEM!

I didn't get to sing any songs the second day, but there were moments when I was very close to having all of my bussing chores caught up. AND . . . I was doing one heck of a job of being a great busboy.

By the middle of my shift on the third day I was ahead of my curve, and asked if I could sing a song. The manager was quite certain that I was leaving something unattended (no busboy had ever asked before). But about two hours later, he told me that if I kept doing the same level of work that I had been doing that day, I could sing . . . tomorrow. I didn't think that was fair, but at least I had something to look forward to the next day, and hoped that the restaurant wouldn't be packed.

The next day was a Friday and it was packed, but my system held up and by late afternoon, I was, once again, all caught up, and I got to sing. One song. "I Left My Heart In San Francisco." I remember it was a request of a table of ten or twelve, a birthday party for a daughter who was, maybe eight or nine, and the mother was a charcoal portrait artist. As a tip for my singing she offered to do a portrait of my three-year-old daughter. It was a $300 tip! But I never found time to take Jennifer to go sit for the portrait. Two weeks later I became the newest member of The Doodletown Pipers, thus ending my busboy career.

But I got to sing a number of times in those next two weeks.

Another remarkable thing happened in that restaurant that month, as well. By the end of my second week, because I was doing such an amazing job of bussing, the tips of the waiters and waitresses who had me as their busboy had risen dramatically. They all noticed it and got together and voted to give me 25% of their tips rather than the standard 10%. It was pretty much unheard of in the food service business. They were all REALLY bummed when I quit.

Years later, in my studies of goal setting, visioning, and positive psychology and spirituality, I learned that what I had done was a classic, metaphysical practice in accomplishing any major task. By concentrating on what I wanted rather than what my "problem" was, I set into motion a series of thoughts and actions that otherwise wouldn't have come to me. By seeing myself "singing" rather than just "working harder as a busboy," my dream for myself in that restaurant came true very, very quickly.

Who would predict that learning how to carry bread and butter and water at the same time could ever be an important part of making a dream come true?

LA STRADA

In the early 70s on Mondays I was singing in Santa Monica at a club called The Horn, and the other six nights a week I was in Glendale at La Strada. La Strada was a fine Italian restaurant and was known for always having three or four opera singers working every night. The show was on the stage and in the audience; arias, Neapolitan songs; fine singers, lots of divas.

I could sing opera, but I was better at Broadway. The owner, when he hired me, admitted that none of his singers were "Broadway types," and that I might not fit in perfectly, but what he wanted me to do was MC the show, sing a few arias each night, and intersperse four or five Broadway songs among the opera singers. He thought it would work and so did I.

My first rehearsal with the pianist was memorable. He shall remain nameless but he was a very fine pianist, an accomplished accompanist, and had worked all his life in movie and recording studios. I was to soon find out that he was also opinionated.

As we were going through my first aria, "Avant de Quitter Ces Lieux," from *Faust*, by Gounod, we'd gotten about halfway through it when he stopped and said, "No, no! This is the way it goes," and proceeded to play it differently than I'd sung it. That had never happened to me before and I responded by saying, "But this is the way I do it," to which he responded, "But THIS IS THE WAY IT GOES!" and played it again.

He wasn't playing any of the notes differently—he was interpreting the phrasing differently. We were at a momentary artistic impasse.

I came back at him as gently as I could, considering the fact that he was really pissing me off. "Mr. [Nameless], I understand you've played this many times for many different singers, but the tempo and the phrasing is sort of an artistic choice that I'm making here, and I've done this aria many times, and this is what seems to work best for me."

He didn't care what worked for me. He continued to insist, "Young man, I have played this many, many times, for many, many very fine baritones, and this is how it goes!" He played it again. His way. And then with his greatest finality, stated, "I'm a musician, and I know!"

I squatted down—I was on a stage about 4 feet above him—to get a little closer to him, and said with an enormous amount of calmness, "OK, here's the deal. We are BOTH musicians. Your instrument is the piano. My instrument is my voice. Most people refer to us as 'singer' and 'piano player,' but trust me, *we are both musicians*. I appreciate the same qualities of music that you do, I always attempt to interpret music in a way that's consistent with the genre and the composer's intent, and I always try to sing so my listener can understand what I'm trying to convey. It's just that I'm up here in the spotlight and you're down there working with less notice. I'm the one getting the applause if we're good, and also I'm the one who takes the heat if it DOESN'T go so well. So, as one musician to another, how about making a compromise with me? I'll move a little your way and you move a little my way, and we'll see how it goes."

He was silent for a few moments, then spoke. "You know, young man, I've been in this business for many decades, and no singer has ever before referred to himself as a musician. I would never have considered it, but, of course, you're right. We ARE both musicians. Thank you for pointing that out to me."

I stood up, took a big breath, and said, "Let's try it again from the top and when we get to this section, if you'll be kind enough to play it a tiny bit faster, I'll do my best to sing it a tiny bit slower, and let's hope we can stay together this time."

We began again. We got through it. It was perfect. I worked, happily, with him until I got a job in "Hallelujah Hollywood" and moved to Las Vegas. (See HALLELUJAH HOLLYWOOD)

"GAAAAAHUHLEEEEEE!"

The Horn was one of better-known nightclubs in Southern California in the sixties and early seventies. It wasn't very big, but they always had great acts there and it stayed busy. Mondays were the slowest night and I got lucky enough to get a short-lived but semi-regular slot on Monday nights. I'd usually go on for about twenty minutes some time between ten and eleven o'clock. I got paid $25.

It was an opportunity for me to hone my craft as an entertainer and also to try out a few of the songs I'd been writing. They weren't very good songs, but I didn't know it.

One night I decided I would try out some of my impressions. I think I did Kirk Douglas, and I might have done Boris Karloff or some other old actor, but my best impression at that time was Gomer Pyle. I did a really good Gomer. That night I got to what I thought was going to be the big laugh, a place where I could go on with my act, and no one laughed. So, being new at this, I had no idea what to do and I just kept on doing Gomer, and the laughs were definitely not what one would want them to be when one is trying to be funny. I realized I was dying. Once I realized that, I was REALLY dying.

Suddenly, from the back of the room, at the end of the bar, in an amazingly good Sergeant Carter voice, one of the comedians who was there that night, Glenn Ash, yelled, "All right Pyle! Cut the crap! Now get back to singing!" The crowd laughed heartily, I yelled back in my best Gomer Pyle voice, "GAAAAAHUHLEEEEEE, Sergeant Carter. Thaaank yoouu! You have just saved my life!" They laughed again, and I WAS saved, and I got back to singing. After my closing song I got a rousing ovation.

Several months later, I was working with the Doodletown Pipers at a big fairground in Santa Barbara and saw Glenn. I went up to him and told him how very much I had appreciated what he had done for me at The Horn a few months earlier, but he didn't remember doing it. He remembered ME, but he didn't remember SAVING me. I can understand that. He had been at the bar, drinking. I had been on stage, dying. He hadn't needed to be saved that night. What we do for others can seem insignificant to us and be monumental to them. Or . . . visa versa.

RESPECT FOR THE DEAD

I read about an audition in Los Angeles for "The Unsinkable Molly Brown." There's no part in the show that I was right for but I wanted the director to hear me sing, so I went. I sang, "All the Things You Are.. I did a nice job and after I finished I stood there waiting for a response.

Usually, one hears, "Thank you very much." Or, "Thank you. That was great. Can you come back in on the 19th, and sing a song from the show?" But one hardly ever hears silence. That's what I got. A *looonnng* silence. I continued to stand there. I didn't quite know what to do.

Then, in a slow, measured, very respectful voice, the director asked, "Would you sing at my funeral?" No one knew whether to laugh or not. There was more silence.

Then, amidst my total surprise and confusion, there was silence on MY part. After a moment, I asked, in a slow, measured, very respectful voice, "Are you planning to die soon?" at which time everybody laughed, including the director, and he stood up.

"No, I'm not. But that was the most beautiful singing I've ever heard, and even though you and I both know there's nothing in this show for you, I just kinda wanted to cast you for *something*."

I replied, "Well, when you get ready to die, give me a call. My number is on my resumé. Thanks for the compliment—I think. Hope to see you again before too long. Or not." And I left.

So far, he hasn't called.

AUDITIONING FOR THE DODGERS

Ever since I went to an Atlanta Braves game while I was in college, I thought it would be really cool to sing the National Anthem at a major league game. I had always been a huge baseball fan, collected thousands of cards when I was a boy, still know the rules and the nuances of the game, and wow, how neat would it be to sing the Star Spangled Banner in front of a whole lot of other baseball fans?

When I moved to Los Angeles, I decided to call the Dodgers and ask about it. They told me to send a photo and resumé. *"How very 'Hollywood,'"* I thought. But I sent an 8x10 and a resumé and about three weeks later I got a call from them asking if I could come over to Dodger Stadium on a Wednesday afternoon at 2pm.

I was still working at Blue Cross at the time so I had to get some time off. My boss said, "Go ahead. I guess it's not like you're getting a real singing job and quitting Blue Cross."

I arrived at Dodger Stadium close to 2 o'clock, parked my car, and went to the gate they had told to go to. A man who told me he was one of the electricians for the Dodgers met me there. He escorted me around the stadium and then, while carrying a microphone stand with a mike on it, took me through a very wide gate onto the outfield grass.

"Wait right here until someone tells you to sing." Then he went back through the gate and I was, OHMYGOD, alone in the outfield of one of the newest, grandest stadiums in the world. The grass was really, really green. The seats were clean. The sun was shining. I was standing in the outfield of Dodger Stadium. My reverie was broken by a raspy voice, coming from somewhere in the left field stands.

A man hollered, "OK, kid. Let's hear it!"

I began to sing. "Oh, say can you see . . ."

There was a pretty long delay between the time I sang the words and the time I *heard* the words in the sound system. It was very disconcerting, but I got through the anthem without repeating any words or notes. I guess it was good enough.

I heard, "That's great, kid! Come up to my office!"

Immediately, the electrician reappeared, swept the stand and mike off the grass and I followed him through the gate. He put the equipment into a little room under the bleachers and I went with him to the club level of the stadium where the executive offices are. As I walked into the office of the man who had listened to me, I could see the inside of Dodger Stadium through immense picture windows. I thought, *"Man, if I don't make it as a singer, I want to work for the Dodgers."* That was the most beautiful view from an office I'd ever seen.

I shook hands with Red Patterson. He was the Vice President of the Dodgers (and later went on to be the number one executive for the California Angels). We exchanged pleasantries, talked a little baseball, and then he said, "So, how many times would you like to sing this season?" I was flabbergasted. I had hoped for *one* time. He was offering much more. I stammered, "Well, I guess I'd like to sing as often as I can. Thank you!"

I got to sing three times that season. Two days before I was to sing the first time, I had all of my clothes stolen from my car. I had very little money but knew I had to look good at Dodger Stadium. I went to one of the big men's suit chains and bought a gray glen plaid suit for $55. I felt and looked like a million bucks. It was an amazing experience AND I got great seats for the game.

The next season I sang two or three times, but I remember most clearly the Old Timer's Game. This was a pre-game exhibition between the Dodger Old-Timers and the "rest of the major leagues" old-timers. In those days, they let the anthem singer hang out in the dugout before he or she had to sing. I WAS IN THE DUGOUT

WITH MY BASEBALL CARDS! Whitey Ford, Mickey Mantle, Yogi Berra, Dale Long (8 home runs in 8 consecutive at bats). As I got up from my seat to walk to the other end of the dugout and go around the track to the outfield, I walked past Satchel Paige. His sleeve touched mine. I almost passed out. In my lifetime, I've shaken hands with three Presidents of the United States. I think that's kind of impressive for a regular citizen. But nothing has ever thrilled me like having Satchel Paige's sleeve touch mine.

Shortly thereafter, the Dodgers discovered they could use the National Anthem as a marketing tool, and unknown singers got fewer and fewer opportunities to sing. However, I was honored to be allowed to sing at least once a season for 32 years in a row. Then I missed a year, sang the next, and missed all the years since. It was a good long run, and though perhaps others have eclipsed my "record," I am absolutely certain that no one enjoyed singing there more than I. Baseball and singing—two of my most favorite things to do—combined. WOW!

I guess it pays to always have a picture and resumé on hand.

JOE COOL TIE

After I'd sung the National Anthem for many years in a row, some time in the early to mid 90s, I wore an item of clothing that I later regretted. I always wore a jacket and a tie when I sang, just out of respect for the job, I guess. That night, after I'd sung, and I came back to our very, very fine lower level box seats, my wife said, "Look at me, and don't look down." I did as she requested. "Now," she said as she put her hand over my chest, "do you know what tie you have on?" She was laughing. I had to think for a few moments and then I realized what she was laughing about. I had worn one of my Snoopy ties. It was red with a tiny image of Snoopy near the bottom and was totally covered with the words, "Joe Cool."

Dodger Stadium has what they call Diamond Vision. It's a 40-foot high jumbotron. While the National Anthem is being sung, a man with a television-quality camera gets right under the singers nose and puts the singer on the 40-foot screen.

Joe Dickey was advertising himself to 50,000 fans as Joe Cool. The necktie was twenty feet long and three feet wide and "Joe Cool" had been pretty easy to read. I was embarrassed for my lack of awareness. I can't say that I felt humiliated, but I most certainly was self-consciously uncomfortable. I put the tie in my coat pocket for the remainder of the evening.

SUGAR RAY ROBINSON

After singing the National Anthem at Dodger Stadium for several years in a row, I thought it would be cool to sing at a Lakers game. I didn't realize it would be even more difficult to achieve that goal than my original dream of singing for the Dodgers, but pro basketball teams play fewer games and LA is pretty enthusiastic about the Lakers, so the competition was quite stiff.

I called the Lakers and got in touch with the man who was in charge of the anthem singers, Eddie Parr. He set an appointment for me to come audition, and when I arrived he took me to a long, narrow concrete-walled room in the bowels of the Forum. He sat in a folding chair near the door and told me to go to the other end of the room and sing. I did.

As I belted out the final note, he applauded and asked, "Have you been to a lot of Lakers' games?"

I answered, "No, I've never even been to the Forum before today."

"How'd you know how to sing the anthem, then? That's *exactly* how I ask all of our singers to do it."

"Well, I guess that's just how I think it should be sung. I've always sung it like that."

"OK, Joe! I know you'll sing it just like that next month. Since the season's more than half over, the only games I have left are playoff games. It looks like the team will definitely make the playoffs this year, so I'll put you down as the singer for the first home playoff game. Don't know who that'll be yet, or the date, but I'll let you know. Congratulations! Good job, young man. You'll get two tickets and a parking pass, and I'll give you all the other instructions you need when I call you. OK?"

I was really happy to be singing, AND for a playoff game. "O-K!"

It turned out to be the Lakers and the Bucks, but I didn't care

WHO they were playing. I felt honored and lucky and thrilled. I asked my friend Rich if he wanted to go with me and he said, "Absolutely!"

When we got into the arena, I was very disappointed to discover that our seats were up high in the "end zone." We were on the first level, but pretty far from the action. I thought they should've given me better seats like the Dodgers do, but . . . hey! I was here. I was the singer. I was very excited.

At the appointed time I made my way down to the floor, sang well, and climbed back up to my seat. About two minutes later I realized I was sitting three seats away from one of my childhood idols, Sugar Ray Robinson. During his illustrious career he had been referred to as the best boxer, pound for pound, in the world. He had a streak of 91 fights without a loss. I had been in awe of him and I didn't quite know what to do. I wanted to be respectful of his celebrity and not bother him, but I also really wanted to meet him. All during the first half of the game I was at odds with myself.

As the half ended, he left to go get something to eat. I switched seats with Rich and moved over beside Ray's wife. I introduced myself as the guy who had sung The National Anthem, told her that her husband had been one of my childhood heroes, and also told her that I had a story to tell her that might amuse her. She was kind enough to say, "Well, tell me. I wanna hear it."

I began. "When I was five years old, your husband had a title fight in London, with Randy Turpin. My brother and I were big boxing fans—we listened to Archie Moore defeat Ezzard Charles to win a heavyweight title, we heard Rocky Marciano fight many times, and we loved Sugar Ray Robinson more than any other fighter. So we were talking to our uncle about this fight coming up in London and were absolutely certain that your husband was going to win. Our uncle asked us if we'd like to make a bet on the fight. Our parents were not gambling types and my brother and I were pretty certain that gambling was a sin, but when our uncle said, 'How 'bout a dollar each?' which was a LOT of money to us, all we could think about was WINNING. The odds were 3-1 in our favor. We agreed to the bet. As it turned out, and I'm sure you remember the night, it was a *sweltering* night in London, hot and very humid, and it was a tough fight, and Ray was tired going into it, and Turpin just kind of beat up on him all night. It was your husband's first loss in a very, very long time. My brother and I were devastated, but even worse, we'd lost the bet. The next day we saw our uncle and he insisted that we pay up. We had to give him a dime a month for the next ten months."

She was thoroughly tickled by my rendition of this tale, and enthusiastically responded, "Oh, Mr. Dickey, you HAVE to tell that story to Ray when he comes back." A few minutes later he arrived with food and drinks and she switched seats with him so he could sit by me. "Ray, this is Joe Dickey. He sang The National Anthem before the game tonight. He has a story he wants to tell you."

We shook hands, he said, "Nice to meet ya," and then he gave me his full attention. "Go ahead. Let's hear it."

So I told him the same story I'd just told his wife. When I got to the end, the part about having to pay our uncle a dime a month, he laughed really hard and grinned as he asked, "So, whaddaya want? Your dollar back?"

Getting to sit beside him for the rest of the game was priceless. Sometime later that year, I was proud to get to sing at NBC on the Sugar Ray Robinson Foundation Telethon. I suspect he and I at least broke even over the years.

HALLELUJAH HOLLYWOOD

I wish I could remember who told me about the audition for Hallelujah Hollywood. I owe that person a huge thank you. I hadn't read anything about it, and when I heard about the auditions, I called immediately. The man I spoke with was actually the producer, Donn Arden. He told me the auditions were over, that I had missed them by about 10 minutes. It was ten after four on a Wednesday afternoon. The auditions had been held at the MGM studios in Culver City.

I was incredibly disappointed, but I didn't hang up. I thought that this was a job I was qualified to do. I didn't want to accept Donn Arden's declaration that the auditions were over. I begged him for an opportunity to sing for him. And he reluctantly agreed. "Well, young man, I have to stay here at the studio until six o'clock. My piano player is gone for the day, so it'll have to be a cappella, but if you can come down here right now, I'll meet you in Studio G and you can sing for me."

I was elated. It was about a 25-minute drive to Culver City and I made it in fewer than 20. When I walked into the cavernous studio, I saw him sitting in a director's chair at the end of the room. He had a drink in his hand and was reading a sheaf of papers. He put them down but didn't rise to meet me. I walked to him, introduced myself, shook his hand, handed him my photo and resumé, and said, "Thank you VERY much for allowing me to come down here so late. I didn't hear about the auditions until late this afternoon, just before I spoke to you on the phone."

He replied in a raspy but cultured voice, "Well, I had to stay anyway, so I'm here. Now, go over there and let's hear your best song."

I walked to where he was pointing, turned around and announced, "I'll sing 'I've Gotta Be Me' from *Golden Rainbow*."

I had never sung it a capella before, but did a good job and he said, "Do you have a ballad you can sing for me?"

"WOW! A second song!" I stayed right where I was. "Yes, sir. I'd like to sing 'Mama, a Rainbow' from *Minnie's Boys.*"

It's a beautiful song with a very touching ending and he was impressed. "I've got a little more time before I have to leave. Got anything else you want to sing for me?"

I could hardly believe this. Two entire songs already, and even though they were without the power of a pianist, it was a wonderful opportunity to show my versatility. "I think I'd like to sing 'All the Things You Are.' It's by Jerome Kern and Oscar Hammerstein, and was in the film *Broadway Rhythm.*"

"I know. You don't have to tell me where show songs came from."

I thought I'd offended him, but he still sat there.

I sang "All the Things You Are" and expected a "Thank you very much. We'll call you if we want to see you again." But I didn't hear anything. He just sat there.

After a few moments he asked, "Anything else? Anything else that'll show me something different?"

It had only been a few years since I'd won the Air Force Talent Contest singing "Alfie" and "Where Do I Go." The latter is a rock song from *Hair.* "Yes, sir. I'd like to sing a song from *Hair* called, 'Where Do I Go.'" I rocked it.

OHMYGOD! FOUR SONGS!

He stood and walked to me. "Well, Joe Dickey, I'm glad you called and I'm glad I had an extra hour, and I'm glad you came down." He began to walk me toward the door that went into the offices. "Last chance, now. Got anything else that's different than what you already sang?" This was UNBELIEVABLE!

"Well, actually, I can also sing a little country/western. I realize this is a show that is all movie musicals, but it DOES show off another facet."

He stopped walking and said, "Well, OK, then. Go ahead and sing me a country/western song." We stood five feet apart and I sang "Help Me Make It Through the Night." He shook my hand, and told me, "We will definitely set you up for a callback. I have your number here on your resumé. Nice to meet you. Nice to hear you sing. You have a beautiful voice. We'll call you."

He went through the door; I practically skipped across the studio floor back to the door I'd originally come through, and as soon as I had gotten outside, let out a whoop! What an audition! "YES! A CALLBACK FOR 'HALLELUJAH HOLLYWOOD!'" It was the best opportunity I'd ever had to get a part in a big show. It was going to be the biggest show in the world! I was one happy dude.

I waited a week. No call from "Hallelujah Hollywood." I waited another week. Then I thought I'd better call *them*. It was exactly two weeks to the day that I'd met Donn Arden. I dialed the number for the production office, and the receptionist said, "I'm sorry. Mr. Arden is in a production meeting right now. Can I give him a message?"

"Yes, you can. My name is Joe Dickey. I auditioned for him two weeks ago and he promised he would call me for a callback. I haven't heard from anyone and wondered what's going on."

"Oh, Mr. Dickey the callbacks were yesterday. I think they've seen everyone they wanted to see."

"But that's impossible. He heard me sing FIVE songs. He said I would DEFINITELY get a callback. Do you think it'd be possible to speak with him?"

"Well, ordinarily I wouldn't interrupt them, but under these circumstances I'll put your call through to their meeting room."

I waited for what seemed like several minutes, and she came back on the line. "Mr. Arden says he doesn't remember you, but if you can be here within half an hour, you can sing for him one more time."

I hung up, wondering how I could get my clothes changed and

down to Culver City in thirty minutes, but I grabbed a photo, a resumé, and a small stack of sheet music and dashed to my car. I parked on Washington Blvd., taking a chance on getting a ticket, and ran into the building. The receptionist knew who I was and ushered me into a large conference room. About 10 or 12 people were sitting around a huge oval table, artists' renderings of sets and costumes strewn about. Half-filled coffee cups, and a group of tired people.

The receptionist announced, "Mr. Arden, this is Joe Dickey," and left. He looked at me vacantly. "You say you sang for me two weeks ago?"

"Yes, sir. In Studio G."

"Really? I don't remember you."

"I called after the auditions had finished and you told me to come on down and I could sing a capella for you. You let me sing five songs."

"FIVE SONGS? I NEVER LET ANYONE SING FIVE SONGS. Well, never mind. You're here again and this time we have a piano player. Marvin, will you play for Joe Dickey?"

A young, lean man got up from the other end of the table and walked to the upright piano against the wall to my left. "Sure. What do you have?"

I handed him two pieces of music and asked the group, "Would you rather hear a ballad or an up tune?"

Donn Arden answered, "We're all too tired to listen to an up tune. Sing us a ballad but don't put us to sleep." The group chuckled along with him. Marvin Laird, the show's Musical Director, began the intro to "Mama, a Rainbow." He turned out to be an amazing pianist and accompanist. I could tell this was going to be fun. I sang about eight or ten bars and the producer waved his hand for me to stop. I thought, *"Oh, shoot! Not good."* I was wrong.

He waited a moment and then admitted, "Well, I don't know how I forgot about YOU, Joe Dickey. That's a beautiful voice! AND . . .

we've hired six boy singers and we need seven. You're the seventh! Do you want to be in Hallelujah Hollywood?"

"YES, SIR!"

"GOOD! You're in. Go out to see Francine and she'll give you a contract to sign. Send it back in a few days. Sure don't know how I forgot about YOU."

No audition had ever been stranger, or more providential, or more successful. I had a job that was scheduled to last for seven months—a month of rehearsal and six months of show, prior to a contract renewal or dismissal. As it turned out I was in the show for almost eight years. But when I walked out of that conference room I had no notion about the future. It was the present that was making me delirious. Hundreds, no, actually it was thousands, from Los Angeles, Chicago, and New York, had auditioned. Seven men got a job. I was thrilled to be one of them. I'm just lucky that my telephone calls had come at exactly the right moments.

Several months later, I figured out why Donn Arden didn't remember me. He was a long-time alcoholic and if he'd been drinking he had little recall. As rehearsal dragged on I learned when to stay away from him. Before he'd had any drinks he was quite civil. After one and a half drinks he was utterly charming. After two or more drinks he was one of the most abusive men I ever met. I was one of the few who never incurred his wrath, but I was always afraid of him.

When I finally left the show in 1980, I left on very good terms with everyone. Donn told me that he had never said this to anyone who had ever worked for him. "Any time you want to come back to this show, you'll have a job." It made me feel really good, even though I was certain I'd never want to come back. When I left Hallelujah Hollywood, I was leaving for a bigger life.

∞

ELVIS' CAPES

Cottroneo's was one of the finest costume makers in the world, and they had the contract for all of Hallelujah Hollywood's initial costumes. I was in one of their large shops in Hollywood getting measured for everything I was to wear in the show. When the show opened I had a set of black tails, a set of lavender tails, a set of white tails, a caliph's costume with cape and headdress, an odd, skimpy, "pirate" costume, and several different vests to make the sets of tails look different.

But the tailor at Cottroneo's was mainly interested in measuring my inseam. He measured very slowly and carefully. I was slightly amused, but not totally amused. After three measurements he asked in a rather wispy, nasally voice, "Which side do you hang on?"

I'd never been asked that question before. "Pardon me?"

"Which SIDE do you HANG ON?" It was obvious that my answer was important. These were going to be very tight pants.

By the time he'd measured three times he should've known which side I hung on. The question had been moot but he had asked anyway. Professional obligation, ya know? I laughed and said, "Actually, I don't think I'm big enough to hang on *either* side." End of measuring.

Now I WAS amused.

We finished the other measurements (sleeves, neck, head, waist, chest, and feet) and as I turned to pick up my belongings I noticed an entire rack full of capes. The rack was perhaps fifteen or twenty feet long. There were 30 or 40 capes, they were full length and they were magnificent. "What are THOSE?" I was amazed at what I was looking at.

"Oh, those belong to Elvis. We store them for him when he's not on the road and they just came in this morning. We haven't had time to put them away yet. Would you like to try one on?"

I hadn't been thinking that I wanted to try one on, but when he asked and implied that I COULD, I said, "Sure!"

He walked over to the rack and took one off. I had actually SEEN this cape before on one of Elvis's television specials. It had thousands of beads and sequins and many hundreds or even thousands of jewels. There was a huge eagle on the back. The tailor put it on my shoulders and I could hardly stand up. It weighed at least 45 pounds! I was struggling just stay upright. And Elvis would wear those things for two or three songs before he took them off.

As we hung it back on the rack I said to the man, "Now it's easy to see why Elvis sweats so much on stage. Man, most of us never have a clue what it takes to look like a star."

COUNTING CARDS

When I first moved to Las Vegas, the one month of rehearsals turned into seven. I was living in an apartment and had lots of spare time. I thought learning how to count cards and making money playing blackjack sounded like a very fine idea, so I began to play at dollar tables and practiced counting cards. It was not difficult to keep an accurate count in a single deck or even a two deck shoe, but it WAS difficult to keep an accurate count *and* carry on a simple conversation with those at the table *and* drink something alcoholic *and* not make noticeably larger bets when the count was in my favor. Then it became increasingly difficult to keep ANY kind of count when most of the casinos went to four deck shoes.

After about six months of playing nearly every night, I was a good card counter, a way-better-than-average blackjack player, and I had gotten to the point where I was breaking even overall. However, I was smart enough to realize several things: first, this was obviously not a great get-rich-quick scheme; second, I was spending an awful lot of time making no money; third, I was creating a huge amount of adrenaline and wasting a helluva lot of energy, just breaking even. By that time, most of my colleagues suspected that I was totally addicted to gambling, but when I decided to quit, they were surprised. I just quit.

I loved creating more efficient use of my time, and I haven't played ten hands of blackjack in the ensuing 35 years.

OSHA

The rehearsals for "Hallelujah Hollywood" seemed endless. There was a lot of sitting around waiting for something to get constructed or changed. When we finally got around to staging the opening number, the chorus singers (of which I was one at that time) were instructed to go up to the side stages and get ready to sing the opening number as we were to come out onto some narrow walkways that would be mechanically thrust from both side stages above the audience. We were standing up there, about twenty feet above the tables and seats below, looking down at the producer and his staff sitting in a center booth.

The music started and we were very excited to finally be getting to "walk through" a number. The curved walkway began to move out in front of us and finally stopped, locked into place, and the three of us looked at each other, scared to even put one foot on this little narrow piece of wood and metal.

There were no rails, only some chains, drooping between four flimsy looking metal posts. I put a foot on this "outrigger" ramp and felt it bounce. They wanted us to go out on this thing and sing and dance. The producer yelled, "GO! GO!" I wasn't going anywhere. The girl beside me wasn't going anywhere. And the young man on the other side of her wasn't going anywhere either. The producer yelled, "CUT! CUT! CUT!" The music stopped and he stood up in his booth pointing at my side of the room. (The other three on the opposite side of the room hadn't moved either, but he was pointing at us.) "ON THE FIRST BEAT OF THE THIRD BAR YOU MOVE OUT ONTO THE RAMP. YOU CAN COUNT, CAN'T YOU? NOW, LET'S START FROM THE TOP AND YOU KIDS GET OUT THERE!" He sat down. We had been told. I was pretty sure I still wouldn't be going anywhere.

I wanted this job. I didn't want to be fired. I also didn't want to die falling twenty feet onto concrete or the corner of a table. This wasn't going to be safe.

Before the music began again, I stepped very gingerly out onto what felt like a high dive springboard. It wasn't much wider, and it felt almost as bouncy, but there was nothing soft or liquid down below. It looked and felt VERY dangerous. The chains were NOT going to keep someone from falling off if they were to lose their balance. I retraced my small steps, considering how scary it might feel to actually have to DANCE out there. I got back to the solid side stage with the other two and knew that I was not going out there again that afternoon.

The music was now playing, we came to the first beat of the third bar and the three of us stood where we were and sang. We were doing the choreography and we were singing, but we weren't going out there. I didn't even look to see what they did on the other side. I was too scared of what the producer was about to do. He was still looking up at us. Tyrants are always unpredictable: sometimes he screamed profanities; sometimes he shut down rehearsals; a few times he had fired people. He was seldom civil. I steeled myself for the onslaught.

He had seen that we were not doing what he had told us to do. "CUT! CUT! CUT!" He spoke quietly with the company manager and the choreographer. We couldn't hear what they were saying. They were not in disagreement; they just weren't letting us know what they were discussing. Finally, the choreographer called up to us. "What's the problem? Is there not enough room for the three of you to go out together?"

I assumed the role of spokesperson for the chorus singers and replied, "There's enough room. There's not enough safety. Those chains are NOT high enough or tight enough to keep us from falling off, especially if we're out there dancing."

The producer yelled something about the set design having

been totally approved and got ready to start again. Before he could signal the music to begin, the choreographer spoke to him again. Then he turned to us again. "We'll change the choreography if it feels dangerous, make it a little simpler. For now, just get out there and do what you've learned. Mark it if you have to, but let's start again from the top of this number."

I paused for what felt like a long time to me but was probably only a second or two. "NO!" I hollered. "We won't go back out there until it's safer." If a note had fallen off a page, you could've heard it hit the floor. No one even breathed. I had not only defied the producer, I had set up a very definite confrontation. At this moment I was truly afraid that my tenure in "Hallelujah Hollywood" was not to last until opening night.

He yelled, "WE'RE WASTING VALUABLE TIME. YOU'LL GET OUT THERE. NOW! Now, without the music, all six of you walk out to your spots and let's see your choreography to my count instead of the music. OK. ONE, TWO, THREE, FOUR. ONE, TWO, THREE, MOVE!" Not one of us budged.

I had allies.

The producer was silent. It was an instant of quiet before the storm. Everyone in the theater knew he was just about to drop an atomic bomb on another chorus singer. We'd already seen him get mad before, but no one had EVER confronted him like this. Before he could start screaming, while there was still a hush in the room, I rather quietly asked, "Donn, do you know how to spell OSHA?" There was a titter of laughter from one of girls on the main stage, but there was deadly silence after that. Most of the cast didn't know what I'd meant.

Donn did.

The storm never came. He sat down. No one breathed as he whispered something to the company manager and the choreographer, and after a few more moments of huddling together, he announced, "That's all for today kids! We start at 10 o'clock tomorrow morning."

The next morning we went up on the side stage to rehearse the opening number: there were solid metal railings on both sides of that curved platform.

OSHA. Occupational Safety and Health Administration. This agency often strikes fear into the hearts of many corporate executives. It most certainly got Donn Arden's attention. It probably saved a terrible accident from occurring. Invoking its name undoubtedly saved my job.

THE RINGMASTER

Eric Michael Gillette is one of the superior entertainers I've known over the years. I met him when I was in the Los Angeles Civic Light Opera Workshop. He was a fine singer and a pretty good dancer, and the instructors stayed on him the entire 13 weeks about his weight. None of the rest of us thought he was too heavy, but they did a really good job of convincing *him* that he was.

I'd been in Hallelujah Hollywood about a year and a half when there was to be another audition for chorus singers. I got a call from Eric, asking if I could put in a good word for him, and get him an audition with Donn. I, of course, said I'd do what I could. I did tout him very highly, and he got an audition slot, and he got the job. He was appreciative of my part in it, but it was his great talent that got him the job.

One of the parts Eric began performing was The Ringmaster. It was an important, small role in the show, where—dressed as a ringmaster in tails and top hat—he was one of the first people the audience got to experience. A few years later Eric quit Hallelujah Hollywood to go into a big show at the Hilton, where he *starred* as . . . The Ringmaster. He was there for quite a few years before he quit to go to the *real* circus, Ringling Brothers Barnum and Bailey Circus as . . . The Ringmaster! He was the first SINGING ringmaster that circus had ever had, and for a number of years Eric lived on a train and entertained audiences all over the country. It was a choice job, he was terrific in it, and "ladies and gentlemen, boy and girls, kids of all ages" loved him.

What an interesting career. Small part: ringmaster. Big part: ringmaster. No part, real thing: ringmaster. Life once again imitates art.

∞

EGO, THE DOUBLE EDGED SWORD

I've always believed that to "make it" in show business you need to have a pretty big ego. From everything I've observed, those of us who do not exhibit over-sized egos have had a governor on our career vehicle. And, conversely, those who see themselves as bigger than life, BECOME bigger than life. I suppose it can be a slippery slope, but for those who manage their egos well, doors open and curtains part and audiences stand and applaud.

However, when one cultivates and builds and feeds the ego until there is an exaggerated sense of self-importance and an excessive appreciation of one's own worth, it can become truly obnoxious. We had a guy like that in our show. I shared a dressing room with him and another principal male singer for several years.

This man was actually a great guy. He had lots of friends. He was tall and handsome and charming and sang well. It was just that . . . his ego was bigger than anything else about him. After about two years of putting up with this overblown sense of importance, the other singer in the dressing room and I decided that Bob (not his real name) needed to be "put in his place." Tom (not his real name either) and I concocted a plan that would take a number of weeks but we thought it might work.

Bob had Wednesday nights off. I did his spot in addition to my own spots on Wednesday nights. One Thursday night, after Bob had come into the dressing room, Tom and I had a brief conversation about how small the audiences were the night before and that it seemed like they had been dwindling on Wednesday nights for quite some time. The audience wasn't really smaller; we were just *saying* it was. We didn't go on and on but we made certain Bob had heard us.

The next Thursday night, Tom and I had sort of the same

conversation. And this went on for several weeks in row. Then something happened that Tom and I hadn't even planned on. Contract renewals.

After about six weeks of hearing Tom and me talking about the small crowds on Wednesday nights, when Bob went in to the Entertainment Director to discuss his new contract, he asked for a lot more money. The Entertainment Director was surprised. Bob said, "Well, I *should* get more money. I'm the one bringing in the people. As you well know the audiences on Wednesday nights are much smaller; that's the only night I'm off. So I think I should be getting more money."

Now the Entertainment Director was *really* surprised. "I don't know where you heard that Wednesdays were any different than any other night. They're not. We have the same number of people *every* night."

Bob had been had. He knew it. Score one for the tricksters. Score another for "the devil made me do it." And score one for the power of the ego to allow us believe almost anything about ourselves that will feed it.

THE EGO ZONE

The same guy ("Bob," the one with the ego) drove a 280Z. He was extremely proud of it and took great care of it. He was so careful to not get it dented or scratched that he would park it WAY far away from the hotel in the part of the parking lot where there were no other cars.

But because of his I-love-how-everybody's-always-looking-at-me attitude, he was just difficult to have around. And even though he was fairly likeable, hardly anyone actually LIKED him. One night, after Bob had parked way out in the hinterlands, two of the other men in the show parked their cars about three inches on either side of Bob's car. After the show they got rides home from other people. At two in the morning Mr. Ego went out to the parking lot and, of course, couldn't get in his car.

He never knew who did it. I'm not sure he ever even knew WHY. The next day the two men came and got their cars, making it look like nothing had ever happened. Maybe nothing DID happen.

Doo ^{doo} DOO $_{doo}$ Doo ^{doo} DOO $_{doo}$. You have just entered . . . The Ego Zone.

IRVING

In the mid-1970s I purchased an old Chevrolet truck with 120,000 miles on it and paid $200. The pipe rack alone was worth more than $200 so I thought I got a pretty good deal.

I used it to do all sorts of things, including transporting 19 French windows to Las Vegas that I purchased from a Los Angeles junk dealer. I designed a room to fit the windows with an oversized, deluxe redwood bath, a walk-in closet, and a big indoor spa. It was spectacular. I would never have thought to do that kind of thing if I hadn't owned a truck that I could use to get windows from LA to Las Vegas. I also bought an old oak barn from a farmer on the Pearblossom Highway between Los Angeles and Victorville, and hauled all of those aged, tongue and groove boards back to Las Vegas to panel my bedroom.

Oh, and I used Irving (I named the truck Irving) to carry an old Boys' Club basketball floor to my house, refinishing the tongue-and-groove birds-eye maple and laying a brick and maple floor in the same house. I got the entire floor for $100 after dickering with the Boys' Club for almost a year, but I would have never even tried to buy the wood if I hadn't had a way to transport it.

My wife, Diane, was a dancer and choreographer, but she also had credentials as an interior designer, and she had spectacular ideas. I took photos of the brick and maple floors, the brick floors in the kitchen and dining room, the tongue and groove oak bedroom walls surrounding a copper faced fireplace, and the 19 French windows. I submitted the decorating ideas to *House Beautiful* and they said they'd like to do a 4- or 6-page spread on our house. The deal became moot, though, when Diane and I got a divorce. I didn't see any point in promoting a house that was decorated by a couple that couldn't stay together.

I regret having sold Irving. I'm sure "he" would've lasted

another several hundred thousand miles. I drove that truck for six years, put about 90,000 miles on it and sold it for $400 more than I paid for it. It WAS a pretty good deal.

LEON POIROT

After I quit playing blackjack, I discovered that I had a lot more usable time during the days. Most of the "kids" in our show would stay out till sunrise, then sleep most of the day and then come into work again the next night. A few went to college, and few held other jobs, but most were partiers and lived from paycheck to paycheck. I didn't want to be like that, so I developed a habit of turning my brain and body off as quickly as I could after the final curtain came down, and by the time I got home, I was able to go right to sleep. Sleeping from about 2am 'till 10am, it gave me eight hours to do anything I wanted to do before having to get ready for work again. For most of my years in Las Vegas, I was pretty productive.

Not too long after moving to Las Vegas, I got a friend to loan me $10,000 at 8.5% so I could buy a fixer-upper house. I did all the right things to that little house, sold it within a year, and was able to pay back the $10,850 very easily. The next house I bought needed a lot of work, too, and it turned out to be more than I could do by myself. I needed help but a general contractor was going to eat up most of my profits and most general handymen were still a little too expensive. In a conversation with another singer at work, he told me about his grandfather.

Leon Poirot came over to my house the next day. We had a brief conversation about all the things I wanted to do to the house; he told me he was just trying to find something interesting to occupy his time, and he was willing to work for $4.00 an hour. In today's wages that was almost $20 an hour, so he wasn't a total bargain but he was worth it if he could do all the things he said he could do. He was eighty years old, a former Wyoming oil field worker, and I discovered that he was just about as tough and talented as any person I'd ever met. It turned out that he knew how to do a multitude of things and was willing to try to do all the rest.

He was a wiry little man with amazingly strong hands. He had a twangy voice and a wicked sense of humor. He once told me, "That Richard Nixon is so crooked, he has to screw his socks on." One time when we were putting black pipe together, running a new gas line to a spa heater, I asked him how tight I should make the connection. He replied, "Ya git it jest as tight as it'll go, and then ya give it four more turns." The time we had to move a pile of bricks from one side of the yard to the other, when we finally got to the last one, he picked it up and with real joy exclaimed, "Well, here it is!" I asked, "Here WHAT is?" He replied, "This brick. THIS one. It's the one I been a lookin' fer all day!"

After we did all the things with the materials that Irving had transported, e.g. the master bath, the walk-in closet, the fireplace, the barn-lumber paneling, the indoor spa with all the French windows, the refinished maple to create a new living room floor, the used bricks in the kitchen and dining room, the butcher block counter tops, and a gas cook top, I still wasn't ready for him to find other employment.

So, I bought a little house that was going to be torn down to make room for a hospital expansion, and hired a house mover to move it across town. We had to roll it 32 miles around the city in order to go twelve miles across town because the straight trip would've involved raising wires that draped across streets. We built a concrete block foundation, set the house on it, re-plumbed it, rewired it, took out a dangerous brick chimney flue and replaced it with a zero clearance stack, sanded and refinished the pine floors, built a front porch, built a sunken family room on the back, landscaped sprinklers and grass and trees, put a picket fence across the front, and sold it a week after we'd finished painting it. It was a very hot summer of backbreaking work, but I'd kept him employed for another six months, I'd made a tidy profit, and he provided me with stories I would tell for the rest of my life. It felt like if I'd been able to keep him working at jobs with me he might have never died.

NO PROBLEMO

I once took a short vacation to Puerto Vallarta. We wanted to go to dinner at a nice, authentic restaurant that was "off the beaten path," and when we asked our hotel concierge to recommend a place and he told us of a very nice restaurant "up the mountain, away from all the touristy hustle and bustle."

"Perfect," we said. And we got a cab ride 20 or 25 minutes up the mountain, outside of Puerto Vallarta. By the time we arrived it was very dark and the cab driver took off. Let me tell you— in those days, twenty-five minutes outside of Puerto Vallarta at night was REALLY dark. On the advice of our concierge, I had left most of my cash in the safe in our room, and was expecting to be able to pay for our dinner with a credit card.

When we got inside the restaurant we discovered "No Credit Cards" and no English. We spoke virtually no Spanish but no one seemed to be disturbed by that and sign language worked well to get us seated. Shortly thereafter, the owner/chef/maitre d', waiter brought us the menu. It was all the entrees, the actual entrees, on a large wooden cutting board. Holding it at an angle to us, he displayed filet mignon, rib-eye steak, crab, shrimp, lobster, and several varieties of fish. With a sweep of his hand he was asking,"What would you like? Just point."

One of the only words I knew in Spanish was "quantos." I had used it before and assumed it meant, "How much?" He understood the improper word usage and said, "No problemo," to which I replied, "Si. Problemo," to which he re-replied, "No problemo." I pulled out my wallet and said, "No credit cards?" He said, "Si. No credeet carts." I then showed him my paltry stash of bills and he laughed and said, once again, waving his hand, "No problemo." I was really worried at that point and repeated. "No. Mucho grande problemo," at which point he got me out of my seat and ushered me to the door of the kitchen. As I stood there he pointed out a huge stack of dirty dishes. "Comprende? NO PROBELMO!" And laughed a huge, hearty laugh.

Somehow the laugh dispelled all of my fear, I went back to our booth, we ordered the steak and lobster, and it was all inexpensive enough that I had plenty of cash for the meal and the cab ride back to the hotel.

No problemo.

ANCHOVIES

My great aunt taught me how to fish when I was six. I've loved to fish my entire life. But I'm not very good at it. Having grown up in the South, my knowledge about fishing extends only to bass and crappie and freshwater perch like bluegill and red ear. I don't have a clue how to catch a trout. But in 1979, when I read in the Las Vegas Review Journal that fishermen were catching striped bass from the shore in Lake Mead, I thought I was ready for a great outing.

I got my rod and reel and tackle box together, packed a big cooler, and headed for the store to buy bait.

I had asked a few questions before going out: where on the shoreline were the fish biting best, what kind and size hooks were working, what bait was most attractive? The answers were the same from everyone: just around the bend from a certain camping area, medium-sized treble hooks, anchovies.

It was a beautiful late spring evening, just enough breeze to keep it cool, and I found a spot where no one else was near. I felt like my line was weighted perfectly, the anchovies were easy to get on the hooks, and I was getting the bait far enough out to be successful. But every time I'd reel my bobber and hook in, the bait would be gone. I couldn't seem to keep it on the hook.

After about half an hour of frustration, an old-timer came strolling by. We chatted for a moment and then I asked him if he'd caught anything that evening, saying that not only had I not gotten a bite, but I was also having a lot of trouble keeping the bait on the hook.

He asked, "Are you using anchovies?"

I said, "Yeah."

He asked, "Are you putting the treble hook through the dorsal fin?"

I said, "Well, it's really hard to tell."

He said, "What do you mean?"

And I showed him the bait that I was using—canned anchovies from Vons. He said, with a totally straight face, "Hmmm. Well, the guys who're catching stripers are using frozen anchovies that are about cigar-sized. You buy them out of the freezer at the bait and tackle shop. You put the treble hook through the top of their back and when you reel them in they look like they're hurt and stripers love to attack them." Before he walked around the rock outcropping, he wished me "good luck."

I can only imagine that the moment he was out of sight he couldn't stand up from laughing so hard. Can you just hear him telling his buddies about the rube who bought his anchovies at Vons? Oh, man! I felt so stupid! I got nothing that night, but I know I gave HIM a truly great fishing story.

BILLBOARD

Across the street from the hotel where I worked in Las Vegas was a dry cleaner. I didn't get very many of my clothes dry cleaned in those days, but I got a spot on one of my favorite neckties and decided to take it in to be cleaned. When I got the tie back the spot was gone, but they had pressed it so the entire tie was curved. I asked the clerk to have it re-done and he told me that they wouldn't be able to fix it. I said I thought that was ridiculous—they had put the curve in; they could take the curve out. When he told me they would have to charge me again, we began to have a few words and I asked to speak with the manager. He told me he was the manager. Bad news for me.

Without thinking about it I asked if he would step outside with me for a moment. He might've thought I wanted to fight with him, but since he was a lot bigger than I was, he walked out with me. I pointed up above us and said, "See that billboard?" We were both looking up now. "I can rent that space for $427.82 for two weeks. I can put anything I want to on that billboard as long as it's not a lie. I could put a great big arrow pointing down to your store, and write, 'They ruined my clothing and now they refuse to do anything about it.' There's not a judge in town who would declare that to be slander, but I'm pretty sure it would alter your profit and loss statement."

He considered it for about three seconds and responded, "Let's go back in and we'll do whatever it takes to get your tie fixed."

I had no idea how much that billboard cost. Neither did he. It seems kind of odd that I'm not a very good poker player.

In my everyday dealings I always strive to do the right thing. Because I think the world would work a lot better if all of us always tried to do the right thing, I want *others* to do the right thing, too. It just seems that every now and then, some of us need a little extra help.

∞

COUNT BASIE AND TONY BENNETT

During the years I was working in Hallelujah Hollywood, I didn't always have a day off every week. It was usually my choice, but I was anxious to earn as much money as I could and by not taking a day off every week, I could do other singers' parts as well as my own and my paychecks were (for me) fairly sizeable.

So, when Count Basie and Tony Bennett were headlining at the Desert Inn, and I only had one night off that month, and I really wanted to see them, I called in a favor from our maître d' in our showroom. He was a very nice man and knew all the other maîtres d' in town, and when I told him that I'd like to see Count Basie and Tony Bennett on my only night off, and could he possibly get me a great seat, he said, "Sure, it'll be my pleasure." He made the call, told me just to tell the Desert Inn maître d' who I was when I arrived, to get there fairly early, and he'd take good care of me.

I arrived for the 8:00pm show a little after 7:00, just to be sure there *would* be a good seat available. I was greeted graciously at the maître d's desk and he told one of his Captains where to seat me. The Captain took me right down front, but instead of putting me at a center table, he steered me three tables to the left, about half way in between center stage and stage right. He put me right next to the stage.

I sat there for a few minutes, by myself, and almost let my ego and my negative thoughts get the best of me. I was thinking, "Pete Bella told me I'd get a really good seat. There are really good seats that no one is sitting in yet, and I'm clear over here. Hmmm. Maybe I should go back to the maître d' and ask for something closer to the center." Then I thought, *"That would make me look like a jerk, and I don't want to look like a jerk, so I'll just stay here."* I was disappointed, but kept my seat.

When the curtain opened for Count Basie's set his piano

was directly above me. I could see his hands; I could hear him humming; I could hear him breathing. I could see the sweat and the smallest smiles. I was as close to him as anyone in the audience could get. It was a pretty good seat for Count Basie.

Then Tony Bennett came out. And for the first 45 or 50 minutes of his set he stood in the crook of the piano. I could see the shine on his shoes. I could see the etching on his cufflinks. I could see his nose hairs. I could hear him talking without the sound coming from the speakers. It was a PERFECT seat for Tony Bennett.

The Desert Inn maître d' knew his room and he knew these two acts. He had promised Pete that I'd get the best seat in the house, and I had come perilously close to ruining it for myself. Had I gone back to him at 7:15, and asked for a different seat—"Something closer to the center, please."—he'd have given it to me. I'd have been a jerk and stupid to boot.

Instead, I once again proved my "theory of management" to be most-of-the-time correct. My theory is that you hire the best person you can find to do a job and then you LET THEM DO IT! You don't question them until you KNOW that it could be done better a different way. You give them the leeway to do what they know how to do. You hire a great arranger? Don't tell him how to arrange. Let him do his thing. You hire a great architect? Don't tell her how to design. Let her do her thing. You hire a maître d' who says he can get you the best seat in the house? Don't ask him for a different seat before the show starts! He DID his thing! There WASN'T a better seat in the house. Thank you, Pete!

GORDON COCKSHOT

At the turn of the steps that led from the dressing rooms to the stage level there was a bulletin board. We were supposed to read it each night to see if there were any notices that might indicate changes in the show. My friend Ray was reading it when I walked up beside him.

He was reading something about some service that was being provided by a person we didn't know. "Look at this guy's *name*! Gordon Cockshot! Boy, if I had a name like that I'd change it!"

Then he glanced over and saw it was I who had walked up beside him and quickly uttered, "OH! Sorry!"

GREAT CHINESE FOOD

Being curious has led me to possess more worthless information than almost anyone I know. While working in Hallelujah Hollywood I somehow got interested in how the human brain works, and particularly in right- and left-brain functions. I read a number of articles by experts, got through a few books, and had a pretty good grasp on the entire subject.

In addition to being curious, I've always thought it very important to maintain balance in all of my affairs, including the way I think. I wanted to be able to view both sides of an argument, to have both masculine and feminine sides to my personality, to keep work and play in perspective, and to be both creative and logical. The last two were direct results of how much I could control my left and right brain activities.

After giving a lot of thought to whether one could actually CONTROL his hemispherical activity, I decided to try it out.

On my way home from work each night I would get off on the Sahara Avenue off ramp. At the bottom of the ramp, before I could turn left, there was a traffic control signal that took an unusually long time to change from one color to the next. If I arrived just after it had turned red it would take two minutes before it changed to green. I knew this because I'd been at this light hundreds of times in the past few years.

One night, it turned red just as I got to the corner. I stared at the light, and then saw, blocking nearly everything else, a billboard on the other side of the intersection. It was advertising GREAT CHINESE FOOD at the Golden Nugget Hotel. It was a black background with huge yellow letters. All it said was GREAT CHINESE FOOD, with the Golden Nugget logo at the top.

Hmmm. Two minutes before the light changes. Enough time to test whether I can control which side of my brain I use. I tried to "feel" which side I was using as I read the sign. Most reading tends to be a left-brain function, and I imagined the left side of my head working to read the words on the sign. Then I consciously shifted my attention to the right side of my head and tried to "feel" that side working to read the sign. Instantaneously, all I could see on the billboard were DISHES of Chinese food. Beautifully prepared, vividly colored, delicious looking—great Chinese food.

I was astounded! The words had disappeared and all I could see were PICTURES. A perfect representation of what should happen when only the right hemisphere is operating. I stayed with the images for a few more seconds and then consciously shifted my feeling back to the left side. Immediately the words appeared again: GREAT CHINESE FOOD.

OHMYGOD! THIS WAS SO COOL! I still had plenty of time before the light changed and I tried it again. "OK, think with the right side. Shift it. Feel it on the right side." BINGO! Same thing. Just pictures. Just dishes of great Chinese food. I'm not certain they were exactly the same ones that appeared to me a few seconds earlier, but they were just as appetizing.

I was totally amazed, not only that this had happened, but that I HAD MADE IT HAPPEN.

I knew the light was about to change, so I shifted it all back to my left-brain. The words reappeared and I was astonished and happy and could hardly wait to do something like that again. I drove home wondering if I could really learn to control ALL of my brain functions like that.

Within a few days, I was very good at it. If I wanted to think about a problem logically, I would just shift my thinking into my left-brain and things would practically "line up." If I needed to be extra creative about something, I'd merely put it in my right brain, and all sorts of images and new ideas would pour in.

I don't remember to do this on a regular basis these days, but

I've used the technique many times over the past three decades. I've since learned that men and women have different sized corpus callosums (the band of nerves that connects the two hemispheres of the brain) which accounts for unequal abilities to multi-task, but we are, after all, from Venus and Mars, so it shouldn't surprise anyone to find out that we actually are NOT alike. Equal for sure. But not alike.

ONWARD AND UPWARD

"They" say that all good things must come to an end. I've never believed that, but things *do* change.

After Robin and I began spending all of our time together, it was a fun, happy, easy life. We both worked in the same show, so we were able to be together nearly 24 hours a day, we understood the demands that the other was under, we had time to dream about our futures, and we were making pretty good money with few expenses.

At contract negotiation time, I asked to see the Entertainment Director, Bill DeAngelis. He was a former stage carpenter who had progressed up the corporate ladder and was now Entertainment Director and Vice President of the MGM Grand Hotel. It was a powerful, choice job. My request to meet with him was granted, even though he didn't know why I wanted to talk with him.

When we met—after a bit of small talk—I suggested to him that I knew a way to make the show better than it was. He was interested—at first. I sat across the desk from him and said, "Bill, the kids in this show are always scared. We're scared of Donn, we're scared of you, we only get corrections and never compliments. Fluff sits in the light booth with her binoculars and then comes downstairs to tell a showgirl that one of her eyelashes was crooked. Never does anyone say, 'Nice show,' Or 'Good job.' I believe you could take fifteen minutes a week to go through the dressing rooms and tell individuals, 'I saw the show last night. You looked great. Thank you for doing a terrific job.' I think if you did that, you'd be surprised at how quickly the show would improve."

He didn't understand one word of that. "These people make a damned good salary and I'm not about to waste my time telling them they did a good job when they're getting PAID to do a good job."

I interrupted. "But Bill, you don't understand. Most of these people aren't in show business to make lots of money. They're in show business because they love to perform, and they love the applause, and they love how it feels to be appreciated. I promise you, a few compliments here and there, the word gets around that you're paying attention to both the bad *and* the good, and you'll see kids busting their asses for your kind words."

"Too damned bad. They're not gonna get 'em. They get their paycheck every week, and that's all they're gonna get from me."

He stood up. The conversation was over. As I walked out I realized it was contract renewal time and I hadn't asked for a raise or anything for myself. I'd only asked for him to try to understand how neurotic we all were and to make a few minutes of concessions each week.

It had been worse than talking to a brick wall.

About a week later I noticed that I had a little stomach ache as I went into work. About a week after that I noticed that I was getting a stomach ache every night about the time I had to go into work. I knew what it was about. I was sick of working for a company that had no compassion and for a group of managers who only mentioned the negatives. It was showing up as pain. I never actually said the words, but this place was making me sick to my stomach.

Robin and I talked about this dilemma in the same conversations that included dreams of a different life. It wasn't too long before we both decided that we should quit "Hallelujah Hollywood" and move to Nashville. It was an odd decision, but one that excited us, and when you're young and in love and can see a wider horizon, odd decisions seem rational.

The thing that was really odd was that she and I were walking away from a combined income of around $95,000 a year, which in 2012 dollars is over $315,000. I think that's a heckuva lot of money to walk away from, when you know your next paycheck is going to be from the Unemployment Office. But money was not part of the decision-making equation. And we left.

Barstow, Albuquerque, Amarillo, Oklahoma City, Little Rock, Memphis. All cities between Los Angeles and Nashville. The first time we drove the 1836 miles we didn't stop in one of them. We had a new destination!

ASHLAND CITY

Most of us have "chapters" in our lives: I lived for seven years at Maxwell Place. I went to college for four years. I was in the Air Force for four years. I was married to Juli, then Diane, then Robin, and finally Mary. Each of these could be a chapter. Sometimes there are sub-chapters within a job, or a marriage, or a living location, like my four years in the Air Force, with sub-chapters like Basic Training, Officers' Training School, Denver, Biloxi, Victorville. I'm not certain that the number of chapters or sub-chapters one has indicates a more interesting life, but I seem to have had a lot of chapters and even more sub-chapters, and I've always contended that I've lived a *very* interesting life.

Ashland City proved to be one of the most interesting and also one of the most instructive chapters in my life.

Robin and I decided to move to Nashville after a brilliant—but pie-in-the-sky—brother-in-law convinced me that I could make it there as a songwriter. Though I was able to make most of the decisions in my life using logic and common sense, the decision to move to Nashville, in retrospect, put me on equal footing with the living-in-dreamland brother-in-law. Looking back on it all, psychologists and psychiatrists have told me it was our need to do a bit of "nesting" that drove us away from Las Vegas and into rural America. That makes sense. We most certainly altered and simplified our lives dramatically.

When we first arrived in Nashville in a Mustang hatchback filled to overflowing, we moved into what looked to be an OK place according to the AAA Guide, The Music City Inn, a cheap motel that had kitchenettes. We were paying by the week to save a few dollars. On our fifth night there, we were watching a local news program on television, and they were doing an exposé that featured the most prevalent locations for hookers. About two minutes into the segment, we realized that we were viewing our own motel. We'd been oblivious to all of the women standing around the parking lot, but suddenly realized this wasn't the place for us to be staying.

The next day, we went to a realtor and began a search for a place to rent or lease. Within three days, and after about fifty property viewings, we fell in love with a little place in the country, 35 miles from Nashville. It was a land—sale contract, it was affordable, it needed TONS of work, but it looked perfect. It was built of uninsulated concrete block, had four rooms—a kitchen, a living room, two bedrooms, and a bath (and an outhouse still standing about 100 feet from the back door)—one window air conditioner and no heat. It had a fireplace that worked, but this was June and heat was not on our minds at the moment. What we loved was that it was on five acres, and it could be OURS. We even thought we might turn a profit if we "fixed it up."

And fix it up, we did. We hauled (carried on our shoulders) old oak barn lumber from a neighbor's property (about a quarter of a mile from our back door) and paneled the living room with burlap and bleached oak, with insulation between the concrete and the old boards. We wallpapered every other wall in the place. We installed an opening from the kitchen to the bath, so guests wouldn't have to go through two bedrooms to get to the bathroom. We had the property bush hogged (a term I'd never known before), and we repaired door hinges and window sashes, and dug and planted a 20' x 20' garden.

All of this is a preamble to what was "instructive" about this chapter of our lives.

The most important lessons we learned in our two years there had to do with priorities: the way to view life in general, the most effective ways to treat others, and what is truly important and unimportant in the great scheme of things.

I could write several thousand words describing all the kindnesses that we were shown. They far exceeded our ability to ever repay them. We seemed to have angels *everywhere*.

But part of our success was due to our own ingenuity. The first day we moved in we went to a pay phone (seven miles into Ashland City from where our house was) and called Bell South to get a phone installed. When the lady asked me what I did for a living, I very proudly told her I was a singer and a songwriter. She informed me that they could put in a phone in about two weeks, but I would have to first give them a $150 deposit. After exhausting all the ways I knew to get her to change her mind, I finally hung up and told Robin that they wanted $150 as a deposit and we didn't have $150 at the moment. (We actually *did* have some savings, but we were trying to live on what we had in our checking accounts and we were pretty certain that food and shelter were more important than long-distance communications.) However, the next day, we made another trip to the pay phone, and when a different lady asked me what I did for a living, I told her, "We have independent investments." It was true. Every one of our few meager investments was independent from all the others. She was quite satisfied with that answer, and our telephone went in the very next day, without any deposit.

Lesson Number One: Don't brag about what you do unless *everybody* thinks it's a big deal. Actually, just don't brag about what you do at all. If you do your job well, others will find out on their own.

One day we came home from Nashville—we drove into town about three or four days a week to meet with producers and agents and other people who were anxious to help us—and our entire yard had been mowed: front, side, and back. At a garage sale I had purchased a little gas-powered mower, but it had taken me three or four hours to mow even the front and side yards.

As we got out of our car we couldn't believe it. It looked great! We wondered who had done it. The next day I saw my neighbor, Earl Bogle, and shouted out to him, "Do you know anything about my yard getting mowed?" He laughed as he walked toward me. "Well, it was the darndest thang. I got thew mowin' my yard, and that darned ridin' mower of mine jes' had a mind of its own. It drove itself right over to your yard and it wouldn't stop goin' round and round till it was all completely mowed." He thought that was a pretty funny story and I thought it was pretty remarkable. I thanked him profusely; asking if I could pay him, and he acted insulted and laughed at me again. "Naw. You guys are such great neighbors, I'll do it again any time I have time. I mean . . . whenever that darned mower thinks it needs it." He laughed again. It was the beginning of a wonderful relationship with a most wonderful couple, Lois and Earl Bogle, two of the finest human beings I ever knew.

Lois worked at the shirt factory, sewing on buttons. She'd been there for many years. Earl drove a truck, but was unemployed much of the time. Their reading and writing skills were minimal— maybe first grade level. They had three boys, one of whom had already left home, three dogs, a large garden (which helped keep them fed throughout most of the year), and a much better-manicured lawn than ours.

Robin and I were both getting unemployment checks and felt very poor, but we were probably making more money than anyone on our road. It was most certainly more than the Bogles and perhaps even more than our across-the-road neighbors who had a 150-acre farm and what looked like a 5-acre garden. He invited everyone in the neighborhood to "just come pick anything you want, any ol' time." At first, I couldn't bring myself to just walk over there and take things out of his garden, but he told me, "Hey, it only takes a day to plow it, we probably don't spend $50 on seeds, we just toss 'em in the furrows and cover 'em, and then everything grows by itself. We can't eat all that food. I plant that much so we can share it." I was amazed and impressed. Plus, that fall, I discovered that the apple tree in our side yard was pretty special, and after that it wasn't so hard to take advantage of his offer . . . I had something to trade.

We had three apple trees and two peach trees on our property. The two peach trees were old and didn't bear a lot of good fruit any more. Two of the apple trees were fairly small and bore a few bushels of apples a year. But the delicious apple tree beside our house, between the Bogles and us, was almost forty feet wide and fifty feet tall, and produced five inch apples that were as crisp and tasty as any I've ever eaten, in such quantity that we couldn't give them away fast enough. I traded an electrician as many apples as he wanted for 50 feet of cable. We told all of our neighbors to "just come pick as many as you want, any ol' time," and we STILL had to eat apple butter, apple sauce, and apple pie, and put up with the wasps that loved to get into the apples that fell to the ground.

Each time I'd see someone walk away from the tree with a sack full of apples I'd feel a little more comfortable about going across the road to get some fresh vegetables.

Lesson Number Two: Give away what you have plenty of. You'll not only get more of what you give away, you'll get offered more of everything. Actually, give away whatever it is that you have. Whether you think you have more than enough is immaterial. You'll always get more in return.

While standing next to a neighbor at the gas pump, just to make conversation, I asked him, "How many times a week do you get into town," meaning Nashville.

He paused for a second and answered, "Oh, maybe once every two weeks."

"And what do you usually do when you go into town?" I asked.

"Well, we just usually buy groceries."

I was amazed. "You go all the way into Nashville to buy groceries?"

"Oh, no. Heavens no! I thought you meant Ashland City. We prob'ly don't get into Nashville more than twice a year. It's jes' too far to drive."

Lesson Number Three: Distance is always relative. Actually, everything is always relative, except maybe mathematics. I'm pretty sure that's absolute.

The Bogles had three dogs: Bar, PayWay, and Chrissy. Bar was a hunting dog. He was an indistinguishable mixed breed, but he could hunt and was their favorite pet, probably because he "paid his way." He looked like a miniature bear, hence his name, "Bear," which the Bogles pronounced "Bar." PayWay (whose name was spelled PeeWee but pronounced PayWay) was a "snake dog." He killed snakes. He LOVED killing snakes. The other dog was Chrissy. More about her later.

One afternoon I was out back mowing the grass, my old mower making a huge racket, and Robin couldn't make me hear her as she was yelling to me that there was a big snake in the tree right above me. She didn't want to get near where I was, so she ran clear around the yard and waved her arms at me. I turned off the mower and she calmly and urgently explained to me that right above my head was a *really* big snake. I looked up, and OHMYGOD, it was a REALLY big snake. When I say really big, I mean it. It was between four and five feet long and as big around as a baseball bat. It was black, and I was out o' there. I moved about 20 feet away and looked intently at it. It didn't seem to be going anywhere, so I went over to the Bogles and told them what we had in our tree. Earl said, "Do you wanna shoot him with my 30/30 or my shotgun?" I didn't think I wanted to shoot the snake at all, but he was already getting his gun cabinet unlocked. "Here.

Take this .410." He loaded it and handed it to me. "You can't miss with this."

We walked to our back yard together. On our way over he hollered to Lois and the boys to "Come lookit what's in Joe and Robbie's back yard." By the time we got there, their entire family had joined up, including PayWay.

I wasn't comfortable handling the shotgun, but Earl insisted, "It's your snake. You get to shoot it." Oh. OK. "But it's your gun. YOU shoot it."

"Naw. Go ahead. If you miss, I'll take a second shot."

I really didn't want to kill that snake, but I also knew I didn't want it around, and I didn't know any other way to get rid of it. So . . . I put the gun to my shoulder, walked up as close as I could without being too terrified to pull the trigger, and fired. The snake fell out of the tree—it was just as big on the ground as I'd thought it was in the tree—and before anyone could even say, "Nice shot," PayWay tore across the yard, grabbed that snake right behind its head and began one of the most violent and lengthy attacks I've even seen, thrashing his head from one side to the other, rolling and growling. He never let go until almost forty-five minutes later; the snake was totally motionless. The snake was dead and PayWay was totally exhausted.

I put the snake in a black plastic garbage bag and took it the next day to the county dump. PayWay slept for over twelve hours.

I saved telling about Chrissy till last because she turned out to be the best. She discovered us about three months after we moved in. At first it was just short, infrequent visits. But after about a month of kind of "checking us out" she began to come over nearly every day. Eventually, she began to sleep on our side porch. As the weather turned colder, we thought we should bring her in at night, but she wasn't our dog and we didn't feel exactly right about that. When we heard a weather report that it was going to go below freezing that night we finally gave in and brought her inside.

We'd known she needed a bath, but until we brought her indoors it wasn't apparent how much she needed a bath. She smelled so bad we could hardly believe it. We bathed her. Then bathed her again. And after the THIRD bath, she was acceptable. Earl had told us she was a Schnoodle: half miniature schnauzer and half toy poodle. She was about a ten-pounder, gray like schnauzers, whiskers like schnauzers, playful, didn't shed, had a long, wispy tail that went around like a propeller when she was happy, and she was very quiet. We later found out—when we took her to our vet in Las Vegas—that when she had been spayed the veterinarian in Tennessee had sewn her up with huge sutures (the kind they use on cows), and they were still IN her. It was a wonder she hadn't gotten infected, but it was no wonder why she was so quiet; it was painful to her when she barked. Our vet was so embarrassed about a fellow doctor being so negligent that she repaired Chrissy for no charge.

That first year in Tennessee, we went back to Las Vegas for Christmas. Upon our return to Ashland City, Earl came over to greet us. During that conversation he said, "Lois and I was noticin' that Chrissy's been spendin' an extra lot of time over here at your house, and while you was gone she come over here every single day jus' waitin' fer you guys to come home. An' we was wonderin' if you'd like to have her?"

I didn't know how to respond. "Well, we really love Chrissy, but she's your dog and we could never take your dog." He interrupted. "Well, actually, you'd be doin' us sort of a favor by takin' care of her. She doesn't *do* nuthin'. We just have to feed her. Now Bar and PayWay, they're good fer somethin', but Chrissy . . . see somebody give her to us two years ago and we like her OK but she just costs us money to feed, and if you were to take her. . . ."

Robin had come out on the porch and heard the last part of what he was telling me. She looked at me with hope in her eyes. We both really liked Chrissy, and it *would* be doing the Bogles a favor. After a few awkward moments, I asked Earl, "Well, how could we pay you for Chrissy. How much do you think you'd want to sell her for?"

"Oh, nuthin'. Nuthin' at all."

"But we would have to give you *something*. We can't just take your dog."

He paused for a second and then looked over at our garage. "You know those two radial tires you got in your garage? Are you gonna do anything with them?"

They had come off of our Mustang when we bought new tires. They were worn, but not worn out. "No, actually, we don't have any plans for those tires. They were too old to sell and too good to give away, so as you know, they've just been sitting there. I guess they were waiting for the right family to adopt them."

He chuckled and finished his sales pitch. "Well, if you don't want 'em, I think they'd fit our son Roger's truck. Actually, I've checked 'em out and they're *exactly* the right size fer his truck."

I motioned toward the garage. "They're yours. But we'd still like to pay you for Chrissy."

"Nope. Two radial tires is way more than enough fer a dog, even one as fine as little Chrissy."

He was happy. We were happy. And Chrissy was happy. We had her for the next ten years. She turned out to be one of the all-time greatest dogs, ever.

Two years after we'd moved there, we finally came to realize that Nashville was *not* the place to make our fame or fortune. We decided to move back to Las Vegas, and try to become lounge stars. A garage sale seemed to be in order.

In those days we enjoyed doing garage sales. We way underpriced nearly everything, we had lots of boxes of free stuff, and we were always willing to negotiate to make our customers happy. Garage sales weren't about making money; they were about getting rid of stuff (and having fun). One of the best things I used to do was to put a little ceramic mouse in among all the other things. On the bottom was a price tag: $860.00. People would come along picking up one thing after another, checking the price, and putting it back down. When they would turn over the $860 mouse, their mouths would fall open, they would VERY CAREFULLY place the mouse back on the table, and ask, "What . . . IS . . . that?" I'd say, "It's . . . a . . . JOKE!" It always got a good laugh and I was able to use that mouse in several garage sales . . . till I sold it for $800. Nah. Just kidding. I think I finally gave it to a little girl.

Almost without exception, the people who came that day to our Ashland City yard sale would ask, "Are you selling your dog?" Or, "How much you askin' fer your dog?" Or, "You gonna give your dog away or sell her or what?" Each time, we'd reply, "No, no. She's not for sale. We're keeping her."

Later that afternoon, as we were driving somewhere, I half-jokingly asked Robin, "If we WERE to sell Chrissy, how much do you think would be enough money to actually get us to DO it."

"I have no idea. But we're not gonna sell her anyway."

I had a curiosity about this, so I asked, "What if somebody offered us a thousand dollars?" She shook her head, as I immediately noticed an awful feeling in my stomach. I mentioned this to her, and then said, "What if we got offered ten thousand dollars?" Immediately, the same awful feeling in my stomach. I laughed, and said, "It happened again, the same feeling. It's telling me, 'No way.' OK, what about a HUNDRED thousand dollars?" Once more, no way. By now she and I were pretty amused. Chrissy just wasn't for sale. Then I said, "What if somebody offered us a

MILLION DOLLARS for Chrissy?"

No feelings. I waited. Still no feelings. I really laughed this time. "Nothing happened that time. A million dollars! My stomach tells me it would be OK to sell Chrissy for a million dollars." Wow. What a moment. To think we had a dog that was worth that much to us. It was all just made up, but from then on, whenever we'd get into a conversation about our dog, we'd tell people, "She's a million-dollar dog." And mean it.

Lesson Number Four: Always pay attention to how your body feels when making an important decision. Twenty-six years later, a very wise man told my wife, Mary, to always be aware of how her "center" feels when confronted with a choice. "Does it give you a feeling of expansiveness or a feeling of contraction?" That "indicator" is never wrong.

One more story about Ashland City. I don't think I can get thrown in jail this many years later, particularly with no evidence left.

We became extremely good friends with a couple who lived in Nashville. I wrote radio-advertising copy for him. In the year and a half I worked with him I wrote over 500 spots. They would occasionally come out to our house, but most of the time we'd go to their house because he had a small recording studio in a spare bedroom and we helped each other with little recording projects. We also smoked a lot of marijuana together. Every time we'd get together, we'd all get loaded. Robin and I, both, were good dope smokers. It made us feel great and we'd become even funnier when we smoked. Some of our friends would get morose when they smoked pot, but not us. It just made us feel good and *everything* was funny.

We realized, after we moved back to Las Vegas and had quit smoking that it had really slowed us down a lot and we hadn't known it. With no feelings of a hangover, we weren't aware that our thinking had been just a little fuzzy, 24 hours a day. One of the primary reasons we quit was the story that follows.

Even though in those days a bag of grass wasn't very expensive, we figured to save money if we could grow our own. We had these five acres, mostly overgrown, and it seemed like a perfect thing to do. We planted seeds along a fence that ran diagonally beside a big blackberry patch, a part of our property that was difficult to access. I kept the seven healthiest plants, they were about five feet apart, I pruned them and loved them, and they each grew to be about four feet tall and were VERY bushy. As we would pinch them back, we'd dry the leaves in our attic and smoke what we'd harvest, and it was really good @#$&.

One afternoon, we pulled into our driveway and there was a Tennessee State Trooper car up near our house. Neither of us could breathe. We didn't even say a word to each other. I pulled around his car, parking closer to our garage and we both got out.

All I could think about was going to prison. In those days, Texas and Tennessee were putting people in prison for any marijuana infractions, and I'd heard that some guys had gotten *40 years* for growing it. As I spoke to the state trooper, I was hoping to at least be able to have some sound come out of my mouth. I surprised myself with my calm approach.

"Hi, can we help you?"

"Well, I hope so. We've gotten word that some folks around here are growing marijuana (My heart rate went to around 6000!) and I wanted to know if it'd be OK for me to walk toward that holler over there and see what I might find." I thought I might faint. He pointed in a direction that was past where our plants were.

I said, "Sure. But, you know, I think the best way for you to get over there is to go down by our garden and then go to your left when you get to those trees." I pointed a slightly different direction for him to go, and walked with him toward our garden instead of toward the marijuana.

He thanked us and walked the way I'd recommended that he go. Robin and I went into the house and totally panicked in a very controlled way. We were truly terrified. We couldn't think straight. We couldn't breathe. We couldn't do ANYTHING about this. We just waited for him to come back. When he *did* come back, he walked back into our driveway from a different place than when he'd departed, and I realized he'd walked *right by* those plants. They were up against a wire fence and there was other vegetation near them, but they were clearly visible to anyone who knew what they were looking for.

I can't begin to describe my fears.

I walked out of the house and casually asked, "Did you find what you were looking for?"

"Well, no, I didn't, not exactly. But before I leave I'd like to tell you that if you KNOW anyone who's growing marijuana around here, tell them to get rid of it."

He'd seen it! He was giving us a break! He liked us and didn't want to see Barbie and Ken go to prison. He was an angel sent by a state police dispatcher.

I mumbled something about, "Yeah, you bet. We don't know anyone like that, but if we hear of anyone, we'll tell them to get rid of it. Thanks for the advice. And thanks for watching out for all of us."

"Well, thank you for letting me park in your driveway. Just be sure to tell anyone who's growing marijuana to get rid of it.'"

"We sure will! Bye." We waved as he backed out of the driveway.

Ten minutes later, Robin and I got in our car and drove all over our rural neighborhood, looking through binoculars to see if he was still spying on us. After thirty minutes of driving around we decided he was really gone and we drove home. With my heart still pounding, but feeling so heavy with sadness about having to do this, I dug up all seven plants, hauled them to the back of our property, dug an enormous hole, threw them all in, and covered them up. It was a hard labor job, but I wasn't about to quit until everything was several feet underground. It was dark by the time I finished. In the meantime, Robin had gone up to the attic, gathered together all the limbs and branches that had been hanging upside down, got all the filled plastic bags that were stored up there, and brought them downstairs. Without any formal ceremony, but with huge amounts of regret, we stripped all the leaves off the stalks and in about 20 flushes of the toilet emptied our house of all remnants of the evil weed.

Sadness and relief were about equal. Eventually, relief won out. Eventually, gratitude became the victor. Thank GOD for the generous spirit of that state trooper. What if he'd been a different kind of personality? What if he'd had a particularly bad day that day? What if he hated his sister who always played with Barbie dolls? What if. . . . We had gotten a break of a lifetime. We were enormously grateful. And we never smoked pot again.

Now, THAT'S a story you won't read in any other book!

BLOWING THE FUSE

Robin and I drove back and forth between Las Vegas and Nashville a number of times during the two years we were residing on the little "farm" outside of Ashland City. We always took I-40, a grand stretch of Interstate that paves the way between Barstow, California and Wilmington, North Carolina. I was a good daytime driver and Robin was a good nighttime driver, so on a few trips we just drove the entire 34 hours without spending a night in a motel.

On one such jaunt, though, we both got really tired about midnight and decided to stop at the next place we could afford. That turned out to be almost an hour later, but we finally pulled into a cheap one-story motel that had a sign out front that said, "MOTEL." You know. One of THOSE kinds of motels. But we were totally worn out and didn't feel safe going any farther.

We checked in with the night clerk and realized we were not only tired, we were also hungry. But there was not a restaurant within a hundred miles that was open at that hour of the night. So, we took a suitcase out of the back and also unloaded our electric skillet. We knew we had two pork chops in the cooler, so we took the cooler in with us.

We immediately put the pork chops into the electric skillet, hoping they'd be done in 10 or 15 minutes, and starting getting ready for bed. We got our pajamas on, got out two paper plates and two forks and knives, and about 12 minutes after we'd put the chops in the skillet, the fuse in our room blew out, shutting off the lights and shutting down the appliance. After lighting a candle and seeing that the pork chops were "just about" done, we ate them, set a mechanical alarm clock that we always carried with us, and went to sleep for the next four hours.

When we quietly crept out of the motel at 5:30 it was still dark and we saw not one light burning anywhere. Not even the MOTEL sign out front. I don't know how, but we had, it seemed, blown out the entire electrical system of that little dumpy motel.

As we drove away we were laughing at how "bad" we were, wondering how many of our fellow travelers didn't get out of bed on time that morning. And we felt lucky that the slightly undercooked pork chops didn't make us sick, considering our dharma, karma, or whatever universal retribution system was working for and against us.

MORE ABOUT CHRISSY

We owned a piece of property in Las Vegas that had a normal-sized three-bedroom house and I converted what had been a carport and a detached office into a tiny guesthouse. For a few years, while we were back and forth between Nashville and Las Vegas and Las Vegas and Los Angeles, we rented out the front house and lived in the guesthouse. (It was *really* small—485 square feet—but I had created a small living room with a fold-out couch, a TV, and an antique drop-leaf dining table; a 9 x 13 bedroom with a walk-in closet on one end and a nine-foot mirrored closet on the other; a very functional 25 square foot office with shelves on three sides; a full-size bath; and a little kitchenette and front hall. We also bricked a patio for barbequing and lounging outside during the few weeks of the year when it wasn't too hot or too cold. We papered nearly every wall with a very expensive string cloth that had been given to us by a decorator friend, we installed new carpet and tile, and it was one of the coziest places anyone ever lived. Ask my mother-in-law, who lived there for five months. Ask my daughter, Jennifer, who lived there for two years. Ask our friends who would come over and not want to leave. It was cozy beyond cozy.

One night, Janet and Jim Blaine came over for dinner. I barbequed some good steaks, we opened a bottle of red wine, and sat down at the dinner table, which—when opened big enough for four—almost eliminated the rest of the living room. We never fed Chrissy from the table. We didn't want her to get into the habit of begging while we were eating. Consequently, she never did and she never even came over near us at mealtime. Before we could object, Jim had cut a piece of fat from his steak and put it down by his side for Chrissy to come grab it. We immediately told him to stop, that we didn't feed her from the table, but it was too late.

She had already taken it and gobbled it down.

During the subsequent six months Chrissy never came over to the table while we were eating. But one night Janet and Jim came to our house for dinner again. I can't recall what was on the menu that night, but we all will never forget that the very moment Jim sat down, Chrissy ran right to his side and sat there waiting for a handout. It had been a one-time piece of steak fat, SIX MONTHS previous. In the interim Chrissy had never come to our table once, not even when we had company. But the moment JIM sat down, she was THERE. No barking, no whining. Just sitting with her chin up, waiting to be fed by someone she remembered.

She remembered him very clearly. And believe it or not, there are actually some people in the world who still say that dogs don't have very good memories.

PUTTING HER DOWN

Chrissy was undoubtedly the best dog in the world. Since there's no real rating system for that title it could be debated by some. But we had her for almost a decade and no dog ever gave any owners more pleasure or more love. So, until someone proves otherwise, I'm still calling her the best dog in the world.

As she aged she developed some physical problems and began to get feeble. The vet said it was just natural old age, some renal failure, some arthritis, maybe a few other infirmities, and some day soon we'd have to think about putting her down. We couldn't bear the thought, not even after we had to start picking her up to take her outside to pee or poop. In retrospect, we let her suffer a few weeks too long before I finally took her to the vet to "let her go." Robin was in bed for five weeks with pregnancy complications and I had to do it, by myself.

It was tough. If you've ever had to put a pet down, you know. I held her in my arms, speaking gently to her, telling her it would "be OK," and she looked at me, totally trusting me, as the vet gave her an injection. Ten seconds later she was gone.

I handed her to the assistant and walked out of the office. When I got to my car I leaned against it and sobbed. I couldn't stop for almost fifteen minutes. It wasn't all about Chrissy. It was about everything I hadn't cried about in almost 20 years. Her death had released a torrent of emotion that I didn't even know I'd been hiding. It was really, really sad, but amazingly cathartic.

God bless that little dog. She gave us way more than she ever knew.

TOPIARY

We were driving in Nashville with Betty Cox Adler, another angel who had sort of taken us under her wing. We passed a large house with lots of shrubbery trimmed in recognizable shapes. Though it was a term we all knew that we knew, none of us could remember what that type of landscaping was called. We drove for a few minutes without successfully recalling the word, and Betty finally said, "When you think of it, call me."

That night, about two in the morning, I woke up and the word came to me. I gently woke Robin up and told her what I was doing, as I dialed Betty's number.

Groggily, Betty answered, "Hullo."

I said, "TOPIARY!" And hung up.

The next day I most definitely "heard" from her!

AGENT ORANGE AND THE BIG-TIME COUNTRY STAR

This is another of those "can't say the real names" stories, but it really happened.

Robin and I were in the office of a big-time talent agent (I'll call him Agent Orange.) in Nashville, discussing our possible careers. He wanted to send us on the road with a "tent ministry" tour, knowing that Barbie and Ken would be a great attraction in that enthusiastic evangelistic market. He told us that he really thought we could earn a hundred thousand dollars in our first year doing that, and we were slightly tempted.

While we were in his office that day, he got a phone call from someone who wanted a particular big-time country star (I'll call him "Big-Time Country Star) to perform at a birthday party in Little Rock, Arkansas. Agent Orange had represented Big-Time Country Star for many years, and he began to discuss the details as Robin and I waited.

The caller said it was his own birthday party, that he'd be happy if Big-Time Country Star could even come for half an hour, but that he really wanted him and he'd be willing to pay whatever it would cost, and that he was willing to schedule the party to fit into Big-Time Country Star's schedule. Agent Orange told this client that Big-Time Country Star's fee for a personal appearance like this was expensive whether it was for an hour of work or a minute of work; he would need all of his travel costs covered, and that they would have to figure out a way to do this in between a few other commitments that were already on the books.

In about fifteen minutes they had it all worked out. Unbeknownst to the Little Rock birthday boy, Big-Time Country Star had a job to do in Los Angeles the same night the client had wanted to hold his birthday bash. We heard Agent Orange say, "Big-Time Country

Star can come to Little Rock on that date, but you'll have to have the party in the afternoon, like between one and two o'clock." (We learned a few minutes later that Big-Time Country Star had a private jet that would need re-fueling in Little Rock, on the way to Los Angeles.) We heard Agent Orange finalize the deal so Big-Time Country Star could go to this guy's house (while his plane was being refueled), do twenty or twenty-five minutes of playing and singing and schmoozing, get back on the plane to Los Angeles, *and get paid thirty thousand dollars to stretch his legs.*

After hanging up the phone, Agent Orange turned back to us and said, "Now, THAT'S what a good agent can do for you!"

We ended up not doing the tent circuit thing, but he *did* make us *think* about it.

RODNEY LUCK IN THE BALCONY

Near the end of 1980, Robin and I both got parts in a musical, *Promises, Promises*, that was to play in three different dinner theatres, for a few weeks at a time. Neither of us had big parts and the pay was miniscule, but it was work, and we wanted to work.

The cast of 13 rehearsed for two weeks prior to our opening night. During the next to last rehearsal before the dress rehearsal, one of the actors, Rodney Luck, said to the director, "I've changed my blocking in this scene. It just didn't look right."

We all stopped what we were doing to hear the response.

"Well, I don't actually mind if you want to change the blocking. We can discuss it and try it, but what do you mean it didn't LOOK right?"

Rodney said, "I looked at it and it just didn't look right."

None of us knew exactly what he meant.

The director asked again, "What do you mean, you LOOKED at it? When did you LOOK at it? Has somebody videotaped this thing?"

"No. No. I just went up in the balcony and saw it and it just looked awkward. So I'd like to change it."

By this time we had all moved a few steps closer, I guess thinking maybe if we weren't so far away from him we'd get it. The director, again, spoke for all of us.

"OK, now I REALLY don't understand. What do you mean, you went up in the balcony and looked at it? How could you see your blocking if you went up in the balcony? And when did you go? I thought you'd been *here* the whole day." We were all very curious to hear Rodney's answer. But HE seemed to be the one who was confused.

"Don't you guys do that?"

Several of us spoke at once. "Do what?"

"Watch yourselves. Go out there and watch yourself so you

can see how to fix things and make 'em better. Haven't any of you ever done that?"

We all shook our heads. The director paused for a few moments and then inquired, "I can understand *wanting* to do that. It seems like a great idea. But HOW do you do that? What do you actually DO?"

Rodney was surprised. "Wow, I thought *everybody* did that! I'm the only one?"

One of the girls said, "Yeah, I guess so. So . . . what is it that you DO?"

Rodney composed himself for just a moment and explained. "I go out of my body. I go somewhere where I can get a good view of the stage, like the balcony if there is one, and I just watch myself . . . and you guys. I stay up there while my body is down here and I can see everything that's going on on stage while I'm up there."

We were silent. Nope. None of us had done that.

(Well, that wasn't quite true. Once, during an intense acting workshop I'd gotten out of my body and had gone to the ceiling of a twenty-foot high room and looked down at the class and my own body lying on the floor. And the next time I tried it I got part of the way out of my body and couldn't go any farther. I never tried it again after that. It had happened to me under the direction and tutelage of an instructor. But Rodney could, evidently, just do it any old time he wanted to.)

So, essentially, none of us had done that.

"OK! WELL! Good job, Rodney. Thanks for being an extra set of eyes for me. Let's take it from the top of Scene three, and everyone just be aware that Rodney's blocking will be different. HOW different, Rodney? Oh, never mind. Let's just see it."

Rodney's blocking turned out to be better.

THE CHRISTMAS GOAT

Promises, Promises was to run over the Christmas holidays, but as we weren't able to afford to drive back to Las Vegas for Christmas that year anyway, we thought it'd be OK to just work. Our first venue was in what was called the Tri-Cities area—where the states of Virginia, North Carolina, and Tennessee come together—the booming metropolises of Bristol, Virginia, Kingsport, Tennessee, and Johnson City, Tennessee.

Our rooms were tiny, the food was average, the play was pretty good, and most of the time most of us got along pretty well. The company manager and his wife (the leads in the play) went out and bought a tiny Christmas tree and we all decorated it with things we purchased. These two actors were better than average singers and dancers, nice people, devout Christians, and they were both pissed when someone in the cast replaced the star at the top of the tree with a small, clamp-on Christmas Goat. The next day the star was back on top and the goat was located deep inside the boughs of the tree. Late that night, the star came down again and the goat went up. The two in charge demanded to know who had switched the ornaments, but no one would confess. After a week of back and forth, and a good amount of useless bickering, the goat disappeared. Some of the cast members were angry, but the company manager would not admit to having it, and we all finally just kind of let it go.

We were having too much fun to worry about a missing Christmas goat.

One day we had a snow so heavy that by mid-afternoon the shows for that night were officially cancelled. With no responsibility that evening, five or six of us snuck into the kitchen, "borrowed" the big flat aluminum trays, and used them as sleds until darkness made it too dangerous to continue. We took the trays back, washed them, and returned them to their storage racks. We never heard a word from the staff about the dents that had been inflicted by rocks. That probably wouldn't be a normal thought process by a chef who needs to put three hundred soft rolls out on the buffet. I can't exactly hear a guy yelling, "Hey, who used these trays for sleds? And was so careless as to bang them on rocks?!"

After the run of this show was finished, the husband and wife moved to New York to try their hand at the "big time." We never heard anything about them, but who knows? They may have become very successful. Most Broadway actors aren't exactly household names.

Anyway, they buried the hatchet the next Christmas. We were back in Las Vegas by then, and we got a football-size package in the mail, heavily taped. When we unwrapped the layers of bubble wrap, we found . . . the goat. They knew all along that we had been the culprits who kept switching the ornaments. We laughed, wished them well, and were very happy to top OUR tree that year with The Christmas Goat.

BARBIE AND KEN

When Robin and I first started working together we were, immediately, a good duet-singing couple. When we started putting an act together we decided we should play up the fact that we reminded everyone of Barbie and Ken. So, as part of our act we would talk about other duet teams and compare ourselves to them: "Steve and Eydie: no, we're younger and much less expensive. Donnie and Marie: no, they're brother and sister. Sandler and Young: no, they're two guys. Actually, the closest comparison we can find is . . . Barbie and Ken." Then we'd just stand there and wait for the laughter to roll. The longer we'd stand there, the more obvious it was that we *were* Barbie and Ken.

After one performance at a conference on the Monterey Peninsula, a member of the audience came up to us and said that she was in the marketing department for Mattel, that they were planning a big employee recognition banquet—about 850 or 900 employees—and she would like for us to be the entertainment . . . as a singing Barbie and Ken. I told her that I would write a special parody for the occasion, and we were hired on the spot. A month later, after having joked about it on stage for months, we were Barbie and Ken, AT MATTEL. It was a big success. Talk about "the word becoming flesh."

A week later, I called the lady who had hired us and told her that I thought Mattel could profit by using a live, singing Barbie and Ken in the Macy's Parade next Thanksgiving. She agreed, was very excited about the concept, and said she'd get back to us about it. The next Thanksgiving there was a live, singing Barbie and Ken in the parade. But it wasn't us. So much for not protecting a good idea. I was devastated. But as it turned out, the couple that played Barbie and Ken that year didn't exactly become famous. It made no difference in anyone's career, except for the fact that it clued me in to the notion that in show business contracts are preferable to promises. It took a few lessons, but Barbie and Ken, the singers, wised up.

CHOO YOURSELF

Part of our decision to try our hand at lounge work was based on the response of one my friends from The Ray Charles Singers. We asked Jim Blaine if he'd be our arranger, conductor, third singer, and comedy foil, and he agreed to everything, including the remote possibility of co-stardom.

One afternoon the three of us were rehearsing a new song to put into the show. It was a medley of "Chattanooga Choo Choo" and "Atchison, Topeka, and the Santa Fe." It was an up tune, it was going to be clever and cute, and we were rehearsing diligently. Robin was singing the melody at one point and Jim and I were making up a backup part. We'd gone over it four or five times, with Jim and me changing it a bit each time. Mostly what we were doing was harmony parts that went, "Choo Choo."

Finally, with a bit of exasperation that "the boys" weren't able to figure something out more quickly, Robin said, "Oh, CHOO YOURSELF!"

To which Jim immediately responded, "If I could do that I'd never leave my room."

End of rehearsal.

YOU'RE FIRED (AGAIN)

Robin and Jim and I hired a bass player and a drummer, and set times to audition for some hotel entertainment directors. We were doing a "main room" style act in lounges. No other act in town was doing that. We got two jobs fairly quickly, one for two weeks at the Imperial Palace. Our next job seemed like a huge success. We got two weeks in the Riviera lounge, a major hotel, the place where Frank Sinatra was currently headlining. We were excited about our future.

The first night, the entertainment director told us we were the best act she'd had there in a long time and it was fairly crowded. The next night the place was packed and people were standing around the outside of the waist-high wall between the casino and us. Wow! SRO! The third night the President of the hotel, Mr. Becker, came in and sat through two sets. Again the lounge was so full that no one could get in, and everybody was staying for more than one set. We were REALLY excited.

The next night we went in a little early to get a paycheck from the Entertainment Office and we saw different instruments and a different sound system on the stage. Our equipment was off to the right of the stage, on the floor. We immediately asked what was going on, and were told that we had been fired. Mr. Becker had seen what was happening in the lounge and he didn't like it that people were staying; he wanted them to come in, have a drink, and go back out to the gaming tables. HE FIRED US! The entertainment director, once again, reiterated that we had been her best act, that we had done everything she had hoped for, and she was really sorry that she had no control over what happened.

We were devastated. Fired for being too good? How could that be? Was somebody pulling our leg? Who ever heard of being fired for attracting a big crowd that wanted to stay? We felt like total losers for a month and a half. Then, gradually, we began to get over the blow to our egos and our careers and decided that perhaps Las Vegas was no longer the basket into which we should be putting our eggs. We began to dream bigger dreams and look at different ways to express our creativity. Not long after that we made the decision to go to Los Angeles.

Getting fired turned out to be the best possible thing that could've happened to us. Heck, I could still be there today, singing, "Tie a Yellow Ribbon 'Round the Old Oak Tree" (not that I ever actually sang that song). However, a jolt to our Las Vegas career, even though it seemed terribly negative at first, was exactly what was required to get us to reassess our lives. It just took us a while to understand that.

BIG BAND SINGER

I got an opportunity to sub for a friend as a "big band singer" in Las Vegas. Though it was my first time at this kind of work, it was a great band, I knew enough songs to make it work, and I was very excited about the evening.

As the event promoter was escorting me across the huge ballroom floor to the bandstand, he handed me my paycheck. As I put it in my pocket, I said to him, "Thank you, Nigel, but you're paying me without even having heard me sing one note. Aren't you taking a bit of a chance?"

He put his arm around my shoulder and laughed as he answered, "Son, I've been in this business long enough to know how to put a Stop Payment on a check."

Every time I get paid in advance, I remember (and tell) that story.

THE UNFORTUNATE HANGUP

In this story, I will use a fictitious name of the star out of respect for his/her privacy.

Robin and I were regular volunteers at public broadcasting television stations for a number of years. We did a lot of on-camera work during pledge breaks, doing our best to get viewers to make contributions. It was work that we did well, we felt good about volunteering, and we always had fun when we did it. (We did this in three different cities so don't try to figure out the station or the star this way.)

One night, as we were sitting in our dressing room waiting to "go on" again, the lady who managed the phone banks poked her head in and laughed as she announced, "We just got a call from someone who said it was Pat Famousperson. S/He said s/he wanted to make a large pledge and would like to speak with either Robin or Joe, that you are friends. Our volunteer called me over to handle this special situation, and I figured it was a crank call and you didn't know Pat Famousperson, so I hung up. You *don't know* Pat Famousperson do you?"

We replied, almost together, "Yes, we DO know Pat Famousperson. We ARE friends."

"Oh, my! I just figured you *didn't*, and that it was just someone who would be wasting your time, so I hung up on them. I guess maybe I shouldn't have."

Little did this lady know how MUCH she shouldn't have.

The next day we called Pat Famousperson to find out what had happened and s/he said, "Yes, I called last night. I thought you guys were doing a terrific job, I really do love the shows on PBS and I was going to make a pledge of $10,000 in your names. I actually just wanted to tell you that I was watching and that I thought you were both doing a GREAT job. But since that lady hung up on me, I've decided I won't write the check after all. It was one of those spur-of-the-moment, emotional things and I'd have been happy to make a big contribution like that last night, but I'm not watching you guys right now, and I'm not going to do it today."

It was no big deal to us. S/he was still our friend. But we hope it was a lesson to the lady who was managing the phone bank. That night we told her they missed getting $10,000 because of her erroneous assumption. It was certainly a memorable lesson for ME.

First of all, you never know who knows whom. You don't know who has a cousin or a brother or a friend. Even if you're face to face with someone, it might be a mistake to summon up too quick of an opinion about him or her. (The story about Leland Stanford and Harvard is legendary.)

Secondly, you can never be absolutely certain who's actually on the other end of the line. In that same vein, it's a good idea to never assume that others aren't also hearing your conversation (See SAMMY LISTENING IN) nor should we ever assume that the recipient of your email is the only one who will read it.

But maybe most importantly, never push away your good. A ten thousand dollar pledge that night would've been significant. We should always allow for larger, more important possibilities to occur than those to which we are accustomed. That lady *wanted* to get large pledges, but she wasn't *expecting* them, and she also didn't have a clear picture of who was in the viewing audience. Her picture was the typical viewer: a 50ish woman, slightly higher than average education, slightly higher than average income. The person who had called had WAY higher than average income and was ready to be extremely generous in a moment of friendship and admiration for younger entertainment business colleagues.

Though that particular star made other contributions to that public broadcasting station, there was never another offer of $10,000. A missed opportunity because of small thinking.

COUNTERFEIT 100s

When I first began to work in Las Vegas my weekly paycheck was between $400 and $500. Every now and then I would cash the check at the cashier's cage in the casino. One night, after doing that, I noticed that the four one hundred dollar bills I'd received just somehow weren't quite right. At first I couldn't figure out what was wrong with them, but when I got home I inspected them closely.

They had a slightly waxy feel to them, and the words "ONE HUNDRED DOLLARS" at the bottom weren't absolutely lined up straight. I knew they were counterfeit.

I called the Las Vegas F.B.I. and reported that I had four counterfeit hundreds, "What should I do with them?"

Their immediate answer was, "Just bring them to us and we'll take care of it from there."

I asked, "So, you'll give me four hundred in good bills in return?"

"Well, no. These are counterfeit bills and you're not supposed to have them in your possession, so we'll take care of them for you."

I was incredulous. "REALLY!" Realizing I had not yet told them my name, I hung up. I hoped for the moment that they didn't automatically trace every call.

That night I cashed them in at the same cashier's cage in exchange for twenty twenties. Never another word about them from anybody.

There's a joke about a counterfeiter who ran off a bunch of $18 bills. He took them up to Eastern Kentucky to pass them off. The first place he went to, he asked, "Could you please give me change for a few $18 bills?"

"Shore," was the reply. "Do ya want three sixes or six threes?"

CHOOSING A CAREER

Some stories I tell are probably not exactly the way other characters in story might tell them. We all see situations from differing points of view and occasionally facts get blurred. So, if you run into my daughter, Jennifer, and you ask her about how she and her dad made some important decisions about what she wanted to do with her life, she might tell this story differently. But this is how I remember it.

She was fifteen and had asked me what I thought she should do for a career. I had no idea what she should do, but I had an idea of how to begin considering that important decision and sorting through the possibilities. This was several years before the shelves of books were written on choosing a career, and other decision-making paradigms. At the time I did what most parents do: I just made it up.

I said, "Go get a piece of blank paper and draw four columns. In column one you'll list all of the things you love to do. In column two you'll list all of the things you hate to do. In column three you'll list all of the things you are really good at. And in column four you'll list all of the things you are really bad at."

I knew that we would pay no attention to columns two and four, but I thought it was a good part of the exercise to get her brain working in complete ways.

After she had done that, we sat down and compared columns.

"OK, see if there are any things in column one that are either the same as, or relate to, things in column three." This took a few minutes of comparison and she finally found several. "Now, write those things on a separate piece of paper."

These items included;

- Draw well
- Creative

- Good at puzzles
- Like to think in complex terms
- Like to play with miniature dolls and dollhouses and furniture
- Enjoy looking at house plans
- Want to make a difference in the world

After a while the list looked like it could possibly fit into one large category: architecture. She had never mentioned wanting to do that, and I knew it was a field populated heavily by men, but I brought it up anyway.

"What do you think about becoming an architect?"

She studied the list some more and admitted that many of those items were important aspects of that particular career field, and said "I've never really considered becoming an architect."

We talked about it some, admitting that it was a field dominated by men, and that it might be tough to break into it, and the academic requirements were pretty tough, but, "Hey, it looks, right now, like something you might really LIKE."

Three years later, she graduated from Central High School, in Little Rock, second in a class of over 2000, got enough scholarships, grants, and loans to afford the tuition, and entered Princeton University. Before long she declared her intention to acquire an undergraduate degree in architecture.

Now, two decades later, she is one of a handful of female architects in Seattle, Washington, and has designed many lauded buildings in her brief career. She is becoming a national expert in regenerative architecture and biomimicry.

I haven't asked her recently if she still likes to play with miniature dollhouses and tiny pieces of furniture.

HANK SNOW'S TRIBUTE

This is one of those stories that's just a wee bit hazy in my memory, so I know I don't have the entire quote exactly right, but the last line is precisely preserved, permanently. (I even found it corroborated in a blog by a country music historian.)

In 1979, Hank Snow, famous and beloved country artist, was inducted into the Country Music Hall of Fame. During his remarks, he was very gracious to those who had helped in his career and toward the end he especially wanted to give greatest praise to his wife.

(I'm putting words in his mouth, but it was close to this.)

"There is one person who is the most important. She stood by me and encouraged me, and was a rock of salvation in my life. She was the best thing that ever happened to me, and I owe everything in my career to this woman. I'd like to introduce to you to this wonderful person . . . Mrs. Hank Snow."

MERVYN'S CHARGE OFF

We were buying a new Honda station wagon in Las Vegas. The price was agreed upon and the financing was not going to be a problem. However, after sitting there for longer than we thought it would take (Isn't that *always* how it works when you're buying a car?) the Sales Manager came back into the cubicle and said that the Honda financing company wouldn't do the deal, that there was something really wrong with my credit.

I couldn't believe it. My credit was great. I asked him to go back and find out very specifically what the problem was.

When he returned he said, "They said you have a charge off on your credit report and they won't finance anyone with a charge off." I didn't even know what a charge off was, much less think I had one.

"Will you either let me talk with them or find out more about this, please?" I couldn't believe that any of this could be correct.

When he came back he had a more complete answer. He told me, "The charge off is with Mervyn's. They say you have a bill that you've never paid and they finally "charged it off." If you want to finance the car through Honda, you have to get it fixed."

The Honda dealership was only about five minutes from the mall where there was a Mervyn's. I didn't know how to fix this, but at least I could talk with someone at Mervyn's. I left my wife with the car salesman and drove over to Mervyn's. On the way over, even though it only took a few minutes, I figured it out.

We had moved to Nashville from Las Vegas and then two years later had moved back to Las Vegas. They must've lost track of me during that time and I never received the bill they were talking about. I *always* paid my bills. My credit score was well above 800. I was going to get this thing fixed.

When I got to the credit department, I told the lady that I had come to take care of a delinquent bill that I thought had been charged off when I moved from Las Vegas to Nashville and back to Las Vegas again, and that I needed some help from her so I could purchase a new car. She was a little confused but she looked for my file. When she found it, she explained through the window, "Here it is. Yes, you *do* owe this. You say you want to take care of this charge off?" She paused to look carefully at my records, as I answered affirmatively, also asking the amount that I owed.

"OK, here it is. The amount of your bill is $4.72."

I was incredulous. "Four dollars and seventy-two cents?" I was being kept from purchasing a new car for four dollars and seventy-two cents?

"Yes. That's right."

And then with a totally straight face, and no hint of amusement whatsoever, I swear to God she said, "Do you want to pay all of this at once?"

I reached for my wallet and said, "Yes, ma'am. I think I would like to pay it all at once. And if I can get a receipt for it, I believe Honda will let me buy that car." I gave her a $5 bill, she gave me back 28¢, and after one more phone conversation between Honda Financing Corporation and Mervyn's, we drove home that afternoon in a new station wagon.

"WHERE'S THE SCAR ON YOUR FACE?"

I was getting a reading in the home of an astrologer who had been highly recommended. She was looking at her charts and notes and making occasional statements, then asking me if they were true, to verify the chart she had drawn. Then she was quiet for a few minutes and looked puzzled.

"I may have made a mistake. I don't see something that I always see when I look at a chart like yours. Hmmm." She looked intently at my face. I sat still and looked back at her.

"Where is the scar on your face? I don't see any scar on your face. When I see a chart with your aspects, by the time someone gets to your age they always have a visible scar on their face." She continued to examine my face from her side of the table.

I chuckled and said, "You haven't made a mistake. I have TWO scars on my face. You just can't see them easily." I pointed to my left eyebrow. "I had fourteen stitches here when I hit heads with Lyle Walker playing basketball in our back yard." And then I raised my chin and pointed to the bottom of my chin bone. "I split my chin open when I was around nine, and there's a scar here, too."

Both scars were visible. You just had to be looking for them to find them.

She was very relieved and went on with her reading. Some of it was right on the money, some it was a little off, but I was pretty darned impressed with her question about the scars.

How do they know THAT kind of stuff?

JANET'S AND JIM'S DOGS
(ASHLEY)

Dogs are great fodder for stories. Everyone has dog stories. Rupert Sheldrake, one of the world's most noted scientists, has written an entire book about dogs and their extrasensory abilities. I have a number of dog stories, too.

My good friends, Janet and Jim, have had several very fine dogs, one of which was a beautiful male Sheltie named Ashley. We went to a party at their house and took along their God-child, our toddler daughter, Blaine. When we arrived the party was roaring. Lots and lots of kneecaps for Blaine to look at. As we walked into the living room, Ashley, who had only seen Blaine once before, immediately ran to her and began to circle her, keeping the adults a safe distance away. It was a herding instinct that even Janet and Jim had never seen before. Those of us who noticed were amazed. Ashley didn't stop protecting Blaine the entire time she was in the living room.

About an hour later, when we put Blaine in the guest bedroom for a nap, Ashley stationed himself in front of the door, facing outward toward the hall, protecting her from intruders, remaining there until we got Blaine up from her nap.

Good boy, Ashley. Good boy!

(MOLLY)

Molly was Janet's and Jim's Great Pyrenees. She was white and enormous. She had a very active, huge, strong tail. We learned the hard way not to leave martinis on the coffee table.

There is a park in La Quinta where the local citizens take their dogs. Most dog owners know to keep their pets on a leash. A few inconsiderate boors do not. One particular man and his dog had similar dispositions: they were both bullies. This man allowed his Rhodesian Ridgeback to terrorize every other dog in the park, and not only refused to put the dog on a leash but appeared to delight in his dog's meanness.

The first time Jim took Molly to the park, the Rhodesian Ridgeback was running rampant once again, and Jim heard the other dog owners complaining, to no avail, to this man about not obeying the rules.

Jim observed several dog owners having to "save" their pets from the Ridgeback, picking them up in their arms, or scurrying to their cars.

Then the bully dog decided to attack Molly. Big mistake. Within a fraction of a second Molly flipped the ridgeback over on its back, put her teeth right on his throat and straddled him with her huge body. She didn't bite him, she just snarled and kept him pinned to the ground. The man who had allowed this to happen was furious. He yelled at Jim and cursed and was ridiculously irate. It was obvious that he was embarrassed at his dog's defeat.

Jim said nothing. The rest of the dog owners applauded.

The bully man took his bully dog and left the park. Ah, yes. Sometimes there IS justice in the world.

Good girl, Molly. Good girl!

"IT'S A BOY!"

My parents were visiting us in Tennessee and they asked Robin and me if we would take them to visit the daughter of an old colleague in Nashville. We said, "Sure," and we drove there for the afternoon. The woman and her husband were only a few years older than I, but they were both academicians, extremely bright, a bit arrogant in regard to their enormous intelligence, and—quite frankly—boring as hell. We sat and chatted for about an hour when their teenage child, Taylor, came in. They introduced us, we all shook hands, and Taylor left to go do homework. Taylor was slightly built with long brown hair and soft features. After Taylor had been out of the room a minute or two, Robin asked our hosts, "What grade is she in?" My mother about choked on her cookie and almost jumped out of her chair. "HE! Taylor is a HE."

Without missing a beat, Robin said, "Oh, I'm so sorry. My dyslexia gets me into trouble all the time. I mix up letters and words and sometimes even say the total opposite of what I mean. Of course I know Taylor's a boy. It just came out wrong . . . again."

All was well. In fact, it was charming how Robin had been able to just admit her disability so easily, and explain so clearly how that could happen to anyone with dyslexia.

The visit ended a short while later. We said goodbye to the Barlows and to Taylor. We got in the car and all four of us about busted a gut laughing.

"He's a HE! He's not a SHE! How's your lesdyksia? I mean your lysdexia. I mean, GOOD JOB, ROBIN!!!"

I think those who say a white lie is always wrong are perhaps mistaken.

DA BOYS

This is one of the stories in which the names are changed to protect the guilty. These stories are absolutely true, and some of these guys were really bad. And I don't know any of them any more.

My good friends Patrice Chanel and Al Carter asked me if I would be willing to act as their road manager and call their lighting cues during a stint of performances as the opening act for Bill Cosby and Sammy Davis, Jr. in different venues in Las Vegas, Atlantic City, New York City, Lake Tahoe, and Reno. What they really needed was a white man who owned nice suits and had a decent vocabulary. I was to be the one who went to the front desk of each hotel, and also would interface with the management of the various venues. I was to work with the PBX operators. I made travel arrangements for Carter and Chanel and I smoothed rough waters whenever the tough winds blew. I loved them both. Robin and I had worked with them in earlier years and had always had a stupendous time when the four of us were together.

Carter and Chanel were a really entertaining act: they sang well, they were funny, they had boy dancers, they had very expensive arrangements, they had Bob Mackie gowns and Armani tuxedos. They paid for the creation of their act with money that was loaned to them by some men who were from New Jersey, and who had reputations that were quite a bit less than savory. It was not an unusual way to pay for an act. Frank Sinatra had (allegedly) done it. Sammy Davis had (allegedly) done it. Many, many big stars had gotten their start in show business thanks to money and support from "the boys."

So, one of the first things I did after I agreed to work for them (temporarily) was to arrange transportation for one of these financiers, from a hotel to a restaurant in Las Vegas. He and I spent six hours together that night driving to and from restaurants in a long black limo. His name was Robert (Bobby) Molinero (NOT HIS REAL NAME). He was a little thug. According to some who knew him he was the sixth-ranked mafia guy in New Jersey. He never mentioned anything about what he did. He was also a helluva lot of fun. He was funny and had a great sense of adventure, and he and I became friends. He was banned from casinos in Atlantic City, but we went in them anyway. We didn't gamble, but we sat around and kind of "defied" the authorities. We rode in a lot of limousines together. We drank a lot of drinks together. And we didn't pry into each other's lives.

It was a few months of limousines, bulges under sport coats, comps to lots of shows, and a friendship with a man who had lots of potential in the wrong direction.

Bobby had several guys who worked for him. They were worse thugs than he was.

Early in my association with Carter and Chanel, after an opening night performance at Caesar's Palace, a bunch of us were partying in Al and Patrice's suite—one of the two story suites that stars get. At the height of the party, amidst all the raucous and festive noise, I went behind the bar to refresh my drink and thought I should get something for others while I was back here. So in a loud voice and my very best New Jersey (not even close to my best Mafia) accent, I asked, "So, does anyone wanna another drink while I'm back here, or what?" The room immediately became deathly quiet. It was like . . . Oh, man. You could hardly believe how fast it got that quiet. A few very uncomfortable seconds later the noise picked up again, and I felt like I could breathe again. A few minutes later, one of Bobby's boys went up to Al and said, "So, uh, how duz yer friend know whut we DOO?" Al laughed him off.

"Hey, he was just kidding around. He's a great guy. You're gonna like him."

As it turned out, Buster DID end up liking me.

He had a very raspy, growly voice. It was like Gabby Hays three octaves lower with a Joisey accent. Very distinctive. Kinda scary.

In each hotel as soon as I'd checked us in, the second thing I'd do was make friends with the PBX operators. Sometimes I'd actually go down to the room where they received and transferred calls. Sometimes I'd just talk to them on the phone from my room, but I always made certain they knew my name, that they were to route to me all calls going to Al or Patrice, and that they could also call me any time if they ever had questions or needed help with anything.

One night, after we'd been at a hotel in Reno for about a week, I got a call at 3 in the morning. "Mr. Dickey, this is Annette. I have a call for Mr. Carter. Do you want to take it?"

"Hi, Annette. Who is it?"

In her deepest, raspiest, growliest voice she laughed as she answered, "It's BUSTER!" Though she had to awaken me at three o'clock she had made us both guffaw. I took the call. A year and a half later Buster was in a federal prison for extortion.

In those days I was living in both Las Vegas and Santa Monica, and I kept the old pickup truck in Las Vegas. (See IRVING) Al called me from out of town and, knowing I had a truck, asked if I would do him a favor the next day. "I've got some boxes in a storage room that I need to have moved from where they are to a store in North Las Vegas. Would you have time to do that for me?

"I guess so. Sure."

He gave me the address of the storage room and the entry codes, and I went out the next day and loaded Irving full of heavy boxes. I didn't have time to deliver them to North Las Vegas that day, so I kept them overnight. Before I went in for the night I looked in some of the boxes. They were all XXX-rated videos. I didn't really think much about it and the next day I delivered them to a video store in North Las Vegas, completing the favor for Al. He thanked me, and nothing was ever mentioned again about any of it.

About six months later, when I was living in Santa Monica full time, I opened my daily Los Angeles Times to the Business Section and there, in large type size, was a headline that read, "New Jersey Mafia Boss Indicted for Video Tape Fraud." As I scanned the article, I saw in the third paragraph, "Robert Molinero, New Jersey Mafia boss. . . ."

"OHMYGOD! That's Bobby Molinero." In the short time since I'd met him, the guys above him had either gone to prison or gotten murdered, and he was now the head of the third or fourth biggest mafia family in the country. "OH, GEEZ! And I KNOW this guy! NO! I don't just KNOW this guy, I'm PALS with this guy!" Suddenly it dawned on me that what was even worse than being pals with him was that I had transported some of those videotapes. I was an accomplice or an accessory or something, and could probably be arrested.

As I write this I am thinking that before this book gets published I should double check on statutes of limitations. If it's less than 17 years, I'm OK. I suppose if you're reading this, the statute of limitations ran out. If it hadn't I'd have eliminated this particular story from this book. I've been accused of being crazy but not stupid.

Now, I don't know anything about phone taps, but after that article was printed Robin and I both thought there was something very strange about our telephone. For quite a while we thought we were hearing odd clicks, and sometimes we just "felt" like there was something awry. We talked about it several times, but after about three months we didn't notice it any more and we finally forgot all about it. If anyone WAS interested in me, they eventually found out that Barbie and Ken lived there and they were wasting their time.

STORIES I'VE TOLD MORE THAN ONCE

RAM DASS

Mafia pals and Ram Dass? Back to back? Even I'M impressed with the full-spectrum life I've led.

Before writing this particular story I thought, *"You have to be extra careful when you write things about people who are still alive. First of all, if you like them, you don't want to offend them in any way, and second of all, they might remember the same event totally differently."**

I always wonder how the Bible (particularly the New Testament) got written with so many quotes when some of the stories were written so many years after Jesus' death. I suspect there are more than one or two interpretations that might not be exact quotes. But, once more, I digress.

Robin had been hired to be the host of a show that was going to feature interviews with the most renowned metaphysical authors and success-oriented teachers of the day. The cast included Leo Buscaglia, Ram Dass, Mark Victor Hansen, Brian Tracy, Roger Dawson, and other equally well-known motivators and therapists. A few of them had already done interviews with each other, but on this taping day Robin was to conduct interviews with a number of these "stars."

She and I were chatting as she was sitting in the makeup chair, when a gentleman walked in and began conversing casually with all of us. Robin said she was hungry and they talked about how it wouldn't be a good idea for her to go out on the floor without having had something to eat. But, this man interjected, "You don't want anything that'll stick between your teeth. It can make you crazy when you think you have food between your teeth." We were all amused by his observation, Robin concurring with him totally.

She noticed there was a jar of large dill pickles sitting on the shelf behind him. "Those wouldn't stick between my teeth. Would you hand me a pickle, please?" He was happy to oblige and reached into the jar, passing it along to her in a napkin. She chomped down on it, said thank you, and he left the room.

As Robin ate the pickle, I asked her, "Do you know who that guy was?"

"No."

"That was Ram Dass."

She shrugged. She didn't know who Ram Dass was. He wasn't on her list to interview that day (He had already done his bit with Leo Buscaglia.) and she hadn't studied up on anyone who wasn't on the list for the day.

"He wrote *Be Here Now*. It's a best seller. He's the guy, when his name was Richard Alpert, who did drugs with Timothy Leary at Harvard. Well, it wasn't like he was doing drugs. They were doing research. Yeah, it WAS kinda like they were doing drugs. But now he's, like, BABA Ram Dass. He's one of the great teachers of our day."

"Oh. OK."

She still wasn't impressed. It would be just fine with her if he was famous. It would be just fine with her if he wasn't famous. Right now, though, she needed to concentrate on the men and women whom she was to interview today. One of the things about her that was so great was her professionalism and her utter disregard for fame. Not that she didn't aspire to it. Just that she didn't let it rule her. She lived by a question that sort of went, "If I were suddenly to have $10,000,000 in the bank, would I still keep doing what I'm doing?" Her answer was always, "YES!" She loved her work and worked hard to get better at it.

As she went from the makeup room to the studio floor for a sound check and a few lighting changes, I went and sat in the grandstand. It was a tier of aluminum bleacher-type seats that might have accommodated perhaps 200 or 250 people. That morning there were about 40 or 50 in the audience. I sat on a row with no others about two-thirds of the way up, fairly close to the center.

I'd been there about 15 minutes, the taping was about to begin, and Ram Dass came and sat right next to me. I don't mean he sat on the same row sort of near me. I mean he sat RIGHT NEXT TO ME. There were 200 other places he could have sat and about 100 of them wouldn't have been two inches from somebody else, but he chose that place to sit.

We chatted amiably without introducing ourselves. We had already "met" without exchanging names and we were both comfortable with that. We didn't talk about anything important, just about the show and the weather and stuff. Then the taping began and we stopped the conversation.

About half an hour into the interviews, something happened on stage that caused some dissention. It wasn't about Robin. I don't remember what the actual problem was, but I remember clearly how irritated Ram Dass got, and he turned to me and hissed, "You'd think these guys would've thought of this in advance. What a bunch of idiots!" (*This is where that asterisk at the end of the second paragraph comes into play. Ram Dass is still alive and well and still teaching in Hawaii, and maybe I've put a word or two into his mouth. I don't actually recall his EXACT words. I just remember how upset and mad he was and how clearly he expressed those emotions.)

I let him finish and then whispered a response. "Yeah, I agree. They probably *should* have taken care of that last week, but can you do me a little favor?"

"Sure."

"That lady down there, the one you were talking to in the makeup room, is my wife. She wants to do a really good job on this show, and I want her to do a really good job on this show. And she needs all the good energy we can provide. Do you think instead of being angry at the producers, we could think of ways to resolve this? Or . . . if we can't think of anything positive to do about it, could we just send soothing, loving thoughts down there? I have this belief that our energy is important and powerful and maybe we could help rather than become part of the problem."

He turned toward me, moving his shoulders and chest back a few inches as if to get a better look at me.

"Now I know why I sat by you. I didn't know why, when there were so many vacant seats, that I was "told" to sit by you. I just kind of felt this strong urge to come all the way over here to sit. And now I know why. Of course, you are absolutely right. I'm sorry I reacted that way. We can both do as you've suggested and I DO think we can make a difference. Thank you very much for being my teacher today."

He wasn't embarrassed by his emotions or his words. He had merely momentarily forgotten to practice what he preached. I'm certain he forgave himself as quickly as we both realized there was nothing to forgive. We didn't speak of anything like this the rest of the morning. But I also recall that as soon as he and I shifted our energy the problem on the studio floor dissipated and they almost immediately got back to the taping. Who knows what fixed it? He sat by me for the remainder of the morning and then I never saw him again. We never did introduce ourselves.

HANGIN' WITH SAM

I first met Sammy Davis while I was working in Hallelujah Hollywood. A co-worker in that show, Gary Marshal, had done a film with Sammy and they had remained good friends for many years. One night Gary asked me if I'd like to go over to Caesar's Palace after our second show and play charades with Sammy Davis, Jr.. "He loves to play charades and I'm getting together a little group to play with him. Come on, it'll be fun." I was unfamiliar with all the details of charades, but at Gary's urging and because of his enthusiasm I said, "Sure, OK." Over the next few years, I ended up playing charades with Sammy a number of times.

I second met Sammy Davis when my second wife, Diane, was working as one of the dancers in his act. Diane was a former Rockette, an experienced dancer in both films and television, had been an assistant choreographer for a number of live shows, and was fast becoming a very fine choreographer in her own right. When she had lived in New York City, she had a roommate named Altovise Gore, who later became Sammy's last wife.

I third met Sammy Davis while working as Road Manager and Lighting Director for Carter and Chanel, when they were the opening for him in Las Vegas, Tahoe, Reno, and Atlantic City. I had known Patrice Chanel in Hallelujah Hollywood where she had been one of the lead dancers. She teamed up with Al Carter, a very fine singer, and formed a duet act that rivaled any in the business. She sang and danced, he sang, they did impeccable duets, and they were a first-rate opening act. I was happy and proud to help them when they asked.

I fourth met Sammy Davis when he and Jerry Lewis were sharing star billing at the MGM Grand Hotel in the summer of 1988. Jerry hired five of us (Evie Littrell, Judy Brown, Guy Maeda, Robin Timm, and me) to do a comedy routine where we sang

"Danny Boy" with great seriousness and he got lots of laughs.

So, there were a number of times when I had the privilege and joy of just "hanging out" with Sammy. All of those times were either in a hotel suite or a dressing room. I never actually went to his home until after he had died.

I recall saying during my eulogy for a good friend with whom I had shared a dressing room for a number of years, "When you sit around in your underwear with somebody for a couple of hours a night, you get to know them pretty well." The first time I saw Sammy in his underwear I was totally impressed with how very, VERY tiny he was.

THE CAFTAN GIFT

It must've been the second time we played charades. We always played when he was working at Caesar's Palace. We'd been playing for about half an hour when Sammy left us and went upstairs. (It was another one of those huge two-story suites.) He came back down a few minutes later wearing a caftan. It had many very bright colors, looked very comfortable, and nearly everyone in the room laughed at him. It WAS a little too big, it WAS a bit gaudy, and he DID look kind of silly, but a few minutes later I complimented him on the garment.

"You LIKE it? Really?" He was surprised by my comment.

"Yeah, I DO like. I've actually sewn two caftans myself, I wear them to work quite often, and I LIKE it."

"Hey, thanks, man. I appreciate you liking it."

We played some more charades and then about half an hour later he went back upstairs again. This time when he came down he was dressed in jeans and a normal shirt and he was carrying the caftan, carefully folded in his hands. He walked over to me, laid it in my lap, and said, "Hey, man, I want you to have this." When I mildly protested, he continued, "No, man. It's my gift to you. A lady gave it to me, but you like it and it's too big for me." We all laughed at that. Everyone knew that EVERYTHING was too big for him.

I wore the caftan a few times, but mostly I just treasured it.

THE DENIM PURSE GIFT

In addition to sewing a few caftans for myself, I also made a great denim purse. (Most caftans have no pockets—at least the ones I made didn't have pockets.) If you're going to carry a wallet and keys you need something to put them in. So . . . I took an old pair of jeans, cut them apart, saving the pockets and the band around the top with the belt loops on it. I created an open-top purse with a pocket on the outside and the belt loop band for the shoulder strap. It got admiring looks and positive comments everywhere I took it. Sammy's "envy" was no exception.

I took it to Caesar's one night and he said, "Hey, man, where'd you get that purse?"

I proudly said, "I MADE it!"

"Get out of here! You didn't make it. Where'd you get it?"

"I MADE it! I cut up an old pair of jeans and put it all together myself."

"WOW! That is so cool. Somebody gave me a denim prison cap that I wear every now and then and I really need a purse like that to go with it."

I heard his desire, but didn't respond to it. All I said was, "Yeah, that would be pretty good, to have a purse and a cap that matched."

That week I made one for Sammy and the next time we saw each other I took it with me. He was sitting down, kind of like I was when he presented me with the caftan, and I laid it in his lap, saying, "My gift to you, man."

He totally flipped. He loved it and used it many, many times. For a man who had nearly everything, and at certain times in his life could afford everything else, I was quite pleased to be able to give him something that no one else had ever given him.

SAMMY LISTENING IN

I was working for Carter and Chanel in Atlantic City—they opened for Sammy several times there in their short career. Each night after the second show I would call home and talk with Robin for 20 or 30 minutes. One night after we'd been in this particular hotel about a week, Robin and I spent part of our conversation talking about a particular song that we were thinking about adding to our act, and during our conversation neither of us could remember what Broadway show it had come from. We ended the conversation still not having come up with the answer. (This was before the days of iPhones where you can just "look something up" while you're talking.)

The next night, prior to the first show I was walking down the hall past Sammy's dressing room. He had left the door open and was waiting for me. When he saw me, he hollered, "Hey, Joe, come in for a minute. Do you have time?"

"Sure," I said, turning around and going in.

He stood up as I came in and said, "The show is *Do Re Mi*."

I didn't know what he meant. Obviously I looked puzzled.

"'Make Someone Happy' is from *Do Re Mi*. Comden and Greene. It's from *Do Re Mi*." He smiled a little smile, and suddenly I remembered that "Make Someone Happy" was the song we didn't know what show it was from. I was confused and he hastily went on.

"I have a confession to make, man. Last night after I got back to my room I picked up the phone to talk with Shirley (Rhodes, his manager) and somehow I was hearing you and your wife talking. I know I should've hung up, but for some reason I just couldn't. So I listened in on your entire conversation. I'm really sorry, man. I apologize. I just wanted you to know."

I didn't know what to say. I finally stammered, "You heard

EVERYTHING? Did we say anything bad about anyone? I mean, geez, what'd we say that you remember?"

"No, no, man! It was a GREAT conversation. I'm sorry I couldn't stop listening, but it was really nice to hear two people talk with each other who really care about each other. You guys really love each other, don't you?"

"Yeah, we do. But are you sure it was all good?"

It's pretty easy to speak unkindly of someone or complain or make an off-handed comment that could be misconstrued.

"Oh, yeah. Don't worry. It WAS all good, and I'm really sorry I didn't hang up, but, man I just couldn't put the phone down. It was really weird, just feelin' sneaky and everything for twenty minutes. But I DID want you to know what I did, and I apologize. So . . ." He waved his hand to let me know he didn't have anything left to add.

As I turned to leave the dressing room, I said, "Hey, thanks for telling me about *Do Re Mi*." We both laughed, letting that piece of information be the most important thing about our conversation.

I walked down the hall and up to the light booth thinking, *"Boy, oh, boy. You just never know, do you? You can never be certain who's overhearing a conversation in person, or on the phone."* Nowadays, in addition, you never know who might be reading an email or picking up a FAX that's meant for someone else. Might be a good idea to just get in the habit of saying nice things all the time.

WHO WAS MORE JEWISH?

On several occasions Sammy and I discussed religion and spirituality. After our first conversation on these topics, during which I had expressed many of my views on spirituality, he said, "Ya know, Joe, I think you're actually more Jewish than I am."

After which he followed with the obligatory, "Funny, we don't LOOK Jewish."

Funny.

LITTLE BIT

My eldest, Jennifer, grew up to a total of five feet one and a half inches tall. When she worked as a dresser for Patrice Chanel, while Carter and Chanel were Sammy's opening act, Sammy really liked Jennifer. First of all, she's a very likeable person to begin with. But he especially liked her because, "She's the only person around here I can look eye to eye, without standing on my tiptoes or bending my neck backwards."

He called her "Little Bit."

PHONING WITH THE STARS

I think there should be a TV show where ordinary people get to call stars and have conversations with them. The winners would be the ones who could get the stars to reveal themselves to be either nicer than we thought, or more egotistical than we thought, or more risqué than we thought, or . . . you know . . . just more of something than we imagined them to be. I don't actually believe the show would make it to the pilot stage. I'm just remembering some of the conversations I've had with big stars.

Some of them came because of my personal friendships, and some of them came because of work I was doing as a writer for various PBS stations, and some of them came because of so many other reasons that I can't even remember them.

I had a LOT of conversations with famous show business people when I was helping produce a benefit for Altovise Davis, Sammy's widow. I had to call and speak with literally 30 or 40 big names, one of them was Frank Sinatra, asking them if they would come to Las Vegas and donate their time for what I thought was a worthy cause. Many of them said, "Yes," as is the habit of so many of these good-hearted folk: Rich Little, Debbie Reynolds, Tom Dreesen, Joey Bishop, Steve Allen. A handful said, "No," for a variety of reasons.

My most memorable conversations, though, were lengthy and filled with a variety of subjects and felt like I had known these people well for a long time.

I was writing a "pledge script" for KCET for Robert Wagner to read. I thought I could make the script more personal for him if I knew a little more about him, so I asked my producer if it would be OK for me to call him. She checked with him and he said, "Sure", so I called the next day expecting to have a 5 or 10-minute conversation with him. He and I ended up talking for almost an hour. At first we talked about what I wanted to know: if he wanted to pitch anything for himself—a film or TV show or a pet project; if he was comfortable reading a prompter or would he rather ad lib his pitches; and if he preferred throwing the script back and forth or would he prefer more monologues. He was great. He didn't care. He just wanted to do something good for public television.

And then he wanted to talk about ME. He asked me if I made a living as a writer to which I replied, "No, basically I'm a singer who just happens to have an extra job writing for KCET." Then he wanted to know all about my singing career. And then he wanted to know about my family. And my parents. And my politics. And before long he and I knew as much about each other as any two long-time friends—maybe more. It was a GREAT conversation and he and I pledged to try to get together some time. We never did though. But every time, after that, when I'd see him on screen, I felt like I knew him. Never even shook hands.

Another person with whom I had an unusual conversation was Carol Lawrence. It was when she was still married to Robert Goulet. I had volunteered to help some friends at the Renaissance Faire. They were macramé artists (so you know it was in the early seventies) and they had crafted some large, very comfortable chairs, from telephone cable spools and jute. The macramé was beautiful and the wood was nicely finished, and they were selling them for $400 each (which in today's dollars is over $2000). It would only take one sale for my friends to be in heaven. I was tending their "booth" when they went to get some lunch. Along came Robert Goulet and Carol Lawrence. These chairs knocked them out. Though I tried to get them to purchase the pair, they only wanted one, and we drew up a contract. They said they would come back a little later to pay for it and to make arrangements for its delivery. Then they left.

When my friends returned they were overjoyed with the sale, I left them to finish the deal, and went home. However, a series of circumstances created a need for ME to call Mr. Goulet and Ms. Lawrence. I had inadvertently kept their phone number in my pocket, and they had been unable to return to the booth that afternoon but still wanted the chair. They called my friends to make certain they could still purchase the chair but assumed my friends had their phone number and didn't leave it on the answering machine. Hence, my friends called me and asked, since I'd been the one who originally interacted with them, if I would do them a favor and call Robert Goulet and Carol Lawrence and close the deal. I was OK with that and called late the next morning.

She answered the phone and as soon as I told her who I was and how we'd met and what the call was about, she blurted, "Honey, I just stepped out of the bathtub and I'm totally naked, dripping water all over the place. Can you call back in a half hour?" "

WHOA! T.M.I, Baby!

"Uh, sure. Be happy to." *WOW! Talking to a naked Carol Lawrence! WHEW!* Visions of sugarplums danced in my head! I could hardly breathe for the next 25 minutes. But I finally gathered myself to make the call. She and I ended up talking for almost an hour, about all things under the sun. Well, not ALL things. I never DID ask her why she had told me she was naked. And it never was mentioned again.

Until . . . over thirty years later, I was in a show with her in Palm Springs. I was with the Crew Cuts and she was appearing as one of the stars of the show. After our sound checks I approached her backstage, introduced myself, told her of our conversation in the early seventies, and though we were both amused with the story, she didn't remember it. She explained, "Oh, honey, I most certainly COULD'VE said that to you, but please don't ask me why. I've never known why I do anything."

Just another conversation.

NOW READ THIS

A benefit I helped produce for Sammy's widow, Altovise, allowed me an opportunity to video tape the two best teleprompter readers in the world on the same day. We had asked a number of celebrities to be in the show, many said, "Yes," many said, "No," and a few said they couldn't be there but they'd be happy to send a video. I made appointments with Dick Clark and Ronald Reagan to shoot their tributes on the same day.

Procuring the date with Dick Clark was difficult. Procuring the date with Ronald Reagan was monumentally difficult: background checks for my film crew, special permits to enter his floor of the building, extra signed release forms, and about three times as many phone calls to get it all arranged. But arrange it, we did.

I took a little film crew to Dick Clark Productions in the late morning. He had prepared a script to read, and his first take was a keeper. The backup take was better than the first. What a pro! It took thirty fewer minutes than we had allotted.

Good thing. Getting into former President Reagan's office in Century City took LONGER than we had allotted. However, we were finally led to a conference room where we set up our lights and camera.

When President Reagan came in, he was with four other men, all wearing suits and ties. We were ALL wearing suits and ties. When everyone is wearing a suit and tie you can only tell a secret service man from a cameraman if one of them is setting up a camera. The former President had on a navy suit and a red tie and looked exactly like a life-size cardboard cut-out that I'd had my picture taken with three years earlier, at a convention. Something was amiss, though. He seemed quite distant and distracted. I couldn't put my finger on it, but I noticed it. We were introduced, I explained what I wanted him to do—to sit here and read the tribute to Sammy. He sat in the chair with the camera right in front of him, and when we switched on the lights it looked like the lights had come on inside of HIM. He took total control. He read the entire script flawlessly.

I said, "Mr. President, that was perfect. Could you do it one more time, just for a backup?"

He replied, "Absolutely." And proceeded to read the script perfectly again, this time with even more energy.

I was very happy. "Thank you, Mr. President. We're finished. We appreciate your time very much and it was a great honor to meet you."

Then he stood up and "went away" again.

We posed together for a few photographs, one of which looked identical to the one I'd had taken several years earlier. We packed up our gear and left.

The two videos were highlights during the tribute to Sammy.

Fast forward six months. We learn that Ronald Reagan has Alzheimer's. All of a sudden I realized what had disturbed me when we were at his office: he didn't know where he was. In retrospect, I could tell that he had come in confused, short-term memory totally gone. But when he sat down in front of the lights and the camera, his old memory kicked in and he could not have been more alive. At that stage of his disease, that's how Alzheimer's works.

It didn't take any higher math or any more information about the progression of Alzheimer's to know that he had been afflicted during his final year of his Presidency. My recollection is that he only had three press conferences that year and he answered no questions at any of them, only reading statements from the prompter.

Made me realize, even MORE clearly, how little we all know about what goes on in Washington, D.C.

∞

THE BOOKENDS

Robin and I were working with Al and Patrice while they were opening for Bill Cosby in Reno. On most nights we were the only white people downstairs at Harrah's. He called us "The Bookends." He also, that Christmas, made 15 sweet potato pies and brought them in and gave them as gifts to everyone who was working there that year. He stayed up most of the night making them and they were GOOOOOOOOD.

As everyone knows, Bill Cosby is extremely bright, extremely funny, and very complex. He appreciated that I was the son of a former university President, and we had some truly fine conversations. We both enjoyed the fact the each of us knew a lot about a lot of things. I didn't get to know him well enough to ever say we developed a friendship. It was, however, a nice acquaintanceship.

ALCATRAZ TEQUILA

I had an opportunity once to spend most of a day just wandering through a wine and spirits convention in San Francisco. I was alone, so it probably wasn't as much fun as I might've had with others. Tasting alcohol just seems like a group event to me.

I got to the section of the convention floor where the new tequilas were. Most of them were high end, expensive tequilas and the bottles were beautiful, and I'm certain they all tasted pretty good. When I arrived at that part of the convention center it was empty except for a few vendors and myself. One of them engaged me in conversation, and I decided to stop walking and actually take a look at what he was putting on the market.

It was a clear glass bottle with a light amber tequila in it. It had something sculpted on the outside, almost the entire height of the bottle, and on closer examination I saw that it was a very lovely calla lily. The tequila was named "Alcatraz." It was a beautiful bottle and a beautiful label. He asked if I would like a taste, saying that they were planning to sell it for around $50 a bottle. I sipped a very small amount—it was excellent—and asked him if he had spent very much time in the United States, that his English was outstanding.

He said, "No. I've learned to speak this way without ever coming to the U.S."

I then asked him, "Do you know very much about Alcatraz?"

"Oh, I know ALL about Alcatraz. I know its chemical properties, I know where the plants are grown, I know exactly what temperature to store it at. I can tell its taste from all other tequilas . . ."

I interrupted him. "No. I mean do you know about Alcatraz, the prison?"

He stopped. It was obvious that he didn't know about Alcatraz, the prison.

I went on. "Most companies who introduce a new product into this country do a tremendous amount of market research. Didn't anyone in your company even research the NAME of your product?"

"Oh, yes. We did. There is a legend about it, from the 1800's, all about how thousands of calla lilies sprang up overnight in a hacienda, and there was a giant agave plant, it's quite a story. As you can see, we put a sculpted calla lily on the bottle. It's beautiful, isn't it?"

I agreed with the striking package design, but was confused by his lack of knowledge about what was considered one of the most horrible locations on the face of the earth. I briefly explained to him what Alcatraz represented in this country and thought perhaps they might reconsider the name, or the target market, or SOMETHING: for me, the bottle, the price, and the name just didn't fit.

"Well, at least you're in the right city to do some quick research NOW. Alcatraz is right out there in the bay, and there's a plethora of information in San Francisco about it."

I took the final sip, shook his hand, wished him good luck, thinking this product was a sure-fire failure. As it turns out, Alcatraz Tequila is no longer available anywhere. It disappeared from the shelves almost as quickly as it had appeared. It's impossible to know whether it was the name, or the price, or the quality, or the distribution, or the agave shortage or something else that caused it's demise. But I think I know.

THE CARDIAC OPERATION

There was an alley that ran beside our apartment in Santa Monica, where our garages were. One day, while hanging some new shelves in my garage, I heard the sound of a grocery cart rattling up the rough pavement. I looked out and there was a black man, about my age, pushing a cart full of bottles and cans. Our eyes met and I said, "Hey, how ya doin'?" He stopped, leaned on the bar of the cart, and began what was to be a half-hour conversation.

About a week later, I saw him again. Same alley, same cart; I'm assuming different bottles and cans. We exchanged greetings and we started talking again. This time, at some point in the conversation, I noticed it was about lunchtime, and asked him if he was hungry and would he like a sandwich. He at first refused, but I knew I shouldn't let him off that easily and he fairly quickly changed his mind.

He waited in the shade while I went in and fixed us both ham and cheese sandwiches. I brought out two sandwiches on paper towels and two Cokes, and we sat down under the protection of the raised garage door.

His name was Mustafa. He had a girlfriend with whom he'd been living for seven years. They had three children, two of whom were hers before he knew her. The two older kids attended public school in Santa Monica. And they all lived in a somewhat hidden tent down near the beach. They'd been there for almost three years. He played the bells at the Bahai Temple in Culver City, walking the six or seven miles down and back every Sunday morning. Mustafa referred to himself as an aluminum recycler and was proud that he was able to support his family.

After that, as often as I would see him (and sometimes I'd actually wait around for him to show up) we would share a sandwich in the alley and have great conversations. We talked religion, and parenting, and education, and racism, and business. He and I really liked each other. I thought a few times about visiting him and his family, but we never actually decided that would be a good idea.

A few months before we moved to Granada Hills, he stopped coming around. I missed him, and looked for him several weeks in a row, but he had either changed his route or something had happened to him. Finally, though, the week we were packing to move, I saw him again. Same shopping basket, same loud rattle coming up the alley. I was really happy to see him, and gave him a hug. "I've missed you for all these weeks. Where've you been?"

"Oh, I was in the hospital and then had to recover. I had a cardiac operation."

I was shocked. "A cardiac operation! Wow! That's really serious. How're you doing now?"

"Well, you can see I'm doin' fine. But it's been tough gettin' back in shape. They took cardiac out of both of my knees."

I don't think he saw my reaction, but I just said, "Yep, that's a pretty tough operation, all right. Looks like you're doing great, though."

I was too busy to get a sandwich that day, and we moved the next week. I never saw him again. But I "use" him when I write my biography. One part of it says, "I've met three Presidents of the United States, and I regularly shared sandwiches in an alley with an aluminum recycler." Neither part of that sentence is more important than the other.

COPYRIGHT INFRINGEMENT

During the early 1980's I created and produced a series of cassette tapes called "Power in Your Words." They were affirmations with a classical musical background, designed for the listener to repeat the affirmations. They were produced in such a way that the listener would not go into an altered state of consciousness, so they were suitable for listening in the car (or anywhere else). A lot of people gave them high marks for that type of program.

I took them with me when I sang at churches, to sell along with my vocal cassettes.

One Sunday, after doing two solos for each of two services at a fairly large church in Redondo Beach, I was standing by the product table selling these cassettes when a lady walked up and said, "I want to thank you for saving my life." I didn't know her and must have looked puzzled. She continued. "Last year, when you sang at this church, I came to the second service with the full intention of killing myself on the way home. I had a place, and a method, and was fully determined to do that. After you sang, I stopped by this table to see what you had for sale. I'm not sure why I did that, seeing as how I wasn't going to get much use out of anything I bought, but you and I spoke for a few moments and I bought one of these cassettes," pointing to one of my "Power In Your Words" tapes. "I put it into my cassette player on the way to my planned suicide, and started to do the affirmations. Within a few minutes, my attitude was changed, I drove around a little more, and I ended up NOT killing myself that day. I was so impressed with this cassette that I've made many, many copies and have given them to my friends." It was apparent that she was proud of her decision to spare her own life, and she was equally proud of her charity in giving all these tapes to her friends.

I was quiet for a moment. Then I said to her in a most light-hearted way. "Well, you're the only person whose life I ever saved and then I wanted to kill 'em." It was HER turn to look puzzled. I went on. "I am incredibly happy that you made such a good decision for yourself to NOT commit suicide. I'm very proud that you think this cassette had something to do with the decision. On the other hand, I make part of my living by selling these cassettes and by copying them for all of your friends you're taking money out of my pocket." By the time I finished the last sentence I was laughing and so was she, with her hand over her mouth in chagrin.

She apologized; I forgave her; we both left the church that day feeling really good about our lives.

PARACHUTING INTO BIG SKY

After producing 19 yearly retreats at the Jackson Lake Lodge, the board of The Grand Teton Retreat was informed that due to scheduling conflicts we would no longer be able to hold our retreat there. We found a new place for the following year, Big Sky, Montana.

One of the attendees, a former Army Ranger, told me during our final hours in the Tetons that he had always wanted to parachute into the park to begin the retreat, but it was government property and he couldn't get permission.

But next year . . . "Since Big Sky is PRIVATE property, I'm certain that I can get permission to do it. Would you like to do a tandem jump with me?"

"REALLY? We could DO that? You think you could really get permission? Oh, man! That would be so much fun! Yeah! I'd LOVE to do it. How much do you think it might cost?"

He said he'd get back to me on the exact figures: we'd have to rent a plane and a pilot, but he owned the chutes, and we'd come right into the big open area next to the hotel so we wouldn't have to hire anyone to pick us up. It wasn't going to be too expensive, and I was already feeling excited.

My daughter, Jennifer, had attended the retreat that year and she was in the car with Robin and me as we were driving home through Wyoming. From the back seat Jennifer said, "Dad, I heard you talking with Cliff about parachuting into the retreat next year. How much is that going to cost?" The last word had barely escaped her lips when Robin blurted, "HALF OF EVERYTHING HE OWNS!"

We almost wrecked the car laughing.

Unfortunately, during the next year Cliff died a tragic, early death. Fortunately, I never had to give any further consideration to the 50% statement.

∞

PRETTY MUCH A NEAR GENIUS

We were "baby sitting" for our nephew, Stephen, when he was eleven. He had invited a school chum to come over for the afternoon and they were lying on the floor playing Junior Trivial Pursuit. Every now and then they would ask me a question that was part of the game and each time they asked me, I knew the answer. After about an hour the friend whispered to Stephen, "How does your uncle KNOW all this stuff?" To which Stephen whispered back, "He's pretty much a near genius."

Robin and I both heard the conversation and looked at each other without laughing or making a comment. Later that evening we had a good laugh, and although we told Stephen's parents, Robin and Steve, none of us thought anything more about until about a year later.

Stephen's father and stepmother were about to have their first child and we were attending a baby shower. The men were standing in the kitchen drinking margaritas, while the women were in the living room playing a baby shower game. The rules of the game were to wrap toilet paper around the pregnant woman's stomach three times, and then each of the other women wrote down how many squares of toilet paper it took to go around three times. They were all having a great time and so were the men.

One of the husbands asked the groups of guys, "So, how big IS a piece of toilet paper?" No one responded so I said, "I'd say those pieces are about four and a quarter inches by four and quarter inches."

"Oh, REALLY! Exactly that size, huh?" He was pretending to be derisive but was pretty impressed that I had come up with any size at all. However, just to have an opportunity to poke real fun at me, he went over to a kitchen drawer, pulled out a ruler, handed it to my brother-in-law, the host of the party, and said,

"How 'bout you measuring a piece of toilet paper?"

Steve walked into the living room and tore off a square, brought it back into the kitchen, measuring it as he walked. It turned out to be EXACTLY four and a quarter inches by four and quarter inches. We all died laughing.

The man who had demanded the measurement turned to Steve and amid all the laughter said, "He's pretty much a near genius."

There it was! Two separate estimations of my intellect. Exactly the same comment. Full corroboration. "He's pretty much a near genius."

No further calculations needed. Ever. I have announced myself as being "pretty much a near genius" enough times to totally disprove it, but it remains one of the closely held urban myths in our little circle of acquaintances.

THE TELEVISION GAME SHOWS

Not long after I'd moved to Los Angeles I went on an audition for the television game show, "Password." I got accepted and became a contestant. The show was hosted by Allen Ludden, and during my particular stint on the show, they were having an unofficial contest between two well-known actors who were exceptionally fine Password players, to see which one was "the best." My partners were Greg Morris (of "Mission Impossible" and other shows fame) and Peter Lawford (of "Frank Sinatra's pal" and other shows fame). Both were highly competitive and very bright. It was very tense between them, and each was trying to help me win money.

We taped as many shows as possible in one day, and I kept on winning. After six shows Peter Lawford's brain began to go numb. In the seventh "day" he gave clues that were less and less effective, and I lost. After the tapings had ended he apologized profusely. "I am SO sorry. I know I caused you to lose. I just got worn out and, as you could tell, my brain just stopped working. I really apologize. I'm sorry, man."

I was disappointed. It really WASN'T my fault that I finally had to stop playing, but it didn't actually cost me very much in winnings. This was very shortly after the quiz show scandals had been exposed and television prizes had practically dropped to nothing. For winning six and a half days in a row, my total earnings were . . . drum roll, please . . . a whopping $1100! Nowadays, six days on Jeopardy is worth about $150,000. Only four games in 2000 netted a contestant $1.2 million on the revival of "Twenty-One." And only a few years later several contestants had earned more than $3,000,000 each.

Oh, I'd almost forgotten about the OTHER game show I was on: Joker's Wild. And the show I DIDN'T get on: Jeopardy. First, the audition failure: Jeopardy.

We, about 60 or 70 would-be contestants, took a test that was comprised of all $800 and $1000 "questions"—the hardest ones on the board. I got 48 out of 50 correct, sat there feeling REALLY good about myself, and then didn't get asked to take part in the interview. Now, get this! The only ones who even got to INTERVIEW to be on the show either got them all right or missed only one. Talk about pretty much near geniuses!

The Joker's Wild has caused a few laughs at our house in the years since I was on it. I was losing, couldn't seem to get any Jokers, and then I caught fire, correctly answering question after question, in rapid-fire order. Then the host asked, "What's the tallest animal in the jungle?' I answered, "Elephant!" WRONG! "Giraffe." I lost. For my "delightful parting prizes" I got a $25 gift certificate to KFC, a KFC plastic collapsible cooler, and a LIFETIME SUPPLY of plastic garbage bags.

We ate the chicken, the cooler split apart after one use, and the LIFETIME SUPPLY of plastic garbage bags lasted about three years even though we tried to ration them. The laughs have come whenever I mention thinking about suing the producers of Joker's Wild for more plastic bags. They were really handy. But can you just see the headlines? **"Disgruntled Game Show LOSER Sues for More Consolation Prizes."**

What I SHOULD sue for is that I got kicked off the show for giving a CORRECT answer. The tallest animal in the jungle IS the ELEPHANT. Giraffes do not LIVE in the jungle. They live in the veldt. Elephants live in both the veldt and the jungle, but giraffes NEVER live in the jungle.

Hmmm. **"Brilliant Game Show Contestant Gets Second Chance."**

PLAY IT AGAIN, MOHAMMED

We were sitting on the floor in a fashionable Middle Eastern restaurant in Hollywood. Towels on our laps, eating with our fingers, canned music with words and melodies we'd never be able to repeat. Robin had consumed a half a glass of wine more than her social limit. Just before dessert, she waggled her finger at our waiter to come over and motioned for him to lean down close to her so she could speak to him.

"Do you think you could you get them to play "Ah-ee-uh-ee-ah-ah-ee" again?

SCRUBBING THE KITCHEN FLOOR

One of the most interesting jobs Robin ever did was a part in a pilot that never got picked up. It was funny enough, and the writers were good enough, but the man who produced it refused to allow ABC to put their own line producer on the show, and the pilot died a quick and expensive death.

The part she played was a hysterical combination of several infamous female stars, one of which could have been recognized as Pia Zadora. She was cast as "Mrs. Edgar Rabinowitz", the wife of an ultra-wealthy television czar. Robin had to wear an $8000 Bob Mackie gown with a 14' feather boa; she had four backup singers called the Edgarettes (actually four of the best studio singers in Los Angeles), and she had to sing just a little off key but with great conviction. Robin was a really good singer, so warbling just barely out of tune was a testament to her ability. Her small part included three songs and eventually a fog machine that got stuck in the on position, covering the stage in a mist so thick that Mrs. Rabinowitz could not even be seen. During one take, as she was parading around the set, singing "Swing Low, Sweet Chariot", she slipped by accident on the boa and fell hard to the wooden floor. Before anyone could yell, "Cut," staying totally in character, she struggled "valiantly" to her feet, never missing a note, and finished the number. It was so funny they kept it in the show. No one could have written that into the script. The credit roll listed every single person involved with "the show" as having Rabinowitz for a last name. Director: Bruce Rabinowitz. Lighting Director: Samuel Rabinowitz. Hair: Joyce Rabinowitz. Makeup: Jeanne Rabinowitz. On and on. Over fifty people, all named Rabinowitz. It was a very, very funny few minutes within a very, very funny half-hour show.

For her part in the pilot Robin was paid $10,000.

For a total unknown who might've done it for scale, this was an enormous paycheck.

The taping took most of one day but we got home from the studio around 3pm. I went into the kitchen at 4:00 and found Robin on her hands and knees, scrubbing the kitchen floor. (I wasn't even aware that the floor NEEDED cleaning. I'd have done it myself.) I said, "What are you doing?"

She stopped long enough to explain, wiping hair from her face with her forearm.

"Today, at one point, I had a woman doing makeup on my arms, another woman doing my nails, another doing my face, and a man doing my hair. While I was on the set I tried to go under the curtain and before I could lean down to pick it up a stagehand ran out and did it for me. I had a guy carrying the ends of the boa around the set. I got treated like a huge star all day. I got to wear an $8000 dress. I got to sing with four of the best singers in Hollywood. I got paid ten thousand dollars to do something that was tremendous fun. I can see how some people might get used to that kind of treatment. I'd LOVE to get used to that kind of treatment. I can also see how easy it would be to become a snob about it. I don't EVER want to take this kind of opportunity for granted. So, I'm just getting back to reality as quickly as I can. I thought doing the floor would help."

I slowly nodded. I couldn't say anything. I certainly couldn't have ADDED anything. It was just . . . one of those moments when who she was spoke louder than what she did.

THE MOST NEGATIVE WOMAN IN THE WORLD

A friend of ours had an aging mother who NEVER had a good word to say about anything, and told us, one day, that her mother had finally spoken the most negative thing she had ever heard.

Upon waking one morning the old woman had announced, "Oh, great! The damn sun is up again."

SEVENTH BIRTHDAY

Blaine and Bridges got pretty good birthday parties. When she was seven Blaine wanted to take twelve girlfriends to see "Moulan" and then have a sleepover. Robin took the baker's dozen to the movie while I ordered two GIANT trays of chow mien ("Moulan" / chow mien / Chinese food—wow, how creative!). We also had the obligatory sheet cake from Costco. It was chocolate everything with an oriental motif on the icing.

The girls got home, ate the Chinese food and the chocolate cake and finally bedded down around midnight. Thirteen sleeping bags in the living and dining rooms.

About one in the morning Robin woke me up and said she thought she heard one of the girls crying. She quickly went downstairs and discovered Barbara Parker WAS crying. And for pretty good reason. She had thrown up all over her sleeping bag and herself. Chocolate cake and chow mien all over the place.

Out of the twelve girls Barbara was the only one that Blaine didn't know well, and Robin and I had never met her or her parents. We didn't discuss what to do—Robin just comforted her and then took her upstairs to give her a bath.

I went downstairs in my robe to see if I could get it all cleaned up and discovered that she had also thrown up on the foot of the sleeping bag of the girl sleeping next her. In the dark I could make out that it was Suzy. I put Barbara's sleeping bag in the washing machine and got another out of the garage. I went to the laundry room and got a few damp towels and went into the living room to see if I could clean up Suzy's bag without waking her.

All the while both Robin and I are thinking that Barbara has food poisoning, maybe something in the chow mien. Oh, geez— TWELVE MORE girls throwing up all over their sleeping bags!

I had even worse thoughts—about getting arrested for child

285

molestation. Here I was in the middle of the night cleaning up Suzy's sleeping bag, and was rubbing against her feet and ankles while doing it. I was afraid she'd wake up and freak out and call her parents and they'd call the police and they would come and haul me away and it would be in all the papers and I'd go to jail and have to report to the federal authorities for the rest of my life and get permission to move into any neighborhood I wanted to live in, and . . . well, you get it. It was a pretty odd few minutes.

But Suzy is a very sound sleeper, and life is still good.

Meanwhile, Robin got Barbara all cleaned up and comforted. Barbara didn't want to call her parents to come get her, and said she felt better and thought she could go back to sleep. Which she did.

The next morning, all was well. We had breakfast for 13, the moms and dads came at 10:30, and by the time Barbara left we had found out from her that she had felt sick the afternoon before but didn't say anything to her mom because she was afraid her mom would keep her home and she'd miss the party.

So it WASN'T food poisoning. It was just one girl with a little stomach flu.

But it taught me several small lessons. One: you don't want to ever have to see chocolate cake and chow mien mixed together. And two: if you have to clean up a barfed on sleeping bag, pray that it contains a sound sleeper. I suspect this was one small instance (or maybe a BIG instance) of another answered prayer.

PIME OUTS

When Blaine was a toddler she never seemed to get into any trouble. She DID cause great amusement when she learned that she could climb out of the bathtub and run through the house with her arms above her head, yelling, "NO CLOTHES! NO CLOTHES!" But she rarely did anything that required discipline.

Bridges, on the other hand, was ALWAYS creating havoc. He had so many "time outs" that by the time he learned to talk, he would assign them to himself. He would do something—pull the dog's hair, hit his sister, remove a plant from its pot, take all the CDs out of their cases (he was very inventive)—and then announce to us as he walked toward the arm chair in the foyer, "I go do a pime out." He'd then climb up into the chair and sit there until we told him it was OK to get out.

We are instructed by many great gurus that "self-discipline is a key factor in a successful life." We didn't even know that Bridges KNEW Yogananda.

DAD OVERBOARD

I'm a very poor sailor and I tend to get seasick if the waves are too big, but I always enjoy going out on Janet's and Jim's sailboat. As a matter of fact, it's not the boat, it's them. I've always enjoyed being with them on any occasion.

Robin had come home after her final cancer operation paralyzed from the waist down, and her place of repose in the house was in a hospital bed angled in the corner of the dining room. Since she couldn't get around, we thought that was the best place for her to be "closest to the action." The most she could do was wiggle her toe and after weeks of hard work she could make one ankle move a half-inch. Her paralyzation, her colostomy, and the unbearable pain from her tumors would have been a burden too great for most people, but Robin hardly ever complained and buoyed the spirits of everyone who came to visit her. Her mom, Lorene, and my eldest daughter, Jennifer, had come to stay with us for those months and they were angels.

Jim and Janet sensed that I needed a tiny break and invited Bridges and me to go sailing with them. We drove down to Dana Point and before we could get to the boat discovered a Kettel One exhibit in the parking lot of the marina. Janet and Jim and I had a martini. If I ever have a martini I always drink gin. Though Kettel One is very fine vodka, this martini didn't taste like much. So I had another. And then I finished my third just before we got on the boat. I wasn't feeling drunk but I most certainly wasn't disturbed about anything at that moment.

It was a nice day to sail—just enough breeze to move us along, but nothing that might create a whitecap or even large swells. Jim let Bridges handle the tiller for a while, our conversation, as always, was scintillating, and we were having the afternoon that Janet and Jim had envisioned for me. We had asked Bridges (age four) to put on a life vest, but the three adults eschewed the responsible thing to do.

We were about two miles off shore when I announced that I needed to go below and use the head. Janet shook her head. "You can't. It's stopped up. Sorry." And Jim added, "We're heading in now anyway. You can use the john in the marina."

My three martinis were not going to wait till we got back to the marina. "I think I'll just pee over the side if that's OK with you guys." There were no negative responses. "Sure. We don't care. You're among friends."

Normally, I would've headed for the back of the boat and stood and peed off the stern. But Janet was sitting back there and I thought it would be easy enough to go toward the bow and pee over the starboard side. We were "zipping along" at about 2 knots, and I didn't even consider holding on to a halyard. I got on my knees, unzipped my pants, and began to (as my grandmother used to say) relieve myself. Just about the time I was ready to zip my pants back up, we were hit sideways by a swell that was a little bigger than all the others. It didn't feel big enough to give a moment's attention to, but it caused me to lose my balance and in what felt like slow motion I began an ascent toward the water. Later Jim told me that he thought I was joking and that I would right myself easily. However, I was not joking and as I slowly went overboard I remember having time to think, *"Oh, shit. I'm going overboard."* That thought took just long enough for my next thought to be, *"OH SHIT! THIS IS COLD!"*

The salt water burned my eyes but I could see the commotion on the boat as Jim tried to turn the boat around and Janet scurried to find a life ring. Thankfully she DID find one and tossed it out to me. By this time I was struggling with the weight of my jeans and sweatshirt and was happy to have something that would hold my body above the water. But it sure was cold.

I swam to the stern to get back in but I couldn't reach high enough to grab hold of anything. I swam around to the side, but it was even higher. When I returned to the stern Jim tried to pull me up but my waterlogged clothing made me too heavy for him to lift me. Then they both tried to pull me in but I was still too heavy. I was thinking that this wasn't going to be much fun, having to be towed two miles to shore at two miles per hour. Sixty minutes in this temperature was not the afternoon I had envisioned for myself. Eventually, with true Herculean efforts, they both pulled me in, bruising my ribs as I was hauled over the edge. Janet put a towel around me, and we headed for home.

Bridges moved as close to me as he could without getting wet. In my great distress I wasn't putting the proper amount of attention on him. This event must have absolutely terrorized him. He was four years old with a paralyzed mother who was dying, and now he sees his father go overboard and struggle mightily to survive a few very scary minutes. He didn't speak one word all the way home.

The four of us drove the 120 miles back to Simi Valley, arriving about dusk. I tried to hurry through the front hall and up the stairs, hoping Robin couldn't see my still soaked clothes. But a few minutes later, when I came back down, she raised her eyebrows and asked the group, somewhat accusingly, "So, uh, what HAPPENED today?"

We all knew the jig was up, so Jim stepped in to save the day. He announced with much bravado, "We were out about two miles and suddenly we were attacked by a giant squid!"

Bridges shot a look at Uncle Jim as said, "Unh, unh!"

Jim went on. "Joe put a knife between his teeth and stood on the side of the boat."

Bridges again went, "UNH, UNH!" Louder.

"And Joe jumped in and stabbed the giant squid a hundred

times, and saved us all!" Jim was quite pleased with his triumphant tale.

Bridges was not.

He ran to the side of Robin's bed and repeated. "UNH, UNH! Uncle Jim is lying! DAD WAS PEEING AND HE WENT OVERBOARD!"

It became a pretty funny scene THEN. It had most definitely not been funny a few hours earlier. Had I drowned I'm not certain the newspapers would have called it an alcohol–related death. But it probably would've been.

I keep a bottle of Kettel One in my liquor cabinet for my friends, but I don't drink it.

Janet and Jim still have the same boat. I don't recall hearing about anyone else having ever gone overboard. As for the giant squid, he's still out there. As for martinis, I now only drink them at home.

ROGER'S GPS

I had a friend who bought a top-of-the-line Acura and it included a GPS. This was in the very early days of these systems and neither he nor I had ever been in a car that had one. On the first night of owning this new car he and I were driving to see a play, about 50 miles from Simi Valley. As we got fairly close to the theatre we realized we didn't know which off ramp to take and remembered we had the GPS. It would give us the exact directions.

Unfortunately, by the time I had punched in the address, we had already arrived at the off ramp where we were supposed to get off the freeway. The first thing we heard from this new-fangled contraption was a very Germanic woman's voice, stating, "MEK A U-TUHN NOW!" When you're on a Los Angeles freeway, you don't make u-turns. We drove on looking for the next off ramp. She spoke again, equally demandingly. "MEK A U-TUHN NOW!" Just as we took the next off ramp, she once again blasted us like a Nazi Mata Hari. "MEK A U-TUHN NOW!"

Roger yelled, "SHUT UP, BITCH!"

I got a feeling that he wasn't going to really like his GPS all that much. Sure enough, the next week he had it removed and got a $2300 refund on his purchase.

A GREAT BIG CD

One day after pre-school, Bridges was singing a new song. I listened for a while, then asked him, "Did you learn that at pre-school?"

"Yeah. Miss Cathee taught it to us."

"Did she have it on a cassette?"

"NO! She had it on a great big black CD!"

HEAD OF THE TABLE

We have some good friends who for a number of years would invite their "orphan" friends to Thanksgiving dinner. Friends who either had no family in the area, or were between spouses, or just never seemed to get any great invitations to anything. For a few years after Robin died, we were part of that honored group.

They served a sumptuous buffet, and we were to sit around a table that easily held sixteen. Bridges, maybe seven years old, had gone through the line first and seated himself in the middle of one side. The host and hostess were planning to sit at one end of the rounded oval. Her stepfather took his plate and put it approximately where the hosts were to sit, and Bridges announced, "Uh, uh, uh. Head of the table pays." To rather lusty laughter, Bob moved down four places.

DON'T STEP ON MY GREEN SUEDE SHOES

My business partner and I were delivering some costumes and some new designs to a shop in Hollywood. We had pulled into an alley, backing my van into a space near their back door. Tom went in to talk to the seamstress while I waited with the van.

As I stood looking around, I noticed an open garage door across the alley, and sitting a foot into the garage was a cobbler, working on a pair of shoes. I'd never actually seen a cobbler working on a last and walked across the alley to observe more closely.

He and I spoke cordially and I saw that he was making an enormous pair of green suede shoes. Pea green. Wing tips. With laces. They looked like ocean-going freighters. The cobbler must've seen the size of my eyes and said, "Wanna know whose shoes these are?" I probably gulped and nodded, wondering if they were for a human.

"Shaq."

"Shaquille O'Neal?"

"Yeah. I make MOST of his shoes."

He knew I had more questions and let me ask them. They came out all at once.

"What size are they? How many do you make a year? Is it rude of me to ask how much they cost? Does he ever wear a pair out and they need repairing?" I could have gone on.

He was smiling and before he answered any of MY questions HE asked one. "Would you like to try one on?"

I was totally flabbergasted. "Well, SURE!" What a unique moment in anyone's life. I'm pretty certain it was the first time I'd ever put on ANYONE else's shoe, much less a big star's. I started to remove the tassel loafer I was wearing. He said, "Oh, you don't have to do that. Your shoe will fit inside easily and besides

I still have to do a final cleaning on them." He handed me one of the green boats. It was very fine suede—rough enough to not be mistaken for ordinarily tanned leather, not so rough as to be mistaken for anything less than high quality. The color was even and the more I looked at it the less offensive it seemed.

I carefully laid the shoe on the ground and put my right foot into it. The shoemaker was righ—there was PLENTY of room, and lots left over.

"He wears a size 23." Being somewhat of an NBA fan I knew that this was not the largest shoe size ever worn in the league. Bob Lanier had worn a size 28 during his playing days. But a size 23 is still REALLY big.

I took my foot out and handed the shoe across the bench.

He began to answer my questions. "I make about fifty percent of his shoes, and I charge him $500 for each pair. Some are easier to make than others, but since I make so MANY shoes for him, it's just easier for him and me to have a set price. I don't really know how many pairs of shoes I've made for him, but I can tell you, he LIKES shoes. He has a closet full."

It was the one and only time I'd ever spoken with a cobbler, the one and only time I'd ever seen a shoe being made, the one and only time I'd ever put my foot into the shoe of a star. (It WASN'T the only time I ever tried on a piece of clothing that belonged to a star. See ELVIS' CAPES.) But it was truly another one-and-only experience for ME. It's only fitting—Dr. Shaq is a "one-and-only" as well.

FOOSBALL CHRISTMAS

The Christmas season of 1999 was desperately sad for me. My wife had died that summer and we had always been pretty good shoppers and really over-the-top holiday decorators. But this year shopping alone made me sad. Getting out all the Christmas decorations made me sad. Having had no life insurance, my lack of money, made me sad. My kids had just turned 5 and 9 in November and December, and I wanted this to be a really good Christmas for them. I don't even recall what I (Santa) got for Blaine that year, but all Bridges wanted was a foosball table. I was feeling quite strapped for cash and a foosball game seemed too expensive, but I bought one anyway.

I found one on sale at Big 5, struggled mightily to get the big box up in the rafters of the garage, and ignored it until Christmas Eve. I went to sleep when they did, around nine, and set my alarm to get up at midnight to "do Santa." I got Blaine's major gift taken care of and then went to the garage to get the foosball game. The box was much heavier than I'd remembered it and I had to really exert myself to get it out of the rafters without dropping it. I finally dragged it into the family room where I was to assemble it, so it would be ready for play when Bridges arose at daybreak.

It took way longer to put together than I had thought it would, and around 3am I turned the page on the instructions and it said, "Have someone help you turn the table over and . . ." It was a good thing I was already sitting on the floor. That sentence would've floored me.

I didn't quite know what to do. I was trying to follow the directions very closely, so it would all be put together properly. But this one was a total impossibility. Three o'clock in the morning, Christmas Day. "Have someone help you turn the table over and . . ." I began to laugh. Overpowering the desperate sadness was complete disbelief, and recognition of the irony that was pervading everything. It WAS funny. "Have someone help you turn the table over!" If Robin had still been alive, we'd have been doing this together. If Robin had been alive we probably wouldn't have spent quite so much money on Christmas. No, not true. If Robin had been alive we'd have had enough money to spend all we wanted to on Christmas. It was pathetic. And funny. I think I remember laughing out loud.

The laughter undoubtedly gave me a new view on the situation.

I probably sat there for two or three minutes, wondering how this was going to work itself out. Finally, I realized why the instructions wanted me to get someone to help turn it over. There were bars and handles sticking out of each side and if one person turned it over, the weight of the table would create pressure on the bars and they would get bent. But there weren't any bars at the ENDS of the table, so I placed myself at the end of the table and very slowly muscled it up on its end and then over on it's legs. MY turning was ninety degrees different than the instruction writer's imagined turning, but it worked perfectly well.

A few more handle grips, an automatic counter and scoreboard assembled and attached, and it was finished. Not bad. Only three hours. I was amused as I looked at the instructions laying on the floor. "Have someone help you turn the table over." HA!

The secret of Santa was saved at our house by a little out-of-the-box thinking. Not needing someone to help me turn the table over was a first big step toward independence from my despondency about being alone.

KINDERGARTEN "NAPS"

During one of my parent/teacher interviews with Bridges' kindergarten teacher, she asked me what I did while he was in school. I told her that I was a singer, that I was a single dad with two kids, and that I did whatever it took to keep our household emotionally, financially, and physically afloat.

"Why do you ask?"

"Well, Bridges said you take naps."

I probably had not taken three naps in the past TWENTY YEARS!

Neither she nor I had any idea where that could've come from, and when I asked him about it he didn't even remember being asked the question.

"TAKES NAPS? A SINGLE DAD?"

Parent should never cease to be amazed at what their kids might think.

THIRD GRADE EXPECTATIONS

Robin died in the summer when Blaine and Bridges were eight and four. I have no recollection of my parent/teacher conferences that fall—I was just numb for about six months. But I remember the following year very clearly. They were starting third grade and kindergarten at an elementary school, which was only three blocks away, and it was my intention to actively participate in their education process.

So when it came time in early September for me to attend these first parent/teacher conferences I was actually anxious to meet the teachers. Blaine's teacher was a 30-year veteran, a woman dedicated to her profession, intelligent, but not very much fun. She explained to me all of her teaching methods and philosophies, and laid out her plan for the year. After about 25 minutes of talking, she asked me, "Mr. Dickey, what are your goals for Blaine this year?"

I didn't know that I would be asked any questions and was unprepared to answer this one. But what came out of my mouth was no surprise to me.

"My goals for Blaine this year would be for her to understand that everything that happens in the world relates to everything else, that all the things she learns in school appear to be relevant to her experiences in the real world, that she become the very best reader possible, and that she have a lot of fun." Mrs. Tanner was stunned. I actually saw her recoil slightly, in what looked to me like disbelief.

I followed my statement with, "Did you expect me to say something about STANDARDS?"

"Well, yes, I did. You see, standards are at the very core of how we . . ."

I cut her off.

"Mrs. Tanner, I actually don't care about standards. They're set by people who have created a system of education in this country that I think is quite flawed. I'll leave the standards up to you, because you are forced by the school district to use them as measuring devices. Let me explain in reverse order about my goals for Blaine. If she doesn't have any fun in school she'll hate every day of the year. If she doesn't become a good reader, she can't learn ANYTHING that comes from books. If she doesn't get that what she learns in school relates to the real world, why would she WANT to learn it? And if she doesn't learn that our planet's activity is interrelated, then there's no point in learning anything anyway."

She was without a response. She nodded her head. I finished the meeting with, "I'll leave the standards teaching up to you. You HAVE to do that. It's part of your RULES. But if you can do any of the things I mentioned, I'd sure be appreciative. Let me know how I can help."

The next day I had a meeting with Bridges' kindergarten teacher.

This was to be his second year in kindergarten. His birthday is in mid-November, and his mom and I had decided several years earlier that we would have him attend kindergarten at a school about two miles away for a year, and then he would attend kindergarten again at our neighborhood school and move on to the next six grades with these same children. We had seen relatives and classmates struggle through school because they were the youngest in their classes, and we were determined that we would not force that on Bridges even if he turned out to be the brightest kid in his school. It was a good plan: he wouldn't be stigmatized by being "held back" in kindergarten, he would not be the youngest boy in his class, he would have thirteen easy years instead of twelve difficult years, AND he wouldn't be the last one to get his driver's license.

Toward the end of his FIRST kindergarten, his teacher told me that she thought he was ready for first grade. I agreed with her and explained that I was still going to stick to our plan, to have him repeat kindergarten at the other school. A few days later I was asked to meet with the principal of that elementary school to talk about this same thing. After showing me all of Bridges' records and telling me that he should be going to first grade the next year, I once again explained "the plan." I also once again explained what I considered to be the advantages, ending with, "AND he won't be the last one in his class to get his driver's license."

This principal actually responded, "But Mr. Dickey that's over TEN YEARS from now." To which I responded, "In ten years wouldn't he STILL be the last kid to get his driver's license? Does time somehow change mathematics?" She was embarrassed to admit that her reasoning wasn't all that terrific, and finally agreed that perhaps my plan was solid.

So, the next fall when I met with Bridges' second kindergarten teacher, Mrs. Johnson, the day after I'd met with Mrs. Tanner, toward the end of our meeting Mrs. Johnson asked me the same question Mrs. Tanner had asked. "Mr. Dickey, what are your goals for Bridges this year?" It took about a millisecond for me understand that EVERY parent was getting asked that question this year. I gave her exactly the same answer I'd given the day before.

"My goals for Bridges this year would be for him to understand that everything that happens in the world relates to everything else, that all the things he learns in school appear to be relevant to his experiences in the real world, that he become the very best reader possible, and that he have a lot of fun."

The response couldn't have been more opposite. She pumped her fist, and almost shouted, "YES!" I was mildly shocked and wildly amused. "Mr. Dickey, you are the first parent I've met with who even MENTIONED the word 'fun'. Thank you!" Before I could even say, "You're welcome," she went on. "So many parents come in and expect me to be teaching their five year olds how to pass an entrance exam at Harvard. They're FIVE for goodness sake! I think my job is to integrate them into social situations, give them confidence, make certain they understand how to behave, and give them some notion of what to expect in first grade. AND to create an environment that is FUN. If they don't have fun, why would they want to come to school?" The remainder of our conversation escapes me now, but I remember it was fun.

Were I to be asked this year what my goals are for Blaine and Bridges, now that she has graduated and he's a Junior, my answer would be exactly the same.

BECOMING A MYSTIC

I had a friend named Helen Brungardt Pope. For a number of years we served on a non-profit board together. She was an author, and a marvelous teacher of metaphysics, and before she died she had completed most of her final book, titled, *For the Aspiring Mystic.* After her death, her widower, Mark Pope, determined to finish the book, asked his friends to buy some books in advance to help pay for the publishing. Even though I couldn't afford it, I bought twenty for $10.00 each. A number of months later, I got the box of books in the mail, gave away most of them, and kept four to give away later. Quite some time after that, I decided to actually read the book.

Helen, as a speaker, was very difficult for me to comprehend. I never got most of what she talked about. But as a writer, she was quite profound and easily understood. (Maybe it was Mark's editing that made the difference. I don't know.) She contended that becoming a mystic was a very simple concept but not easily accomplished. Boiling several chapters into one sentence, I understood her to say that to become a mystic all one had to do was to place one's full attention on God, all the time.

That's the preface to my "depression story."

At some point during late 2001, I was working a "regular" job and still trying to take care of a 10-year-old and a 6-year-old. I loved the man I was working for but he was most definitely a type-A personality, his children were grown, and he thought nothing of working 12-hour days. So my 9-to-5 job was turning into a 9-to-9 job, I was getting less and less sleep, my social life was zero, I wasn't being a good dad, and my life was just not working very well.

One evening, driving home, I was flipping through radio stations and heard an ad that asked, "Are you having difficulty sleeping, do you cry often, are you angry, are you sad, do you feel like you're not having any fun, do you have trouble getting out of bed in the morning," and more of these similar conditions. Near the end of the ad it said, "If you answered yes to more than one of these questions, you may be depressed." Oh, geez, I'd answered yes to about twelve out of fourteen. I was asked to call a number to make an appointment with a doctor to see if I was qualified to join a clinical trial for relief from depression. I was dialing my cell phone the moment the ad was finished.

I made an appointment for the next evening at six o'clock, and got somebody to take care of my kids while I went to this interview. I took Helen's book along with me to read while I was in the waiting room. I finished the chapter that I mentioned at the beginning of this story—the one that said I was supposed to put my full attention on God all the time. I sat there and thought, *"Well, I don't know exactly what that means, or what that would feel like, but I wonder if I COULD put my full attention on God?"* Even after many years of trying to figure It out, I still wasn't even quite certain what God was or how to put ANY attention on God, but thought as long I was just sitting there, waiting, I might as well give it a shot.

So . . . I put the book down, closed my eyes, sat there, and for about ten minutes did my very best to "put my full attention on God." After only a minute or two, I could feel myself shifting. It was like I was no longer just a body sitting in a chair. I sort of felt like I had no beginning or end, that I was not a finite being, that my energy extended way farther than I'd felt it before, and that I was literally surrounded by light. Then, not just surrounded, but that the light and I were inseparable, I was infused with it. It was an amazingly calm feeling, and I breathed it in physically, mentally, and emotionally.

Then the nurse called me into the interview.

I followed her into her small office where she proceeded to ask me questions for almost 15 minutes. After the quarter-hour barrage, she left me there for a few minutes while she conferred with "doctor." Then she escorted me down the hall to his office. He was the quintessential psychiatrist—oversized black-rimmed glasses, a van-dyke, and a clipboard. He proceeded to ask me the same questions, only using different words. I gave him the same answers, and while stroking his pointed beard said, "Well, you most certainly qualify for our program. I'm not concerned that you'll kill yourself, but you are what we would call 'clinically depressed'. I think our program can help you. Now please go back and speak with the nurse again, and she'll get you enrolled."

So I went back into her office and told her what she needed to know to fill out her forms. At one point, near the end of the application, she informed me, "Now, this is a seven week program, and during this seven weeks you will not be allowed to take any other drugs, or drink any alcohol."

"OK," I said. Then I held up my hand. "Wait a minute. Seven weeks without alcohol?"

She put her pen down. "Are you an alcoholic, Mr. Dickey?"

"No, I'm not. But I do enjoy drinking, and I'm not certain I want to stop for seven weeks." I was certain at this moment that she thought I was an alcoholic.

She became a bit stern. "Well, that's the program. If you enroll in the program you will be taking medicine that precludes you drinking alcohol."

I paused for a moment, then asked her, "Am I fully qualified for this program?"

"Yes, you are."

"Is it going to be going on for more than seven weeks?"

"Yes, we'll be conducting the trials for almost the entire year."

"And can I get into it any time I choose?"

"Well, yes, I guess you can."

"Then I'll tell you what. I think I'll NOT enroll today, and enjoy my drinks for the next seven weeks, and then if I still don't feel better than I do now, I'll come back, get into the program and not drink for seven weeks. Is it possible to do that?" Now I KNEW she thought I was alcoholic!

"Yes, Mr. Dickey. You can do that. Our program will still be going on in seven weeks. You could come back then."

I thanked her and left. I could just hear her thinking to herself. "That poor man! Doesn't even KNOW he's an alcoholic."

What she DIDN'T know was that the ten minutes I'd spent putting my full attention on God had somehow changed me. Something happened that I will never be able to fully explain. I left that doctor's office that night feeling great and never had another moment of depression, ever again.

Many years later, after thinking many, many times about what happened that evening, I suspect my "healing" was not a miracle but rather a perfect example of how dis-ease cannot exist in a body that is operating at a very high level of vibration. Since then, I have not been successful in putting my full attention on God all the time, and my desire to become a mystic has moved to the back, back burner of my daily affairs. But I AM in the process of learning how to raise my vibration more and more often. Perhaps it will be the entire subject of another book.

BOZEMAN AIRPORT GIANT SUNDAE

Each year for the past 29 years, I have attended a spiritual retreat called "The Big Sky Retreat." It's held in Big Sky, Montana, for six days around Labor Day, and it certainly appears after all this time that it's one of the "must do" things in my life. 13 years ago they made me the President, so I guess it's a good thing that I LOVE going.

To get to Big Sky, you fly into Bozeman. It's a small, attractive airport, things seem to go pretty smoothly there, and it's always a pleasure to come in and out of BZN. Upstairs, there's a restaurant and lounge.

One year, I was returning to Los Angeles, alone, and got to the airport early enough to have time to grab a bite to eat in the restaurant. After looking at the menu I decided that all I really wanted was a chocolate sundae. I asked my waitress to describe it to me and she cupped her hands and said the dish was about that big and there would be some chocolate syrup and whipped cream and a cherry on top. I asked her if there was any way that she could make a sundae that was larger than that. She said she didn't know, but she'd find out.

When she came back she said, "I'm actually the one who MAKES the sundae so I can use a soup bowl if you'd like. But it'll be a lot of ice cream. Do you still want it?"

That sounded GREAT to me. "Yep, I sure do." And she brought it.

When the bill came, it was still $2.75, the price of the smaller sundae. I asked her about it, and she said, "Oh, don't worry. I was happy to do it." So, I gave her an extra large tip, and felt quite pleased about my good fortune.

The next year, I decided to do the same thing. It was a different waitress, but I described to her what had taken place a year earlier, told her that I would be a very satisfied customer ("Do you understand me clearly?") if we could repeat the whole scene, and she nodded: another soup bowl, heaped high with vanilla ice cream, covered completely with chocolate syrup and whipped cream. A thing of beauty AND magnitude. Another extra big tip.

The next year, on the final morning of the retreat, I was telling some of my friends about my two-year-in-a-row triumph at the Bozeman Airport restaurant. They asked if I was planning on doing it again "this year" and I said, "You bet!" They, then, said, "If you get there before we do, will you get us an extra large sundae, too? Do you think you can?"

The final part, the question, seemed more like a challenge than an honest query. I, quite confidently, replied, "I'm sure I can do it," but wondered.

I DID arrive at the airport before they did, and as soon as I got my boarding pass went upstairs to the restaurant. It was closed, but the lounge was open. I went in and was waited on by the bartender, a young man who obviously lifted weights and sported a flattop haircut. I told him of my two-year history in the restaurant, and then, almost under my breath, took him into my confidence by telling him that my friends were questioning my ability to get the same great treatment for them. I finished our little conversation by telling him, "If you could make me an extra large sundae and do the same for my two friends, I would really make it worth your while. Do you understand me clearly?" He responded, "Yes sir! I understand perfectly."

Just about that time my friends arrived and the bartender said, "I'll be back with your three sundaes in just a few minutes."

About five minutes later, he brought two soup bowls full of ice cream and chocolate syrup and put them in front of my friends. They were impressed and thanked me for the favor. I was joking with them about difficult it had been to convince the bartender to help me, but that my negotiation skills were so good that he had agreed. While I was bragging about what I had accomplished the bartender disappeared for about two minutes and then reappeared, with a co-worker. They were carrying a turkey platter, HEAPED with vanilla ice cream, brown with chocolate syrup, whipped cream all over everything and three cherries on top. It was the most ice cream any of us had ever seen. The two guys were smiling, my friends began to howl with laughter and amazement, and I was just speechless.

They placed it in front of me and we all just stared at it. It was truly an amazing sight. We were all laughing so hard by now. I got up, shook the bartender's hand and said, "Buddy, you have just whipped my ass!" He and his friend died laughing. I asked him, "How much ice cream IS that?" And he ushered me into the room where the big freezer was and opened the door to show me the fifteen-gallon container it had come out of. "I don't know how much we put on there, but it was probably about as much as three of those square cartons you buy in the grocery store. Ya know what I mean?" I did know what he meant. He meant he had put about a gallon and half of ice cream on that platter. I was amazed again.

My friends ate their sundaes and thanked me for them. I ate about two thirds of mine and then shared about half of what was left with two others who had joined us. We only left a little of that giant sundae, and when the bill came, it was for three sundaes, totaling $8.25. $2.75 each. I left $30.00 on the table, knowing that a $21.75 tip was a bargain compared to the fun that bartender had provided for us.

The next year, when I inquired about the bartender, he had quit his job in the airport lounge and was selling used cars at the Dodge dealership. We had to settle for the soup bowls.

∞

STATE OF THE UNION

One January morning, the day that President Bush was to deliver his annual State of the Union Address, I mentioned to my son, Bridges, that I would be watching it that night on television. He asked, "What's the State of the Union Address?" I explained that there was a law that each year the President was required to deliver a speech to Congress, describing to them the condition of the United States. It had come to be called the State of the Union Address.

He paused for just a moment and remarked, "Probably gonna be a pretty short speech, huh?"

PINK ARGYLE SOCKS

I had been assisting in producing a show that seemed, assuredly, bound for Broadway, with Tony Awards in the offing, and future profits all around. We had been doing "on-book" presentations for about a year, many rehearsals under our belts, all of us pretty well acquainted with each other.

In this play, I performed the part of Arthur Miller, Marilyn Monroe's writer husband. On an afternoon prior to one of these backer presentations, I showed up, as usual, in semi-costume—grey slacks, 50's-width red tie, and a blue blazer. This particular day I decided to wear a pair of pink argyle socks.

As I sat on my stool next to one of the other principal actors, a man I'd known for over two years, he looked down at my socks. A very handsome, tall, leading man type, a fine singer/actor, married to a gorgeous woman, he said, rather softly, "Wow, it takes a man who's pretty secure in his sexuality to wear socks like that."

Without turning my head, with no inflection whatsoever, I softly replied, "Or not."

I actually saw him move an inch farther away from me.

THE PINK BOW

While standing in a long line at a UPS store, I struck up a conversation with a lady who was carrying a five or six month old baby girl on her shoulder. As we talked the lady confided that, though her child was almost bald, and looked to most strangers like a little boy, she had started putting a pink bow on the child's head so people wouldn't mistake her for a boy. With no hair to pin it to, she had gotten creative and stuck the tiny looped pink ribbon to the girl's head with Karo Syrup.

Very shortly after she had told me about this identification practice, two men in bib overalls left the counter and walked toward us to exit the building. Said one to the other, "Wood ja lookit thayut! 'At woman put a pink bow in 'at little boy's hayer!"

The woman just looked at me and shrugged.

SWEATSHIRT FREE

Blaine was a freshman in high school and we had just attended our first "Drug Free" rally at the school stadium. It had been a long chilly night, filled with one testimonial after another, interspersed by a bad rock band, and really dull speeches by local politicians and police officials.

We were cold, tired, and "drug-freed out" upon arrival at home. Bridges, now nine years old, walked to the middle of the kitchen, removed his sweat shirt, threw it on the floor, raised his arms above his head and yelled, "I . . . AM . . . SWEATSHIRT FREE!"

His little performance made the entire boring evening totally worth it.

SISTER, CAN YOU SPARE A QUARTER?

I'd been a single dad for four years when Blaine began middle school. We hadn't had any discussions about the female anatomy or sex, but I bought her a box of Kotex and on her first day that fall asked her to keep a few of them in her locker. She looked at them and was desperately embarrassed. "Why are you giving me THESE? I don't NEED them."

"I know you don't need them YET, but at some point you WILL need them—next week or next month or next year—and I just think it's a good idea to be prepared."

"DAD! They have machines in the girls' bathrooms."

"Yeah, I know, and wouldn't it just a big piece of bad luck if your period starts while you're in class and you go to the girls' bathroom and the machine is empty! Blaine! I just don't want you to be embarrassed by something that could go wrong with a situation that's totally normal, OK?"

She very reluctantly put them in her backpack and kept them in her school locker for two more years before she actually needed them. I also bought a box of tampons for her to keep at home, truly hoping she would learn how to use them from her girlfriends. One morning, after breakfast, just before she began walking to school, she whispered to me, "I started my period today."

Even though we know something is eventually going to happen, sometimes when it happens we're still surprised. I recovered quickly and asked her if she was OK.

"Yes."

"Do you have any pain with this?"

"No."

"Are you going to be able to handle this OK at school today?"

"Yes, Dad!" Exasperation is a frequent if not constant emotion with fourteen year olds.

Just at that moment, Blaine's best friend Aimee came to the door to walk to school together.

I turned to her. "Aimee, have you had your first period yet?"

She was caught totally off guard, looked down at the floor and stammered, "Uh, uh, yeah."

"Good. Blaine, Aimee knows the ropes. Stick with HER today."

Aimee quickly retorted, "Well, I don't really know the ropes. I've only had one period and that was four months ago."

"Oh." Now I was temporarily stumped. "OK, then DON'T stick with Aimee. Just do the best you can and if you have any problems Mrs. Nordal will help you."

Blaine protested immediately. "I'm not gonna go to Mrs. Nordal!"

"Blaine! Listen to me! You don't have to go to anyone if you don't have any problems, but if something SHOULD happen, she's a good teacher and kind of like a friend and she would actually be honored to help you at a time like that."

Blaine and Aimee had already headed out the door. There was no reason to stand around and listen to a DAD talk about things like THAT! Everything went perfectly at school and even though I asked her twice that week if "things were going like they should", and she gave the typical cryptic, "Yeah," I never heard another word about any of it until one night several months later. About 10 o'clock, Blaine announced that she needed for me to go to the grocery store to get her some tampons.

I was in no mood to go to the grocery at ten at night, but after grousing a bit about "looking ahead" and "keeping better track of things" I got in the car and went to Pavilions. We didn't need any food items, and we had cabinets full of sundries, just no tampons. After picking up TWO boxes of the particular tampons she had asked me to get, I thought maybe I should buy some other things anyway, just so the checkout counter encounter wouldn't feel so embarrassing. Then I thought, *"Who the hell cares?"* And walked right up to the empty cash register line.

The checkout lady was in her late thirties and she and I recognized each other from my many other visits to that grocery store. We didn't know each other's names or any details about each other, but it was a friendly cashier/customer relationship. Out of habit and because of store policy she asked, "Did you find everything you needed?"

Then she looked at my two identical items on the black rubber mat as it moved closer to her. She didn't laugh, but there WAS a certain look on her face that required a comment from me.

"Single dad, teenage daughter."

"Yep. Got it. Good luck, dad."

We both released that ice-breaking chuckle that so many of us have found necessary in certain situations. She bagged the tampons, handed me my receipt, and said, "Have a nice 'next couple of years'." Then we both LAUGHED.

Skip a number of years ahead and it would be time to discuss birth control pills. Thank God by that time I was married again. WHEW! Saved by the "I do!

"OH, NO, NO, NO"

Vin Scully is EVERYONE'S favorite baseball announcer. He should be. He's the best. End of discussion. If you like baseball he makes you love it. It's going to be a VERY empty day when he can no longer describe the Dodgers. "Oh, my," as Dick Enberg would say. It makes my whole body sad to even think about Vic Scully retiring.

One summer night, a friend asked me if I'd like to go with him and another friend to a Dodgers/Braves game and sit in the restaurant, the Stadium Club. I'd never seen a game from that vantage point (It's way out in right field.) but it hardly matters to me where I sit. If it's a baseball game I'm going to enjoy it.

We stayed late after the game having an extra cup of coffee, so late, in fact, that we saw the Braves bus drive through the center field gate and around the warning track to the dugout to pick up the players. I never knew they did that. As we were walking out of the Stadium Club I saw Vin Scully way down the hallway pulling a piece of luggage. The team had just returned from a road trip and it was long enough ago that Vin was still doing all the road games.

I said to my friends, "Hey, guys, that's Vin Scully! He's one of my idols. Wait here. I'm going to go introduce myself and shake his hand." They thought I was being a bit juvenile, but, man, this guy is a legend and I wanted to meet him. I'd sung at Dodger Stadium many, many times, and I'd been in the press box many, many times. But I'd never been in HIS section of the press box, and here was a perfect opportunity to just get close to a man who is revered by millions.

My friends stood where they were, as I practically ran down the hall toward Vin. I slowed as I approached him, and spoke. "Mr. Scully, my name is Joe Dickey. I'm like everyone else. I'm a big fan of yours and I just wanted to introduce myself and get a chance to shake your hand." He extended his hand to me, and in that mellifluous voice of his thanked me for coming all the way down the hall to meet him. Then, as we walked down the hall together I did something that a teenager might do, except I was in my fifties. I asked him if I could help him with his luggage. He chuckled and said, in that mellifluous voice of his (sic) "Oh, no, no, no. I can take care of it. Thanks, though."

"But Mr. Scully, I'd LIKE to do it for you. Please allow me to help you. It looks heavy."

He laughed this time, but once again in that mellifluous voice of his (sic again) said, "Oh, no, no, no."

Just about that time we walked out into the night air. Our car was to the left and his was a short distance to the right, so we parted ways. As he got to his car (the biggest, blackest Mercedes I've ever seen) I hollered so he could hear me, "I really would've pulled your luggage!" We heard from that distance, between chuckles, in that always mellifluous voice of his, "Oh, no, no, no."

Gary and Charlie and I imitated that phrase a bunch of times on the way home that night.

Two years later:

I'm walking down the corridor at the Burbank Bob Hope Airport about 11:30 in the morning on the way to my gate to go somewhere. I see Vin Scully in the gift shop. He's with his wife. His wife walked out of the gift shop while he was still looking at something. Very hesitantly I approached her and introduced myself, finishing by telling her I had a story I'd like to tell Vin about the last time he and I met. "I don't like to bother people like him, but do you think it'd be OK if I took just a minute of his time?" She was very nice and said, "He's kind of hungry right now and we're on our way to this restaurant so he can grab a bite to eat. And he can get a little temperamental when he's hungry, but I think it'd be OK for you to talk to him as we walk that way." So when he came out of the gift shop I approached him and re-introduced myself and began to relate the story about how I'd wanted to pull his luggage and he wouldn't let me. He was enjoying the story and when I got to the part about hollering to him, I said, "And I hollered at you, 'I really would've pulled your luggage, and you said . . .'"

And before I could finish, HE finished in that mellifluous voice of his, with, "OH, NO, NO, NO!" He laughed really hard as he turned into the restaurant and I kept walking down the corridor. Didn't matter to me whether he remembered the incident or not. He sure knew how to finish the story!

TAMPA AT ITS FINEST

Evidently you don't have to be able to spell officious or obnoxious to be them.

A few months after 9/11, when many airports had instituted new security measures, the Crew Cuts were in the Tampa Airport flying back to California. The terminal we were in was a VERY large room with high ceilings and numerous gates around the outer walls of the room. After we had gotten through the security check, there were still some lines to wait in and we found ourselves being "instructed" by a man standing in the middle of the room without a microphone, yelling at the top of his lungs.

With as thick a redneck accent as I've ever heard, he was giving orders to everyone in the room. "Ev'yone goin' on flight four-twayulve to Dallas, git aginst that wall an' stay thar till I tell you tuh moove! Ev'one on flight thirty-fie-sem'teen, goin' to Loo'vull, git aginst 'at other wall, an' you stay thar till I tell YOU tuh moove!"

He was totally in charge!

Someone across the room started toward the bathroom.

"I thought I said tuh STAY there. Git back in 'at line. AH'LL tell you whin tuh go!" The entire room was under his command. He was loving it!

I was standing in line behind a man with a foreign accent who was wearing an ermine hat, the kind with flaps that folded up, and it probably cost $10,000. I was impressed with the hat. I was equally impressed in a totally negative way with the fact that the man in the middle of the room could command hundreds of people to do EXACTLY as he said because we had become a nation afraid of terrorists. Right in our midst was a real terrorist—the guy in the middle—and we were being treated like prisoners in our own country. We were totally amused but still continued to stand in line. How did we know this backwoods monster didn't have a gun? He was most certainly the type to USE one.

It reminded me of Basic Training, when a group could be so cowed by one person in charge, forced to do his bidding for no apparent reason, because we were all so afraid of the imagined consequences. After about 10 or 15 minutes of this, it was our turn to "git tuh moove." As we began to walk toward our gate, I was thinking that this guy at least needed some sort of uniform. As we walked past him I quietly said to him, "Sir, you need a hat!"

He didn't get it.

HOW GREAT THOU ART WITH RECLINING SEATS

The Crew Cuts had just finished a mid-day concert in Cleveland for about 600, many whom had come from out of town on buses. I was standing behind our CD table helping a lady who was perusing the back of each CD. When she picked up our Crew Cuts Gospel "Find Us Faithful" CD, she suddenly exclaimed. "OH! 'How Great Thou Art'! That's my favorite song. Why didn't you sing that one today?"

I replied, "That's one of our gospel songs that we do when we perform as a gospel group."

"Well, why didn't you sing it TODAY?" She was insistent that I be more succinct.

"Well, we did our secular show today. You know, the 50's songs. But if you ever come to one of our gospel concerts, "How Great Thou Art" just happens to be my solo."

"OH! OH! YOU sing 'How Great Thou Art'? It's my very favorite song. Would you come out to bus and sing it for us?"

I was flabbergasted and sputtered, "Well, I don't know. We just finished a week on the road, I just did a two hour concert, I'm hot and sweaty and exhausted, and I'm not certain that's something I really want to do."

"Oh, please, Mr. Dickey. Please. It's my favorite song. Please come out to the bus and sing it for us."

I paused for a few moments, then asked her, "What's your name, and what church do you go to?"

"Ruth. Grace Brethren. Near Akron."

"OK, Ruth. If I come out to the bus and sing 'How Great Thou Art', will you put an extra $50 in the collection plate next Sunday?"

She looked me right in the eye and answered, "Not a problem!" I began to follow her out to the bus.

As we got on, I leaned down to the driver, "Turn off the AC and close the door. We're going to be here for a few minutes." I thought for just a second that I should use the bus microphone, but then thought better of it. The lady began her "announcement."

"Ladies and gentlemen, Mr. Dickey has come on the bus to sing us an extra song. It's my favorite. Here's Mr. Dickey."

It was a long bus, every seat filled. Maybe 60 or 70 people, all of whom appeared to be past retirement age, most of the little ladies had bluish hair. I stepped right into the task.

"Your friend, Ruth, asked me if I would come out and sing something extra for you, and I agreed to do it, provided that she would contribute an additional $50 next Sunday to her church. So, how many of you go to Grace Brethren?"

Not one person raised a hand. I turned to Ruth and laughed. "Oh, so you think you can get away with not putting anything extra in because none of your friends go to your church, and you think no will know?" They all laughed. "Well, I can promise you, Ruth, Jesus'll know. Jesus'll get you. Do you all know the joke about 'Jesus'll get you?'" No one indicated that they'd ever heard the joke.

I told it.

"This burglar goes into a dark house and begins to stuff things into his big sack. From the other side of the room, out of the darkness, comes a voice, 'Jesus'll get you.' He stops. He waits. Nothing. He starts putting more things into his sack. Again he hears the voice, 'Jesus'll get you.' He stops again. This time he turns on a lamp. Sitting across the room is a parrot on a perch. 'Whew,' he thinks. 'Just the bird.' Once more he begins to put things into his sack, and as he walks around behind the couch, he is face to face with the biggest Doberman he's ever seen. The bird quietly says, 'Get him, Jesus!'"

Amidst the laughter I turned to my friend. "So, trust me, Ruth.

I'm counting on you putting in that extra fifty bucks."

As they quieted down, I began to sing "How Great Thou Art." My big ending to the song created true appreciation and loud applause, and as I stepped down from the bus, Bob Duncan (the owner of the Crew Cuts) gave me a very quizzical look and asked, "What was THAT?"

I landed on the pavement and smiled. "I don't really know, but I think I just made fifty bucks for a church I'll never go to."

WHAT'S NEW, PUSSYCAT

Over the years I've sung for many hundreds of funerals. Usually the song requests follow the 80/20 rule: 80% of the time you get asked to sing the same 20% of available songs. With funerals it's probably more like 90/10. But occasionally I have been asked to sing things that didn't make much sense, like the "USC Fight Song," and "Green Eyes," (in Spanish for a person whose last name seemed Scandinavian), "Show Me the Way to Go Home," and "Take Me Out To the Ball Game." (TWICE.) But the best was, "What's New Pussycat?." The Tom Jones hit. A song that you can't sing with any reverence whatsoever. When you sing "What's New Pussycat?," you've got to sing it full out!

I thought it an odd choice, but my job is never to question what might bring comfort to a grieving family. You just do the best you can do with the task at hand. I knew, no matter what, if I did it well all would be right with the world.

The chapel was tiny, the front row fewer than four feet from where the singer stands. I went out and sang the heck out of it. But, as it turned out, the family member who had planned the service was sitting in the second row. From the looks of consternation on the faces of the five front row congregants, they were totally in the dark about "What's New, Pussycat?."

They looked at me with true amazement, a few mouths agape. They looked at each other. They did everything except look behind them, where the "funeral planner" was nodding her head and smiling in appreciation. All the while that I'm belting out the "Whoa, whoa, whoa's," these poor five people are thinking, "What the hell is this?" By the time I finished, it felt like that song had lasted half an hour.

As I drove home that afternoon, I thought, "Well, ya know, maybe life and death aren't so totally different after all. In both spheres, it, obviously, takes all kinds: "Peace In the Valley," "In the Garden," "What's New Pussycat?" The older I get the more often I find myself just . . . smiling and shaking my head.

STRETCHING THE ANTHEM

The Crew Cuts were singing the National Anthem to start a charity golf event at a Southern California country club. It was being headed up by Dick Butkus, the former Chicago Bears defensive star. The man who was in charge of the order of events was a member of the club, and had obviously been chosen for that task because he was an extreme detail man. When he told us "the plan", it kind of went like this:

"At 1:14 your group will move from the patio to the center of the steps that lead to the cart path. At 1:17 I will signal you to be ready to sing. At 1:18 you will begin to sing. You will know it's my signal to sing when I raise my hand and point at you. Be watching for my signal. Please sing in a tempo that will make the entire song between a minute twenty-five seconds and a minute and a half. The moment you finish the anthem, an F-116 will fly by. It's very important that you follow my instructions and be ready to move to the steps at 1:14. If we could please synchronize our watches, I have exactly . . . one oh eight and . . . fifteen seconds."

We looked at each other in amazement and Bob said, "Uh, OK." And at 1:14 the four of us went to stand on the steps. The tempo of the song wasn't a problem. We knew how fast to sing it, and we'd done it enough times to know that it was, in fact, going to be around a minute and twenty-five seconds.

We spotted the micro-manager in the middle of the crowd and waited for his signal. Sure enough, right around 1:17 he gave us a little wave and then a minute later gave us "the point." We began our a cappella version of "The Star Spangled Banner."

Just as we got to the end of the second verse, right before the lyrics say, "And the rocket's red glare," Mr. Do-It-Exactly-My-Way scurried out of the crowd, right in front of us, with great panic on his face, and began using his hands to give us a "STRETCH" sign. Closing his fingers into little circles and moving his hands apart, like stretching taffy, three or four times, with his eyes getting bigger and bigger. He was in trouble. We didn't quite know what to do, but kept on singing. We DID slow it down a smidgen, but even at that the song only lasted about two seconds longer. We finished and the crowd of golfers stood there, waiting for something else but not knowing why they were waiting.

About a minute later the F-116 thundered into the vicinity, descended to about 100 feet off the ground, and zoomed past with all the glory and noise you could ever want. Late. At least it was late according to "the schedule."

A few minutes after the F-116 fly-by, I was walking up those same stairs with Butkus and a friend who is member of the club and they asked me about the little guy who had given us the stretch sign during our song. They knew him, and they knew he was in charge of the ceremonies, and they knew how anal he was. They just didn't know what he had been doing. By this time, the whole thing was almost hysterically funny. I told them what he was trying to do, to get us to make the song a minute longer, and said, "Actually, I figured we had two choices. Either we could sing "And the rocket's red glare, and the rocket's red glare, and the rocket's glare" until he signaled us to proceed, or I could stop the song and declare, "So Saddam Hussein and Uncle Sam walked into a bar together . . ." They both died laughing.

We never heard from our event manager again. He was probably too busy measuring mayonnaise portions on the finger sandwiches.

EARLY MORNING STIFFY

I was singing for a funeral at a large mortuary in Los Angeles. I had sung my first song and was sitting "backstage" with the accompanist, listening to the eulogy, waiting to sing a second number. I knew the accompanist and we were quietly chatting, listening with one ear so we'd know when the eulogy was finishing up and I would go out again.

The eulogizer was the middle-aged son of the deceased man. He was doing a beautiful job of talking about his father, and the accompanist and I were doing more listening to him than talking to each other. I heard him say, "I want to tell you how non-judgmental my dad was. Now, how can I say this so it'll be OK? I'm not sure how to talk about this, but it's important to me and I want you to know about it, so I'll just try to make it OK. I guess I was twelve or maybe thirteen, and I woke up one morning with . . . what should I call it? I woke up that morning with . . . my first early morning stiffy."

The congregation laughed heartily with surprise, maybe embarrassment, and with a lot of past information about the deceased.

"Well, I was fascinated." They really laughed this time.

"I went and got a ruler and was measuring it . . . (more laughter) . . . when my dad walked into my bedroom." The laughs were getting bigger. This time it was on behalf of HIS embarrassment. He went on.

"Instead of making fun of me or saying something sarcastic, he just said, 'Well, son, how long IS it?'" Four hundred people almost fell off their pews. The laughter went on for almost fifteen seconds. People were wiping their eyes. Most tears at funerals come from grief instead of gales of laughter.

My accompanist turned to me and asked, "Did he just say what

I thought he said?"

"Yep," I laughed, "He sure did."

The man at the lectern concluded, "I just wanted you to know what an amazing dad he was." Five or six minutes later he finished his eulogy to thundering applause. And why not? Most great eulogies don't include references to engorged body parts.

CLOWNING

We were driving from Simi Valley around to Thousand Oaks, a little past dusk. We passed a man walking down the sidewalk, dressed as a clown. We weren't 50 feet past him when Bridges, muttered, "THAT guy lost a bet."

"GET A ROOM"

When Mary and I got romantically serious about each other, Bridges was barely eleven. He went with me to the airport one day to pick her up. As she and I were hugging each other, he turned his embarrassed self away from us, and chided, "Get a room!" It wasn't loud enough for the entire baggage claim area to hear, but it was loud enough to be heard by a few. It didn't stop us from continuing the hug, but it made us laugh while we had our arms around each other.

"BAG OF BONES"

As a reading assignment in high school, Blaine chose to read "Bag of Bones," by Stephen King. She had to take an oral exam with her teacher, and stood in front of his desk as he held the book and read the back cover.

After asking her a few easy questions about the characters, he surprised her. "It says here, on the back, that this book is guaranteed to give you at least one sleepless night. Did it give you a sleepless night?"

Without a moment's hesitation she replied, "It sure did! I stayed up all last night READING the darned thing!"

He almost fell over backwards laughing. "You get an A. Thanks for the best answer I've had in a long time."

Good grades can be earned in a variety of ways.

THE VOICE OF GOD

After Robin had endured two major surgeries and six months of chemotherapy, and got reports from her doctors that she was doing very, very well, we discovered that she was NOT doing well, that the cancer had returned, more vigorous than before, and that her prognosis was exceedingly dim. The news devastated us. We had really believed that she could DO this, that she could win, and she had gone through a helluva lot already. For a day or two neither of us could even talk about it. There wasn't much to talk about. Neither of us knew what to say, and neither of us knew what to do.

Then one day right after lunch we sat on the living room couch and even though we knew we were GOING to talk about it, all we could do at that moment was to hold each other in our arms and cry. We both cried a lot. Then we talked about what we might be able to do, what the possibilities were, how bad we both felt, and we cried some more. We were afraid and mad and scared.

Finally, it was time for me to walk three blocks to meet Blaine at school and walk home with her. As I walked out of our house, not being in front of Robin for a few moments, I began to cry even harder. By the time I got to the end of the block I was literally sobbing—big, deep, hard sobs—almost unable to walk and feeling truly unable to control this never-before-experienced emotion. As I crossed the street, I held my arms out in total supplication, and said, out loud, "What am I supposed to do?"

A voice answered me. It didn't have any audible sound, but I heard the words clearly. It was so clear that it felt like somebody had spoken it directly into my right ear, only a few inches from me.

It said, "You're supposed to be God."

It was very matter-of-fact. It didn't "boom." No accent. No

emotion. No second sentence. Just "You're supposed to be God."

I stepped up on the other curb and realized it was the first time I'd ever heard "the voice." Who or what it was didn't seem to matter to me. I'd asked a really important question and I'd gotten an immediate answer.

"Hmmm. Supposed to be God, huh?"

As I walked around the corner I wondered, very deliberately, what it would be like to "BE God." It took only a few steps before I realized that if I were God I could heal Robin. If I were God, I could take away all her pain and suffering. If I were God, I could fix everything!

And the voice told me that I was SUPPOSED to be God. But how? How does one be God? How do you even BEGIN to be God?

Answers came as quickly as the questions were posed. *"One becomes God by PRACTICING, just like anything else, dummy. Hmmm. How does one practice being God?"* I had a few ideas, but none seemed to be a sure-fire curriculum. I walked on, thinking about it, considering what could happen if I could be God, and the idea was quite appealing. Daunting, but appealing. (Jim Carrey's movie, *Bruce Almighty* hadn't come out yet. I was not considering the pitfalls. All I knew was that I had asked what I was supposed to do, a voice had told me and if I could DO it things would be OK.)

I picked up Blaine, we got busy talking about her day, we walked home, and I lost track of "the voice" thing for the rest of that normal, active day. The next morning when I mentioned to Robin what had happened the day before she was not impacted by it as I had been. It wasn't "her" voice, it didn't feel plausible to her, she had her own stuff to deal with, and we actually barely discussed it.

In retrospect it's a bit odd: I had heard what I considered to be "the voice of God" and we barely discussed it! That's how big cancer can be. It can overshadow all other events and activities, including what I had considered to be direct communication from God!

I, however, did NOT regard it lightly. I thought about it a lot. I even began to be enthusiastic about it, particularly the "healing part." I was desperate for Robin to get well. We were willing to do anything. Even being God no longer was out of the question. That's how big cancer can be. It can make you do more than merely consider an impossible possibility.

I still didn't know what to do about it, though. I didn't have a plan to "be God." A month later, I was having dinner with a friend, Terry McBride, and before the meal was finished I had divulged to him this very private and odd matter. (I hadn't told anyone else. Many people who have heard voices have been institutionalized.) Terry has helped a lot of people in his life. He is direct and blunt. He's smart and confident. And a lot of the time, he's right. This time his response was, "What are you going to do about it?" I was hesitant to state anything affirmative, but he was insistent. "You heard the voice. You know what it means. What the hell are you going to DO about it?" He's the kind of guy you don't waffle with.

After a few sentences of equivocation, I finally said, "I guess I'll be God."

"GOOD! I'll help you if you need help."

"That's just like Terry," I thought. *"I'll help you be God!"* Geez! Leave it to Terry McBride, a man who had spoken for years about "being The Christ", to say he could help me be God! It was almost laughable, his positive and confident attitude about what I should do.

We didn't talk very much more about it that night. I just decided that I would do everything I knew how to do, and began to practice. I began to see myself as bigger and more loving, I began to envision myself touching and healing others, I thought often about increasing my own personal power. I was trying to do everything I could to be God. I even gave a sermon at a church where I was a soloist, about the call to be god-like, and I asked the congregation for help. I admitted that I didn't know how to do it, particularly since I had no don't-worry-I've-been-God-I-know-how-to-do-it teachers, and that perhaps if each one of them were to do all they could to become God, we might be able to heal Robin TOGETHER.

I don't know what they thought about the talk. I never asked anyone. But a month and a half later, Robin died. I had failed to heal her. I had failed to become God. I was, amazingly enough, disappointed in myself. Sad, bereft, lost, and overwhelmingly grief-stricken. But also very disappointed.

It never occurred to me that what I had expected of myself was impossible. It merely felt like I hadn't had enough practice, that in trying to learn how to do this by myself I didn't have an experienced mentor, and that my God-skills were not honed. I vowed to keep practicing even though I had failed to help Robin.

As with many resolutions, part of my devoutness to the idea faded with time. I got too busy taking care of a four-year-old and an eight-year-old, while trying to earn a living, while trying to survive my all-encompassing grief. I never forgot what the voice sounded like, and I never forgot what the voice had told me to do. I just didn't have a compelling reason to "keep at it."

Skip ahead seven years.

I had met Mary. We had fallen in love. We had decided to marry.

She had a few good friends who insisted that before she could marry me they had to give their approval first. She had acquiesced to their requests and scheduled a series of meetings for me to meet with these individuals and couples. The first few "inspections" were casual and I "passed."

The first real scheduled couple was easy. They are lovely

people. We had dinner together and they liked me just fine. It was an evening of light banter and no tough questions.

The next meeting proved to be quite different.

We were to meet this man and his wife for lunch in Seattle. He is a businessman and a shaman. He "sees" things clearly, he is not a man to couch his words, he speaks his truth, he's very bright, and he was most definitely NOT going to let Mary make a mistake this time.

On the way there, I got two phone calls, one from a woman and one from a man. Both were best friends with Mary, who knew I was on my way to this "inquisition." The woman said, "Just be careful. He's going to show up kind of like Darth Vader." During the second call the man admonished me, "Don't be scared, but he's a bit like Rasputin."

"OH, GREAT! I'm having lunch with a combo Darth Vader and Rasputin! How lovely. How much joy will THIS be?"

We hadn't been seated five minutes when the direct interrogation began. There were no grilled items on the menu, but there was most certainly some grilling going on in that restaurant!

After two or three questions about me, I interjected, "Ya know, James, I don't really care if you like me or not." He was taken aback. I actually saw his body recoil. He had not anticipated a comment from me like that. I hadn't expected it either! I needed his approval. I needed his grace. But it, nevertheless, came out of my mouth, "I don't really care if you like me or not." I didn't show my own surprise.

But even though he had been thrown a slight curve, he was not deterred from his original quest—to find out who I was, what I was all about, and to make certain that Mary wasn't about to say "yes" when she should be running the other direction. He had me chained to a wall, he had a whip, and I could feel it swishing.

Though we actually had a nice discussion and there was never a hint of animosity, his questions were pretty much non-stop.

About half way through lunch, he inquired, "Are you willing to play full out?" When I answered affirmatively, he went on. "Good! 'Cause if you're going to be married to HER, you're going to HAVE to play full out. If you don't play full out, you'll be left behind so fast you won't know where the rest of the world went!" I told him she didn't intimidate me and he believed it.

Toward the end of the meal, came one of his most important questions: "Joe, are you the one?" I didn't know what that meant and told him so. He explained, "Are you the one who will help her become all she can be?"

As it turned out, just the day before Mary and I had had a rather lengthy and important discussion about sovereignty. So, my answer was, "No. I'm not responsible for what she becomes or how she becomes it. She has total sovereignty over ALL of her life."

He was a bit impatient with me. "That's not what I mean. I understand about sovereignty. I want to know if you are the one who will HELP her, who will SUPPORT her in becoming all that she is meant to become. Are you the one who is PERFECT for her evolution?"

I knew the answer, but gave a long enough pause to make it seem like I was considering it. "Yes. I'm the one."

He looked intently at me, pausing long enough to make it seem like he was about to say something important. Then he did. "Good. Then let me tell you what I've seen. Let me tell you what your heart is like."

I didn't know what he was talking about. "What do you mean, you're going to tell me what my heart is like?"

He leaned in from across the table. "I can see your heart."

"What do you mean you can SEE my heart?" I REALLY didn't know what he was talking about now.

"I can SEE YOUR HEART. I can literally see what your heart looks like, what size it is, how it radiates energy. I can see it."

I was incredulous. "I don't understand. How do you DO that?"

"I just see inside of you. It's not like I can see your blood vessels or see your valves pumping. What I see is energy coming from your heart. It's big and it's bright and it's very whitish pink. And I will tell you now, that you have one of the purest hearts I've ever seen."

I was astounded. I felt complimented. I felt like I could breathe. I knew the inquisition was over. He had laid down the whip without having to use it. I wasn't bleeding anywhere and as a matter of fact the dungeon where he'd put me for the previous hour was now filled with a bright shaft of sunlight. He leaned back a little in his chair and declared, "Ya know, I like you. I think we can be friends."

I, with a bit of humor in my voice but with dead seriousness in my heart, replied, "Ya know, James, I STILL don't care if you like me or not." We all laughed, but we also knew it was the truth. The truth, then and now, is that I DO like him! He's a remarkable man. But I was not going to let him or his questions or his opinions stand between me and the woman I loved.

I was a fine hour for me!

(I'm about to get to my other "voice of God" moment.)

The next day, Mary and I went to a place in Portland called, "The Grotto." It's a Catholic retreat center, with a big cross and altar set back into a thirty or forty foot high natural indentation in a huge rock cliff. There are paths to walk and places to sit among the trees. It was a place of peace for her, a holy retreat where she had gone often to pray during the days when she was going to college. She told me that she had had many conversations with God there. It's beautiful and quiet, people walking silently about, or sitting, meditating, speaking to each other in hushed whispers.

Mary and I walked hand in hand toward the large occlusion in the cliff. As we got closer, I remembered James' "warning" that I would need to play full out. I posed a few rapid questions to myself, *"How do I have to change to play full out?" "Must I get bigger to play full out?" "Is playing full out sort of like 'being God'?" "What will I really need to DO in order to play full out?"* And once again, the nagging old question, *"What do I have to do to be God?"* And once again, but for the first time in seven years, I heard "the voice." It was exactly the same voice! It spoke to me in the same ear, in the same "non-auditory" way, in real words, with identical matter-of-factness. It said, "Just be your self."

I was shocked to hear the voice again. It really was the same one I'd heard as I was crossing the street seven years earlier. Only this time it gave me information that was so EASY. Instantaneously I comprehended, and just as quickly I felt huge relief and joy. *"JUST BE MY SELF! That's all I have to do? Just be myself? WOW! I can be GOD by just being myself?"*

Suddenly, I knew! I KNEW! I had received a universal message of universal importance. We can be all that we are meant to be by just being ourselves. Our TRUE selves. Our true nature. Not our ego selves. Not whom we THINK we're to be. Not who others WANT us to be. Just ourselves. "And God made man. In His own image did he make him."

When I first heard "the voice" in 1998, it spoke to me in words that I needed at that time. It could have just as easily told me THEN to "just be yourself." But I was in such a state of grief and overwhelm, that I wouldn't have been impacted by that—being myself THEN would have meant staying little, staying mad, staying hurt, staying scared, and staying powerless. So the voice told me to become something I'd never considered—omnipotent.

Now, seven years later, after I'd discovered that I really had no way to be the kind of God I'd originally thought I needed to be, it told me the same thing in totally different words. "Just be your self, Dude!" "You are enough, just like you are."

I felt light as a feather, ten feet tall, and relieved beyond all measure. It was interesting to hear the voice again. It was even more interesting to hear It give me an instruction that I could easily comprehend and believe. I immediately told Mary about it and we actually rejoiced as we spent the rest of our time at The Grotto.

My prayer that day was one of immense gratitude. "Thank you, God, for lessening my load. 'My burden is easy and my yoke is light.' Thank you, God for giving me a clear path. Thank you God for ALLOWING me to be more like YOU by just being the one you created in your image!"

Gandhi said, "God speaks to each one of us every day. The voice is as loud as our willingness to hear."

TITLING A CD

A few years ago I recorded two CDs. It was the first time I'd done any of my own recording in almost 30 years. It was to be two albums full of positive-lyric standards, songs like "You'll Never Walk Alone", "The Impossible Dream", "My Way", and "Climb Every Mountain." I, at first, thought I'd call one of the albums, "Familiar Songs With Long, Loud Endings." Then, after hearing the final version for the first time, I thought I should call it, "Boy, That Old Guy Can Still Sing." After some more consideration I entitled it, "FULL OUT!"

Thanks to the right answer during a successfully navigated inquisition.

"DO YOU SING TO YOUR WIFE?"

The Crew Cuts were the final act before intermission on the bill of a Sunday afternoon, multi-group concert at a big performing arts theater in Southern California. We were planning on selling our CDs at intermission and then departing the venue. I took my wife, Mary, and our two kids with me that day as we had other plans for the remainder of the day.

While the first half of the concert was going on they took the car to get it washed and did a bit of shopping and then returned to pick me up. They arrived as I was standing on the patio behind our CD table, and since I was "working" they stood about 10 feet behind and waited for the rush of sales to dwindle.

At one point, a very attractive lady, perhaps in her 50's, walked briskly up to me, flashed a lovely smile, and said, "You have the most beautiful voice! I really enjoyed hearing you sing and watching you perform on stage. Do you sing to your wife?"

I paused for a moment and replied, "Yes, actually, I DO sing to my wife every now and then."

She smiled again and said, "Your wife is a very lucky woman." And she turned and went back into the theater.

A few minutes later, Mary and Blaine and Bridges let me know that they had arrived and we left together. As we were walking toward the car, Mary remarked, "That was a brilliant and VERY cool way to find out if you were married or not."

I was puzzled. "What do you mean?"

She continued. "Didn't you recognize what she was doing?"

I was clueless. "I don't understand. What are you talking about?"

"That woman. That attractive woman who asked you if you sang to your wife! She was finding out if you were married or not."

"You're kidding! You HEARD her? What do you mean she was

finding out if I was married or not?"

Mary was laughing by this time. "We'd been standing there for a few minutes. We didn't want to bother you while you were selling CDs and then that lady walked up and asked you if you sang to your wife. That was a very nice and non-threatening way of finding out of if you were married. When you told her you DID sing to your wife, she left, right?"

"Yeah."

"That wasn't the answer she wanted to hear, but it answered her question."

"Oh, wow! I didn't get that at all. That just zoomed past me."

We walked on to the car, hand in hand. As we all got in a wonderful realization came to me, "You know, it's GREAT being so married, so committed, so in love with Mary, that it never occurred to me that that woman could possibly be hitting on me." I told her that and she appreciated my comment.

It's a well-known anthropological and social fact that most men are clueless about a lot of things that are related to "relationships." We just don't think like women. But in that particular instance, I think it was perfect for me to be clueless.

INDIA

I've never had any wanderlust. In my earlier years I had plenty of opportunities to travel, even to go many places across the oceans, but I never took advantage of them, preferring to just stay home. When I married Mary, I married a woman who LOVES to travel. She takes groups on pilgrimages several times a year—to Egypt, Israel, Bali, Italy, Greece, India, and more.

Even though I've never been an ENTHUSIASTIC traveler, I'm a GOOD traveler. I'm easy-going, flexible, fun to be around, and supportive of those I'm with. And I love Mary, so wherever she wants to go, I say, "Book me, too."

Our first big trip together was to India, in 2008. As plans were being firmed up, she told me, "India can be a little rough at times. There're well over a billion people, and the traffic is horrific, and the pollution is intolerable, and the pace is a bit frenetic. So just be forewarned." Though I know no martial arts, I am aware that when an opponent makes an offensive move, one of the things a martial artist sometimes does is move in the opposite direction, absorbing the blow. So, I decided I would just metaphorically put my arms up, lean backwards, and let India come at me with all of her might. It was a good strategy. By being willing to take whatever it was that she had to give, for the entire two weeks, I literally felt NO blows.

I loved India. I loved the gracious, smiling people, I loved the cows (and what they deposited) in the streets, I loved the ceremonies on the Ganges, I loved the tiny alleys full of shops and kids and dogs and more gracious, smiling people.

On this particular trip, each person in the group brought an extra suitcase filled with school supplies (pencils, pens, rulers, protractors, calculators, paper. etc.). We were donating them to a private elementary school in Delhi. This is a school that is funded by corporate dollars and other charitable donations. Because poor parents in India do not want their kids to go to school—they want them out begging, and going to school decreases the money a family can earn—the school pays the family $25 per month for each child who attends the school. Because the income of these families is so extremely low—often between $200 and $500 per year—this is a huge amount for them. The school also charges each child ten cents a month, so the child will have a sense of ownership in his or her education. When we arrived at the school we saw tattered uniforms, but eager learners. We also saw a dilapidated set of buildings, and a tremendously under-funded institution. But it was open, it was functioning, and we were impressed by the dedication of the staff and the students.

As we stepped from the bus I asked our host if there was a restroom nearby. Actually, in India you just say, "Toilet?" and they direct you. It was a question that needed a quick answer. I was directed around the corner of the building and up the next flight of steps to the left. I found it just in time. As I was standing at the urinal, feeling much better, (I started to write, "Feeling much more relieved", but that was just a way-too-easy play on words.) I heard a sound that didn't sound quite right. Then I looked down I saw drops of liquid on the tops of the toes of my shoes. I suddenly realized that my pee was flowing through the urinal and hitting the floor right below. Here was this thoroughly modern convenience, but it wasn't hooked up to anything. Big surprise! *"OK! This is India. Wipe your shoes off and move on."* Whoops. Nothing in that bathroom would qualify as a paper towel OR toilet paper. "OK. Move on anyway."

I met back up with the group and we were entertained with songs and dances by many of the students. We ordered and paid for pizza lunches, a real treat for the kids and probably the best meal they got all month. Then we put our supplies on the stage.

It was a pile almost as big as a small automobile. Even WE were impressed. We then sang them a song accompanied by a CD by Ken Medema that included handshakes, shoulder rubs, and hugs. They absolutely loved it. It seemed like every one of them wanted to hug every one of us. By the end of the hour there was an awful lot of love going around.

Then the headmaster led our group to the part of Delhi where these kids live. She just wanted us to have a close up look at what their lives were like away from the school. If you saw the movie, *Slumdog Millionaire,* you have a partial idea what this neighborhood was like. But it was WAY worse than any movie could have portrayed. It was close to a square mile of the worst squalor imaginable. None of the houses had complete roofs; the walls were made of cardboard, and scraps of wood; there were no windows and no doors and no floors; there was no running water; no electricity; and whatever cooking they did, they had to use twigs they gathered daily for the fire, and there would never be a way to cook a real meal with the tiny fires they might generate. The smells were horrible. The people were filthy. It was the most deplorable conditions any of us had ever seen or heard about or read about. We couldn't believe our eyes.

And yet . . . and here is the wonderful and amazing part of this whole story . . . there was not one bit of misery! These people — ALL of them — appeared to be happy. They lived in total harmony. Not one of them would've stolen anything from another. Not one of them would have harmed another. They smiled and laughed and played and worked and were happy. Oh, it wasn't that they were unaware of what others had, or even what they might have. But at some deep level I think they knew what real happiness was and it had nothing to do with belongings or conditions.

This was a huge revelation for me. In the United States we pretty much equate poverty with misery. In India there is no correlation whatsoever. And it wasn't just in that huge slum neighborhood. It was everywhere that I looked in India.

I will freely admit that each of us sees every situation through different eyes. What I saw may not be the truth. But it is what I saw. It's what I heard. It's what I felt. And what I experienced that day changed me forever.

WOULD YOU MIND REWORDING THAT?

On an airplane that was only partially boarded, a cute little boy ran down the aisle with his arms extended, shouting, "Grampa! Grampa!" He stopped at a row of seats where there was an elderly man, who, quite obviously, was the boy's grampa.

The little boy was excited—and loud. His volume didn't bother the passengers, rather it amused us all to hear his young voice sounding so thrilled and delighted as we took off. He pointed out clouds. He asked lots of questions. For six rows around we could all hear him.

It was as the plane began its descent that his best lines came out. It became noticeable to him when we broke through the clouds and he shouted, "WE'RE GOING DOWN! WE'RE GOING DOWN!" The whole plane roared with laughter.

We all hoped his verbiage was precise rather than colloquial.

MARRYING MARY

I am often asked, "How did you and Mary get together?" This is the way I reply.

Mary and I had actually met several times in the previous decades. The first time was probably 1984, when she was speaking and Robin and I were singing at a big conference in Houston. Mary and I may have shaken hands but neither of us recalls. We met a few more times at big conferences, a few times in the Tetons, and even once when she was a guest speaker at Big Sky in 2000. All those times, both of us were with other people. In 2005, when she came to the Big Sky Retreat again as our Special Guest Speaker, she and I were both "unattached."

As the President, I felt obliged to pay a little extra attention to her. I emailed her before she arrived, I tried to be sure that she felt "attended to" while she was there, and after it was over I emailed her a gracious thank you note, explaining that a "real" thank you letter would be forthcoming. I did notice that by the end of the week, each time I would enter the main conference room I was scanning it to see if she was there.

Mary's assistant, Ginger, remarked to Mary, as they were driving away from the resort at the end of the retreat, "What about Joe Dickey. Couldn't you get interested in someone like Joe Dickey?" Mary replied, "NO! I'm not interested in ANYONE right now." To which Ginger responded, "Well, all I know is that when the two of you were on stage together, I saw magic."

Later, I told Ginger that I owed her a Cadillac.

It took Mary three weeks to reply to my post-retreat email. She contends that she had computer problems, but I still think it just took her three weeks to get back to me. She was and still is a very busy person.

However, at the end of the email, she asked a question. She

has a great friend who is a 50's and 60's music buff. Colleen knows THOUSANDS of oldies, and can "name that tune" in two notes nearly every time. So, Mary asked when the Crew Cuts would be working again and where they might go to see us. I, of course, was obligated to respond. By the end of September, Mary and I were emailing several times a day, having discovered that we appreciated each other's intelligence, sense of humor, and particularly the ways that each of us "thought."

At some point in October, I wrote something to the effect of, "Even though I really don't like to talk on the phone, we'd be able to get a lot more said in a phone conversation than in emails, and I'd like to call you some time."

She quickly replied that talking on the phone felt a little too much like a relationship, and she was very happy just being friends, that she was not interested in a relationship.

I called anyway.

As it turned out, we were both on the same cell phone plan and could talk for free. (Remember the days not so very long ago when an unlimited minutes plan didn't even exist?) And . . . as it turned out, we found out we could talk for hours and not get tired of the conversation. Because we were both very busy people, the calls started getting later in the day, and finally we were sort of "putting each other to bed" with our phone calls.

We continued our emails, though. Both of us found the other to be a good writer, to have interesting ideas, and we amused and intrigued each other. One day in November, I wrote, "The next time you're in L.A., I'd like to take you to dinner, " to which she quickly replied, "I don't think so. That would be too much like a date, and though I love our emails and our phone conversations, I'm really not interested in escalating this into a relationship."

I wrote back. "Mary, it's just dinner . . . "

She says that her next book should be titled, "It's NEVER just dinner . . ."

Though there is more to tell about the next few months, by the middle of 2006 we were committed to each other, we married in June of 2007, and the commitment continues to grow daily.

After Robin died, I never dreamed that I would be so lucky to get another chance at true love. I have no idea what I ever did to deserve someone as wonderful as Mary. After reading all of these stories that I've told more than once, you may wonder the same thing. But there is a song in *The Sound of Music*, called "Something Good," by Rogers and Hammerstein. It goes like this:

> Perhaps I had a wicked childhood.
> Perhaps I had a miserable youth.
> But somewhere in my wicked, miserable past
> There must have been a moment of truth.
>
> For here you are, standing there, loving me,
> Whether or not you should.
> So somewhere in my youth or childhood,
> I must have done something good.
>
> Nothing comes from nothing;
> Nothing ever could.
> So somewhere in my youth or childhood,
> I must have done something good.

I guess I must've done something good.

ANTIQUES MADE TO ORDER

While driving through a small town in Bali, we saw this sign: ANTIQUES MADE TO ORDER.

As my mother often writes, "'Nuf said."

AFTERTHOUGHTS

So . . . though I know more stories than this, this book is finished. I hope you enjoyed reading it. I REALLY enjoyed writing it.

If you have a story or two that you've told more than once, I'd love to read them. If I get enough of them, and with everyone's permission, I might even write another book called, "Stories THEY'VE Told More Than Once." I'm not certain any of us would make any money, splitting royalties a hundred and fifty ways, but it might be a fun book to compile and read.

Send it (them) to me in a Word format to:

JosephTDickey@gmail.com

If I get a bunch that make me smile, laugh, cry, sigh, or go, "OHMYGOD!" I'll get to work on them. In the meantime, if any of these stories have reminded you of one of your own, maybe something you'd forgotten or hadn't thought about in a long time . . . TELL IT! It's part of your history. And, trust me, history is still very, very alive and well!